Chapters from

Effective Behavior in Organizations
Fifth Edition
&
Organizations: Behavior, Structure,
Processes, Eighth Edition

**For Santa Clara University
Managerial Competencies and
Effectiveness**

IRWIN
CUSTOM PUBLISHING
Burr Ridge, Illinois
Boston, Massachusetts
Sydney, Australia

Chapters were selected from:

Effective Behavior in Organizations, Fifth Edition by Allan R. Cohen, Stephen L. Fink, Herman Gadon, Robin D. Willits, Natasha Josefowitz.
Copyright © Richard D. Irwin, Inc., 1976, 1980, 1984, 1988, and 1992.

Organizations: Behavior, Structure, Processes, Eighth Edition by James L. Gibson, John M. Ivancevich, James H. Donnelly, Jr. Copyright © Richard D. Irwin, Inc., 1973, 1976, 1979, 1982, 1985, 1988, 1991, and 1994.

CONTENTS

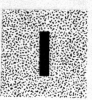

Introduction

"Managers interact with a great number of people. Precisely because they have been assigned to a managerial position, they automatically are expected to form relationships in many directions."

1

In many of our huge corporations we treat people like commodities. And people cannot be managed. Inventories can be managed, but people must be led. And when people are reacting to being treated improperly, they are not doing their best work. And when they're not doing their best work, our international competitors can beat us. That is the core of our problem. It's not robots, it's not technology, it's how we treat our people.[1]

"May you live in exciting times!" In China, this statement is hurled as a curse; centuries of upheaval, revolutions, and counterrevolutions have created a longing for stability and predictability in daily life. Whether excitement is a curse or a stimulant, you are studying management in exciting times. Dramatic changes in global competition, government regulations, work force composition, and employee expectations have led to an explosion of experimentation with leadership and organizational methods. Some of the forces altering traditional assumptions include:

- Tough competition from Japanese companies, some of which are successfully operating plants in the United States, and increasing competition from companies in South Korea, Taiwan, and Singapore with even lower wage rates.

- Crumbling boundaries between industries, as new technologies, loosening government regulations, unprecedented mergers, acquisitions, and spin-offs create opportunities. For example, banks and insurance companies are increasingly in competition to provide financial services, while Sears has entered the credit card business.

- More competition, based on the speed of bringing products or services to market, with organizations searching for ways of utilizing new technologies before they become obsolete.

- Women entering the work force in increasing numbers, occupying (or deserving) jobs that formerly were held only by men. Over half of all married women with children now work full time, and increasing numbers of women have aspirations to rise in management, rather than just provide supplementary income.

- Members of minority groups, some of whom do not speak English, making important contributions to the work force and becoming increasingly ambitious. "The white male share of the labor force will drop to 39.4 percent by the year 2000 according to the U.S. Labor Department, while the share of women and people of African, Hispanic, Asian, and Native American origin will rise."[2] They bring their various

---

[1] Ross Perot, founder of EDS, interviewed after having his shares purchased for $700 million by GM because he was "irritating" to top management and the board. From "Perot to Smith: GM Must Change," *Newsweek,* December 15, 1986.

[2] Julie Solomon, "As Cultural Diversity of Workers Grows, Experts Urge Appreciation of Differences," *The Wall Street Journal,* September 12, 1990.

subcultures' attitudes and behavior to their organizations—or are assumed to, by unknowledgeable or biased whites.

■ Employees becoming more educated, bringing with them expectations that their jobs should be challenging and meaningful. A sense of entitlement to important, fulfilling work and to a voice in decision making is a frequent by-product of higher education. From blue-collar workers to specialized-knowledge workers, these beliefs are now widespread, and unresponsive organizations can no longer count on automatic company loyalty to hold employees who are frustrated at blocked opportunities to contribute.[3]

■ A stubborn economy that manages to combine high inflation with low growth (stagflation), or reduced inflation, large federal budget deficits, and still low growth or recession, making it increasingly difficult to rack up profits and growth by doing the tried and true thing.

What have companies been doing about these changes? Even a casual reading of the business press reveals a great ferment in American industry. New thinking about management, organization, and people has begun to percolate throughout industry:

> So far, what has emerged is a host of management theories and practices befitting an age of global enterprise, instantaneous communication, and ecological limits. Some are familiar: hierarchical organizations being replaced by more flexible networks; workers being "empowered" to make decisions on their own; organizations developing a capacity for group learning, instead of waiting for wisdom from above; national horizons giving way to global thinking. Others may still seem a little far-out: creativity and intuition joining numerical analysis as aids to decision making; love and caring being recognized as motivators in the workplace; even the primacy of the profit motive being questioned by those who argue that the real goal of enterprise is the mental and spiritual enrichment of those who take part in it.
>
> Individually, each of these developments is just one manifestation of progressive management thought. Together, they suggest the possibility of a fundamental shift. Applied to business, the old paradigm held that numbers are all-important, that professional managers can handle any enterprise, that control can and should be held at the top. The new paradigm puts people—customers and employees—at the center of the universe and replaces the rigid hierarchies of the industrial age with a network structure that emphasizes interconnectedness.[4]

The Japanese system of automobile manufacturing, called *lean production,* is being favorably contrasted with American mass production

---

[3] "Loyalty Ebbs at Many Companies as Employees Grow Disillusioned." *The Wall Street Journal,* July 11, 1986.

[4] Frank Rope, "A New Age for Business," *FORTUNE,* October 8, 1990. The Time, Inc. Magazine Company. All rights reserved.

techniques:

- In running the factory, Japanese manufacturers attach great importance to getting it right the first time. U.S. auto-makers devote something like a quarter of their work force and one fifth of their floor space to correcting mistakes.

- In designing the car, lean production stresses a continual feedback process that allows Japanese engineers to bring products to market in half the time of their American counterparts.

- In coordinating the chain that supplies the 10,000-odd parts to build a car, American companies rely on many different suppliers to make the same component, hoping competition will keep costs pared to a minimum. They're surprised when parts don't fit. In contrast, Japanese companies stress a close relationship with suppliers.

- In dealing with customers, American manufacturers still permit dealers to haggle with consumers in a "bazaar" selling system, which most customers despise. In Japan, car companies sell cars door to door in an effort to create long-term relationships. In truth, the Japanese sell cars here the same way the American auto dealers do—because they have to.

- In managing their firms, Western companies rely on career paths that are still highly specialized and geographically narrow. They reward seniority without regard to problem-solving skills. Successful lean-production companies move their managers around less frequently, but select such managers for their experience, which is typically deeper and broader than their Detroit peers.[5]

Experiments in factory organization are proliferating, spurred by Japanese success in rapidly introducing and producing high-quality products at lower costs:[6]

Many American companies are discovering what may be *the* productivity breakthrough of the 1990s. Call the still-controversial innovation a self-managed team, a cross-functional team, a high-performance team, or, to coin a phrase, a superteam. Says Texas Instruments CEO Jerry Junkins: "No matter what your business, these teams are the wave of the future." . . .

A recent survey of 476 Fortune 1000 companies . . . showed that while only 7 percent of the work force is organized in self-managed teams, half . . . say they will be relying significantly more on them in the years ahead.[7]

The A. O. Smith automotive works found that it could double the rate of productivity growth and dramatically reduce defects by evolving to five to

---

[5] From a review of "The Machine That Changed the World," in David Warsh's column, "How 'Lean' Replaced 'Mass' and Humbled Mighty Detroit," Reprinted courtesy of the *Boston Globe,* January 6, 1991.

[6] John Holuska, "Beating Japan at Its Own Game: A 'Quiet Revolution' Is Changing America's Factory Floors," *New York Times,* July 16, 1989.

[7] Brian Dumaine, "Who Needs A Boss? Not Employees Who Work in Self-Managed Teams. They Arrange Schedules, Buy Equipment, Fuss Over Quality—And Dramatically Boost the Productivity of Their Companies," *Fortune,* May 7, 1990.

seven person teams who rotate jobs and essentially manage themselves. Elected team leaders take on many managerial activities, including scheduling production, maintenance and overtime, and when necessary, stopping the line. Even the work standards set by engineers can be revised.

How A. O. Smith Did It

TYPE OF REFORM	RESULTS
1981–84 Quality circles started by management without union support.	Quality improves. But program suffers from lack of union involvement.
1984–87 Problem-solving committees formed jointly by unions and management.	Hostile attitudes begin to change on both sides. More improvement in quality.
1987–89 Work teams set up throughout plant. Unions involved in decision-making.	All workers involved in raising quality. Productivity growth rate doubles in 1988.

SOURCE: *Business Week.*[8]

Volvo has built a plant without an assembly line, where teams of 7 to 10 workers assemble a complete car,[9] while the GM Saturn Plant has teams of workers ride a "skillet" platform together while working on a car, and gives them far more say than used to be allowed.[10]

Even high-level executives are discovering the benefits of teamwork, driven by the speed and complexity of current conditions:

> Richard Vancil, a professor at Harvard Business School, notes the increasing popularity of the "office of the chief executive officer." By 1984, he found, 25 percent of American companies used this arrangement, which melds three to six top officers into a team led by the chairman; that's up from only 8 percent in the 1960s.
>
> Others predict that the trend will continue. "It's getting tougher to run a big organization," says Delta Consulting Group's David Nadler. . . . "There are fewer places where one brilliant or two brilliant people will have all the answers."[11]

Top managers must learn new styles of managing, better suited to the increased challenges (see Managerial Bulletin, p. 8).

Not all of the changes are comfortable for managers. Middle management jobs are not only being eliminated (at least 1 million slashed during the '80s)[12] but top managers are finding that increased use of information

---

[8] John Hoerr, "The Cultural Revolution at A. O. Smith," *Business Week,* May 29, 1989.

[9] "Volvo's Radical New Plant: 'The Death of the Assembly Line'?" *Business Week,* August 28, 1989.

[10] James Treece, "Here Comes GE's Saturn," *Business Week,* April 9, 1990.

[11] Amanda Bennett, "The Chief Executives in Year 2000 Will Be Experienced Abroad," *The Wall Street Journal,* February 27, 1989.

[12] Thomas F. O'Boyle, "From Pyramid to Pancake," *The Wall Street Journal,* June 4, 1990.

MANAGERIAL BULLETIN

A CEO's Checklist for Managing in the '90s

In the more competitive business environment of the 1990s, companies will have to be more flexible, move faster, and tap every last bit of talent in the organization. Case in point: Bob Daniell's reinvigoration of United Technologies Corporation. Here are the secrets of his success.

Flatten the hierarchy

Daniell leveled a Byzantine corporate structure by cutting many layers of decision making. At Pratt & Whitney, for instance, he cut eight levels of management to as few as four.

Empower your workers

Managers pushed decision making down. For instance, field representatives at Pratt & Whitney now make multimillion-dollar decisions about reimbursing customers on warranty claims. Before, they would have to wait for approvals from numerous layers above.

Get close to your customers

Worker empowerment helps, but the imperative goes even further than that. For instance, Pratt & Whitney lends some of its top engineers to customers for a year—and pays their salaries.

Train, train, train

Daniell uses training to revamp the corporate culture. More than 5,000 senior and middle managers are getting at least 40 hours of classroom work. In some classes, customers are brought in for gripe sessions and a problem-solving team gathered from many different departments must come up with solutions.

SOURCE: From "Where 1990s-Style Management Is Already Hard at Work." Reprinted from October 23, 1989, issue of *Business Week*, by special permission, Copyright © 1989 by Mc-Graw Hill, Inc.

---

technology lets lower level workers make decisions, because they have access to information—and the managers are less than thrilled at sharing control.[13]

Also, experiments in pay are going on at many levels. In addition to new "pay-for-knowledge," rather than "pay-for-job grade" systems being introduced at factories, there is renewed attention to profit sharing,[14] incentive-pay systems,[15] and bonuses.

"Everyone is looking at team bonus plans," says an AT&T spokesman. Aetna Life & Casualty Company studied several approaches; it recently began a "star performance program" to give modest bonuses for creative and cost-saving ideas. Xerox Corp. started a small-scale award program for work teams in its upstate New York operations.

"Incentive pay is being pushed down within the corporate organization,"

---

[13] Daniel Coleman, "Why Managers Resist Machines," *New York Times,* February 7, 1988.

[14] "The Promise in Profit Sharing," *New York Times,* February 9, 1986.

[15] "Ohio Firm Relies on Incentive-Pay System to Motivate Workers and Maintain Profits," *The Wall Street Journal,* March 12, 1983.

says AT&T. A survey of 601 corporations by Hay Group, a Philadelphia consultant, says 18 percent have extended their bonus plans to lower levels of management.[16]

A great deal of attention is being placed on finding ways of blending different cultures or changing a firm's culture as firms merge, make acquisitions, enter joint ventures, or face new competition.[17]

Injecting new energy, creativity, and initiative has also become a preoccupation of many large companies that have become bureaucratized and rigid. General Electric, for example, has launched a major change effort, called *Workout,* designed to eliminate bureaucratic fat and administrivia.

> [Chairman John F.] Welch is challenging GE's 300,000 employees to use Workout to fundamentally question the way the company conducts its business.
>
> Through a series of town-meeting-like Workout sessions within the company, GE employees are examining all sorts of company practices, with promises of no retribution and immediate feedback—and action—by management. . . .
>
> Workout is part of a broader effort by Mr. Welch to create what he calls a "boundary-less" company, in which ideas, customer contacts, technology and management practices flow smoothly throughout GE's dozens of disparate businesses.[18]

In turn, organizations are struggling with ways to raise individual and collective performance through management training (companies spent over $50 *billion* on all forms of training in 1986!), other forms of training (another $150 *billion*), new policies, and procedures.[19]

Special attempts are being made to deal with the new, more diverse work force. More white male managers are being made aware of the subtle forms of discrimination that have held back women and other minorities; and they are making attempts to address these problems through affirmative action policies, cultural audits, creating networks to link minority members, training,

---

[16] "Bonus Awards Spread as Employers Try to Reward Effort but Limit Pay Costs," *The Wall Street Journal,* December 31, 1985.

[17] See "Corporate Odd Couples: Joint Ventures Are All the Rage, but the Matches Often Don't Work Out," *Business Week,* July 21, 1986; "Growing Pains: A Spate of Acquisitions Puts American Express in a Management Bind," *The Wall Street Journal,* August 15, 1984; "Cultural Change: Pressed by Its Rivals, Procter & Gamble Is Altering Its Ways," *The Wall Street Journal,* May 20, 1985; and "How Ross Perot's Shock Troops (from Electronic Data Systems) Ran into Flak at GM," *Business Week,* February 11, 1985.

[18] Mark Potts, "Seeking a Better Idea," *Washington Post,* October 7, 1990.

[19] See "The Not-So-Fast Track: Firms Try Promoting Hotshots More Slowly," *The Wall Street Journal,* March 24, 1986; "Keeping in Touch: More Corporate Chiefs Seek Direct Contact with Staff, Customers," *The Wall Street Journal,* February 24, 1985; "Demanding PepsiCo. Is Attempting to Make Work Nicer for Managers," *The Wall Street Journal,* October 23, 1984; Alecia Swasy and Carol Hymowitz, "The Workplace Revolution: Jobs Have Become Far More Demanding and Workers Must Think in Different Ways and Adapt to Unpredictable Changes," *The Wall Street Journal,* February 9, 1990.

and modeling appropriate behavior. This is by no means easy, as feelings run high, attitudes have to change, and even well-intentioned policies can result in controversy or discomfort with whether enough—or useful—things are being done.

> . . . diversity specialists . . . say companies should recognize genuine differences, work to separate them from stereotypes—and value them. Certainly women can learn to talk "militarese or sportspeak," said Avon chairman James Preston. . . . "But . . . why should they have to?"
> But to make changes in day-to-day corporate life, people must get comfortable with their differences. "If I'm a [white male] VP, I'm not going to put a million dollar piece of business in your hands if I don't know you, if I'm uncomfortable with you symbolically or personally," says Barbara Walker, who launched the Valuing Differences program at Digital Equipment Corporation. "We accept that," she adds. "But we say, 'Now, Mr. VP, you have to go out of your way to know people of difference.'"[20]

All of this activity and experimentation can be highly unsettling, knocking cherished assumptions and beliefs askew, but it can also provide a tremendously stimulating challenge. Although this book (indeed, any book) cannot provide you with all the answers to the behavioral dilemmas facing managers today, it will provide you with a way to understand and address the issues and to practice some of the key skills needed. We urge you to plunge into this course. More than ever before, your career success will depend upon your being able to effectively manage the behavior of others—and yourself.

WHAT DOES A MANAGER DO?

We have been looking at the way in which this book tries to reflect some of the complexities inherent in the manager's job. But just what do managers do? How do they spend their time? What makes the job so difficult?[21]

Interpersonal Functions (Building Relationships)

Although some students think of managing as primarily involved with financial calculations, the thing to note is that managers interact with a great number of people. Because they have been assigned a managerial position, they automatically are expected to form relationships in many directions: with those who work directly for them (subordinates), with their boss or bosses (superiors), with others in comparable positions in the organization (peers), and with a variety of outsiders, such as customers, board members, and attendees at industry or professional meetings. Every manager is in a

---

[20] Jolie Solomon, "Firms Address Workers' Cultural Variety; the Differences are Celebrated, Not Suppressed," *The Wall Street Journal,* February 10, 1989.

[21] Much of this section is based on the research of Henry Mintzberg, reported in *The Nature of Managerial Work* and in "The Manager's Job: Folklore and Fact" in the *Harvard Business Review.* (See Suggested Readings at the end of this chapter for complete references.)

boundary position between the unit he or she supervises and other parts of the organization or the organization's environment. In that position the manager is a symbol of the unit as well as the one ultimately responsible for inspiring or leading the unit's members to high performance. Thus, managers are forced into relationships with many people whose goodwill they need in order to be successful.

Outplacement counselors claim most of their assignments involve compe-
tent executives who lost their jobs because of personal incompatibility,
political in-fighting, or corporate reorganizations. Of all the major reasons
for terminating a competent manager, problems resulting from interper-
sonal relationships is by far number one on the list.

Carl W. Menk, President
Boyden Associates, Inc.

Informational Functions (Giving and Receiving Information)

Relationships with others are needed for the manager to acquire information for sensible action. The manager must know what is going on inside and outside the organization—who is performing well, who is having troubles, what competitors are doing, what projects are proceeding well, what opportunities are available, and the like. While some of this information may be available from written material or reports, most managers find that the best sources of current, useful information are through face-to-face or phone conversations. This kind of information requires careful interpretation, since others may be reluctant (or unable) to say exactly what they mean. Thus, the relationships which managers automatically form as a result of their position need to be open and mutually satisfying for acquiring timely information and for passing that information on to others who need it.

Decisional Functions (Making Decisions)

The information is needed, in turn, for the manager to make appropriate decisions. Managers have to decide how available resources—money, people, materials, and time—will be distributed throughout the unit being managed. Even more important, the manager must be a source of, and support to, new ideas, projects, methods, and opportunities. The effective manager cannot wait for innovation but must take the lead in insuring it.

Another important set of decision-making activities arises from problems that others in the organization can't solve. Whether the problem is deciding what to do about a large canceled order or settling a dispute between two other managers who disagree about the potential for producing a new

---

MANAGERIAL TOOLS

Mintzberg's Categories of Managerial Functions

Interpersonal (Relationship) Functions

Symbolic figurehead (represents organization to the world).
Liaison (contacts with others outside the unit).
Supervisor (hiring, training, motivating subordinates).

Informational Functions

Monitor (collecting data within and outside the unit).
Disseminator (circulating information to unit employees).

Spokesman (circulating information outside the unit).

Decision Functions

Innovator (initiating and designing changes).
Disturbance handler (dealing with nonroutine problems).
Resource allocator (parceling out time, money, materials).
Negotiator (seeking favorable conditions from others).

---

product, managers are frequently called on to handle disturbances or deviations from the usual routine.

Finally, managers must often serve as negotiators on behalf of their organization. If they are managers of a unit, they must try to persuade higher management to approve their budget request so they may acquire what they believe to be sufficient resources. They may have to negotiate salaries or working conditions with individuals or groups of employees, contracts with important customers, priorities with other units, and the like.

The activities of the manager can be summarized in the Managerial Tools box on "Mintzberg's Categories of Managerial Functions."[22]

As you can see, managerial work is demanding. The manager must be good at building relationships, gathering information, and making decisions—all of which affect future relationships, access to information, and future decisions! As noted earlier, the manager acts on but is also a part of the organization, and people in organizations have feelings that affect how they respond. They are more likely to provide accurate information or carry out organizational tasks well when they trust their manager.

NEEDED MANAGERIAL SKILLS

We can identify crucial managerial skills by looking at the activities described above and spelling out what it would take to do the manager's job well.

Think about the kinds of skills necessary to do these activities. In order to carry out the interpersonal activities, for example, a manager would need public speaking skills, a sense of how to dress appropriately relative to the

---

[22] These activities or roles are described in more detail in Chapter 12.

MANAGERIAL BULLETIN

Where the Action Is: Executives in Staff Jobs Seek Line Positions

In some cases, ex-consultants and staffpeople have trouble adjusting to the pace of line management, the need to set priorities and make decisions quickly. Dan Carroll, a former Booz, Allen consultant who was president of Gould, Inc., in the late 1970s, frustrated underlings and created minor gridlock in the executive suite when he got too preoccupied with overanalyzing some relatively small investment. "I made a couple of mountains out of molehills," Mr. Carroll concedes.

He later went back to consulting, and now runs his own firm. But most of the ex-consultants and staff experts who have tasted line management have gotten hooked on the action. Says Mr. Sponholz of Chemical, "It's like a boxing match. The bell rings at 8:30 and you just keep punching till 6."

Consulting seems drab by comparison. "I was bored," Geoffrey Dunbar says of his days as a consultant. "After you've done your 10th management study, they all begin to look the same. And the glamour of rubbing shoulders with very senior people wears thin; instead of just being with them, you'd like to be one of them."

SOURCE: Jeff Bailey. Reprinted by permission of *THE WALL STREET JOURNAL*, August 12, 1986, © Dow Jones & Company, Inc. All Rights Reserved Worldwide.

expectations of others, the ability to talk easily with others and to build trusting relationships so that many people will be open with him or her, the willingness to exert power when cooperation is lacking, a sincere interest in others and in listening to them, the ability to inspire others to work for organizational goals, good judgment of others' personalities and capacities, a knack for sizing up new situations, and so on.

To perform the informational functions well, the manager needs to be able to extract information from conversation, observations, and reading; must be able to judge who has the needed information and to whom it should be circulated; and again, be articulate about organizational goals. These, in turn, require that the manager be able to ask good questions, be observant and attentive to what is happening around him or her, and be skillful at reading between the lines, as well as realizing what is not being said or discussed.

The decisional roles call for imagination, openness to ideas, willingness to take risks, courage under fire, analytical ability, logic, intuition, bargaining skills (including the ability to bluff, sense others' positions and boundaries), and a sense of timing.

The list of required skills can be easily expanded; it is undoubtedly easier to name needed skills than acquire them! Yet at the heart of these skills are very human qualities that involve making relationships with many different people. Without good relationships the manager cannot carry out many of the other functions that constitute managerial work.

At this point it might be useful for you to assess some of your own managerial skills, using the various abilities noted above as the criteria. You could take each item (e.g., public speaking, knack for sizing up new situations) and rate yourself in terms of both ability and confidence (or comfort) in that skill. You might even repeat the process from time to time to measure your development in those skills relevant to this course. Finally, you could check out your own observations with those of others to provide more objectivity.

Managing Time: A Key Skill

Forming friendships is not enough, just as merely being technically competent is not enough. The person who wishes to advance in an organization needs to be aware of the implications for action inherent in the job of the manager.

For example, one of the fundamental issues for managers is where to spend time. The research on managerial jobs reveals there is almost always an abundance of work, especially since so much time must be spent interacting with others. Managers seem to prefer to gather their data firsthand by talking directly with others, which means that there are constant short conversations going on. The manager has to decide with whom to talk, for how long, whether to pursue particular individuals or wait for interactions to happen, and so on. At any given time there are likely to be many possible activities for a manager. Furthermore, managerial work is fragmented and variable, with many interruptions. The phone rings; subordinates want answers, attention, and approval; the boss wants the same; colleagues need help. Research on managerial work shows that managers average less than nine minutes on half of all the things they do in a day.

Should the pressing deskwork be completed, or would a walk through the plant reveal something important about operations? Or perhaps a meeting with a friend who works at a bank would uncover some useful information about future interest rates. Or a chat with an unhappy employee might save a valuable person who will be difficult to replace. And the phone keeps ringing with "urgent" calls.

Somehow the effective manager has to learn to manage time, rather than be managed by it. Self-discipline and conscious attention are necessary, as is a definition of "work" that includes a lot of relationship building with a variety of people.

Many managers, especially new ones, think of their work as only the technical decision-making part of the day. They see all the people contacts as intrusions getting in the way of real work. But as we have tried to show by carefully examining what managers do, connecting with other people is an essential part of the job, and not necessarily the first thing to eliminate in order to "save time."

Therefore, effective managers learn how to make activities fold in on one another and serve double purposes. For example, they use lunch time and short coffee breaks to chat informally with people they might not otherwise

MANAGERIAL TOOLS

16 Time-Saving Managerial Practices (Can You Apply These to Student Life?)

Clarify Goals

1. Develop and use clear, long-range goals.
2. Clearly establish what to accomplish each month, week, day, and by each task.

Plan Ahead

3. Use a Daily "To-Do" List to plan and prioritize each day's activities.
4. Before meetings, review agenda, clarify your objectives, get information, anticipate events, and plan actions.
5. Set deadlines for major tasks.

Manage Daily Activities

6. Do important tasks first. Avoid trap of "getting small items out of way." Do tough jobs at your best times.
7. For big projects, divide task into manageable parts and sequence.
8. Handle each piece of paper only once, or note next step.
9. Stick to your agenda. Include restricted moments of relaxation and socializing.

10. Bring work to use during unavoidable idle time while waiting or traveling.
11. Limit interruptions. Close office door, reschedule drop-in visitors, ask secretary to hold phone calls, schedule "thinking time" and honor it.

Organize Your Workplace

12. Clear desk of clutter and other distractions.
13. Develop usable filing system and tickler file.

Spend Time Efficiently

14. Use 80/20 rule: 80 percent of the results are determined by 20 percent of the decisions. Concentrate on those.
15. Review actions to learn from past mistakes, but don't pick at imperfections and waste time on regrets.

SOURCES: Alan Lakein, *How to Get Control of Your Time and Your Life* (New York: David McKay, 1973); R. Alec MacKenzie, *The Time Trap* (New York: McGraw-Hill, 1975).

easily see, yet who have useful tidbits about the company, the market, projects, and the like.

Organizational Politics and Getting Ahead

Similarly, when asked to serve on committees or task forces, alert managers look at the assignment as an opportunity, rather than as a burden. Serving on a committee brings them into contact with people from other parts of the organization, and they use the contact to establish relationships and gather data (often during the "holes" in a meeting—when people are just arriving or leaving, or when a few go to the bathroom during a break, and so on).

Furthermore, managers who want to get ahead realize that committee work allows them the opportunity to "show their stuff," to demonstrate to people who might be their direct boss or subordinate in the future that they are competent, reliable, hardworking, and easy to work with.

MANAGERIAL BULLETIN

Yellow Brick Roadblock

For many new employees . . . reality shock consisted of the discovery . . . that other people in the organization were a roadblock to what they wanted to get done. Others in the organization did not seem as smart as they should be, seemed illogical . . . irrational . . . lazy, unproductive, or unmotivated. . . . [New managers] did not want to have to learn to deal with other people; they simply wanted them to go away. . . . Those who resisted this reality . . . at an emotional level used up their energy in denial and complaint, rather than in problem solving.

(Based on interviews with Sloan School Alumni during the first year after graduation.)

SOURCE: Edgar H. Schein, *Career Dynamics: Matching Individual and Organizational Needs* (Reading, Mass.: Addison-Wesley Publishing, 1978).

Thus, as simple an activity as going prepared to a committee meeting serves several purposes—relationship building, data collection, visibility creation, and the formation of a good reputation, which might lead to future promotions (Cohen & Stein, 1980).

Another way in which managers, especially those new to a particular organization, can create alliances is by observing what social activities, interests, style of dress, and the like are valued by high-level managers in the organization. They can then adapt to those things that do not violate their sense of themselves. Those who do what others in the organization value are likely to more easily form relationships around shared interests and to seem more trustworthy. Was it a coincidence that everyone on President Kennedy's staff "just happened" to play touch football, while those on President Carter's staff seemed to prefer softball? If you worked for President Bush, would you find tennis and speedboat racing more interesting?

The true test of somebody who's really good at power is that nothing interests him or her more than other people's problems, because it's an opportunity to be decisive and to exert authority over another person.

Michael Korda

Of course, all of these things do not make up for lack of ability, but their absence can make those who have the power to help advance one's career uncomfortable. Furthermore, there is no law which demands that you try to get ahead. Many people, including those who study administration, do not place high value on career advancement. But should you want to get ahead, it helps to know how to do so intelligently.

MANAGERIAL BULLETIN

What's New in Office Politics

"We're all equal in this family," said the company president as he welcomed Wiloughby Sharp, then a management trainee, to the employee fold. The two men, along with a beaming personnel manager, rode the elevator down from the president's penthouse. The president was going to the lobby, Mr. Sharp to the second floor.

"As I pushed the second-floor button, I saw the personnel manager's face go red," recalled Mr. Sharp, now head of his own company, Machine Language, which is based in New York City. "Evidently we weren't all equal in this family—I was supposed to ride with the president to the first floor and then back up to the second."

The experience so thoroughly turned Mr. Sharp off to the politics of corporate life that he left the company six months later and has been self-employed ever since. But not all people have the psychological makeup or the financial cushion needed to walk away from corporate America. For them, a realization that corporate futures can be made or broken by the rules of office politics is essential.

Such seemingly mundane matters as choosing luncheon companions, deciding when to send memos and to whom, recognizing who is in ill favor and to be avoided, and learning to deal with the idiosyncracies of the top brass can be as important to success as on-the-job performance.

Indeed, corporate politics are growing ever more intense. Corporations are cutting back on management staffing, leaving lower-level employees competing for fewer promotions. "Corporations are going to keep people in positions longer, and the frustration level will be higher," warned Bill Gould, president of the Association of Executive Search Consultants. The likely result: more maneuvering, buck passing, and backstabbing.

SOURCE: *New York Times*, Sunday, October 14, 1984, © by the New York Times Company. Reproduced with permission.

Problems of Women and Minorities

It is worth noting here that women or members of various minority groups are often at an automatic disadvantage in organizations traditionally run by white males, because their visible physical "difference" from the majority makes some majority members uncomfortable or less trusting. The fewer the minority members in the organization at managerial levels, the greater the difficulty they are likely to have in being perceived as trustworthy—that is, as similar enough to be "one of us" where there are sensitive issues. As unfair as this is to those who are seen as "different" in whatever way, it is useful to understand that in organizations social judgments of individuals are made as well as technical judgments, and these evaluations are often based on such things as dress, sex, color, "style," and the like. It is not accidental that, as more women decided to attempt to move upward in organizations, articles and books began to appear for them on such subjects as "How to Dress for Success," "Office Politics," and "How to Avoid Threatening Your Boss." Even if it is not true that only women who wear tailored blue suits can get ahead in business organizations (as one advisor claims), women, just like any others who choose to try to get ahead, need to be aware of what they can do

---

MANAGERIAL BULLETIN

On the Virtues of Learning Gin Rummy

"I picked up the game . . . with Procter & Gamble. P&G had acquired Folger Coffee and sent me . . . to study the financial structure. The Folger people saw me as an outsider; they gave me the cold shoulder.

"I soon noticed that everybody played gin rummy at lunch and, although that didn't seem very businesslike to me, I decided I should play to see what the attraction was.

"Well, it was fun. Besides that, I got to know the people in a way you don't get to in a pure business relationship. Once I began playing gin, I was accepted by everyone."

SOURCE: Sam Phillips, chairman of the board, Acton Corporation; quoted in *Inc. Magazine*, January 1981.

---

to inspire comfort and confidence in them by the organization's decision makers. Trusting relationships are not a nicety of organizational life—they are fundamental to managerial work.

The Dangers of Gamesmanship

At board of directors meetings, "the one unmatched asset is the ability to yawn with your mouth closed."

Robert K. Mueller,
Behind the Boardroom Door

In many ways the above may sound to you as if we were seeing managers (both men and women) as having to "play politics" constantly or play a phony game. It certainly can, and sometimes does, become insincere and manipulative. But it also can be a matter of doing what will avoid surprises, reduce misunderstanding, increase trust, and encourage cooperation—that is, facilitating good decision making and making it easier for people to work together. The line between effectiveness and "gamesmanship" is vague, and every manager at times must make some concession to playing the game. You alone will need to decide where to draw the line, but we want to emphasize that it is not necessarily all phony and can be both functional and genuine. In fact, since most people can spot insincere and artificial behavior quite easily, getting ahead through relationships usually requires that you be genuinely interested in others. Otherwise, they will be cautious toward you, which is exactly the opposite of what is necessary.

We get rid of anyone who starts in with office politics, plotting, or back-stabbing. If you have to keep looking over your shoulder, you can't play the game well!

Senior vice president,
Fortune 500 company

NOTHING IS AS SIMPLE AS IT SEEMS

As should be clear by now, if you long for a job in which people never get in the way, all problems are easily defined with their causes clear and known, decisions are simple, future events are quite predictable, and you can almost immediately find out whether you made the correct decision, you probably ought to think again about a managerial career. Organizational life is much too complex for a handful of rules, theories, or slogans to be automatically applied to every problem. While the behavioral science theories and concepts in this book should be helpful to you in figuring out what is going on, or even in guiding an action, they are by no means sufficient for all problems you will encounter, nor easy to apply. They are more helpful than common sense alone, but they do not come with 10-year money-back guarantees.

For every problem there is a solution which is simple, direct, and wrong.

H. L. Mencken

Multiple Causality

For one thing, most behavior of any significance has multiple causes and multiple consequences. For example, how can you explain why extremely intelligent, caring managers at NASA decided to proceed with the Challenger shuttle launch on a cold January 28, 1986, when, as tragically proved true, the rubber rocket seals would not hold in temperatures below 50 degrees? Although it is an all-too-human trait to want to find a single villain—a simple cause that explains everything—a combination of many factors allowed NASA to send astronauts to their deaths while millions watched on TV.

Key NASA officials were warned the night before the launch by Morton Thiokol managers and engineers but discounted the data. They thought the evidence was not conclusive. The many delays in this and previous launches had created a sense of urgency about pushing ahead. National media had begun to belittle NASA delays. The string of successful missions may have engendered overconfidence that somehow things would work out as they always had; NASA culture reinforced managers for a "can do" attitude and for cool unflappability. As in other large organizations, mid-level personnel were used to withholding "bad news" from higher-ups, and communications often became distorted as they passed up and down the organization. Internal politics and rivalries probably helped shape what managers and engineers told one another.

At Thiokol, the contractor for the rocket boosters, similar pressures impacted key players. Furthermore, the company was competing vigorously with several other corporations to get future shuttle contracts. It is difficult to continue to say "no launch" to a customer who says, "I am appalled" as NASA official George Hardy did, or to another official, Lawrence Malloy, who reacted to Thiokol's reservations by saying, "My God, Thiokol, when do you want me to launch, next April?" Thiokol's engineers, who fought the decision but were overruled by their managers, backed off out of doubt about how certain they could be, natural fears of continuing to argue with their bosses, and even personal distaste for conflict.

Undoubtedly there are other reasons for the foolhardy decision; the ones listed are just some of those made public after the disaster. If you had been asked right after the explosion to "solve the problem once and for all," think about how easily you could have missed the complexities and focused on "firing the incompetent guy who said to launch" or "replacing the lousy contractor." Though either or both of those actions might ultimately be part of a solution, if that's all you did, the other complex forces would undoubtedly cause similar problems to occur in the future. *Oversimplifying your diagnosis of the cause(s) of problems almost always leads to incorrect or insufficient remedial action.* This kind of leap to hasty, oversimplified conclusions happens all the time in organizations; dramatic events like the Challenger explosion are just rare public glimpses of what happens when diagnosis misfires.

Seek simplicity; then distrust it.
Alfred North Whitehead

Here's another dramatic example: One of the world's largest consulting firms was approached by a manufacturer of tubing made from a rare metal. The manufacturer said that its problem was the *measurement of faulty tubing;* the tubing came out of the extruding machines so fast that, by the time they could examine it, too much product would be wasted if the diameter and tensile strength were off. Could a gauge be devised that would constantly monitor quality as the tubing was extruded? The consulting firm eagerly took on the project, since its quality control division could utilize very advanced

FIGURE 1–1   Many Possible Causes for Any Given Problem

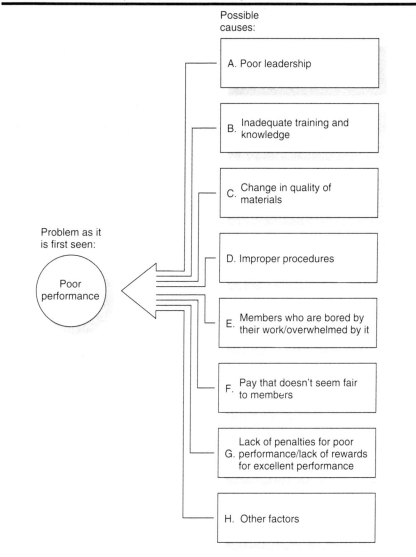

Possible causes:

A. Poor leadership

B. Inadequate training and knowledge

C. Change in quality of materials

D. Improper procedures

E. Members who are bored by their work/overwhelmed by it

F. Pay that doesn't seem fair to members

G. Lack of penalties for poor performance/lack of rewards for excellent performance

H. Other factors

Problem as it is first seen:

Poor performance

technology to devise an entirely new kind of measuring gauge. One year and several hundred thousand dollars later, a new gauge was perfected, to everyone's delight. The new gauge was installed but, unfortunately, within another year the manufacturing company went broke, because such an extremely high proportion of the tubing produced had to be scrapped.

Although with the new gauge they were immediately aware of quality problems, the *real* problem was that the extruding machines were inadequately designed. The scrap problem was not primarily one of measurement but one of *faulty production* in the first place due to poor equipment design! An improper problem definition led to an elegant but not very relevant decision.

As a manager you will have to learn to see many, often interconnected, causes for behavior. Let's say you encounter a work group that is not performing well. How will you decide ways to improve its performance? More important than the "perfect, latest and greatest technique," which may not fit the particular problem, will be to trace backward from the problem to find its overlapping and reinforcing causes (see Figure 1–1). Behind any important problem is a tangled web of forces that together form a fabric of causes. In the case of the poorly performing work group, some of the causes might be a combination of *(a)* poor leadership, *(b)* inadequate training and knowledge, *(c)* a change in quality of materials, *(d)* improper procedures, *(e)* members who are bored by their work or overwhelmed by it, *(f)* pay that doesn't seem fair to members, or *(g)* lack of penalties for poor performance or lack of rewards for excellent performance, or both.

Though the problem may stand out clearly, its components will require careful analysis. If all the causes aren't identified, it will be easy to overfocus on one cause, make the same kind of mistake as the consulting firm, and "go down the tubes." *In analyzing cases in this course or in actual organizational problems, beware of the temptation to oversimplify your explanations.*

Uncertainty

Another problem facing managers is that they must make decisions under uncertain conditions, often before all the desired data are in. Quite often there is insufficient time for thorough study, or the roots of the problem are not accessible to the person who must decide. For example, employees are often afraid to tell *any* boss all they know, especially if what they say might include criticism of the boss. And even if they were to be completely open, they might not fully know their own motivations or other necessary information. Finally, the conditions at the time of the decision can change by the time it is implemented, so that what looks sensible at one time may seem foolish later. When energy planners decided to create a large underground oil reserve for the United States in the Utah salt domes, they had no reason to expect it would be needed before 1980. Therefore, they delayed installation of pumps to get the oil out in order to save taxpayers' money. They could not foresee that in early 1979 the Shah of Iran would be forced to leave Iran, Iranian production would stop completely for several months, and that they would look foolish with millions of barrels of oil stored underground and no way to pump it on short notice. Because it takes over three years to design, build, and market a new car, numerous automobile manufacturers have built gas-guzzlers when consumers wanted economy, or produced compact cars when family-size was preferred.

I can live with doubt and uncertainty. I think it's much more interesting to live not knowing than to have answers which might be wrong.

Professor Richard Feynmann
The Economist
December 26, 1981

Living with Consequences of Decisions

Managers must also live with the consequences of their decisions. They do not have the luxury of leisurely tinkering with something inside a sealed vacuum flask and being able to put aside the experiment when it is not going well. As suggested earlier, even deciding to do nothing is a decision that can affect a manager deeply, since that will not stop a chain of consequences from following, including changed perceptions of him or her by subordinates, colleagues, and boss.

Because the manager lives in a complex world of multiple causes and effects, makes decisions under time pressure and uncertainty, and must live with the consequences of decisions made under imperfect conditions, a specific ability is needed. It is the knack of thinking in terms of probable outcomes, rather than certain ones, of figuring and playing the odds. Anything managers can do to predict likely outcomes more accurately, to increase the possibility of correct action, even when they cannot be *sure* about what will happen, is a great asset. If even "no decision" is a decision, the ability to take risks when outcomes are not certain becomes an important managerial attribute.

The pressures of managerial work lead to a relatively high degree of stress for managers as they struggle to cope with all the demands placed upon them. For some, the stress leads to physical or psychological problems. Yet successful managers are apparently people who thrive on the challenges inherent in their work; they consistently report in polls a greater degree of job satisfaction than, for example, hourly workers, who have less control, responsibility, and challenge in their work. In studying organizational behavior, you will have the chance to practice being a managerial decision maker and also to see whether you enjoy being in the hot seat that managers sit in.

You may be placed in a position of having to act and live through the consequences of each action or decision. For example, you may be asked to participate in group projects; if you decide not to say anything to the members of your group who shirk their responsibilities for fear of hurting their feelings, you will be one of those who will live with the outcome. And conversely, should you decide to confront them you would have another set of consequences to cope with. Which way you choose to handle such a dilemma and which consequences you are willing to accept depend upon your *own* personal values; no one else can tell you what is worth living with. Even in a class discussion or case analysis, you must decide whether or not to express your views and must live with the consequences (both good and bad) of the choice you make: for learning, clarifying your ideas, gaining credit for contributing to class discussion, or for your relationships and reputation with other students.

When you analyze cases, try to think of the people in them as being, like you, real individuals struggling to do the best they can in accordance with their values. The more you can project yourself into their positions, imagine yourself to be in their shoes, the better you will understand why things are happening—and the more interesting the cases will be.

Through this continual process of being placed in organizational situations where you must make decisions about how to behave and then see what happens, your skills and organizational effectiveness should be improved. Most often you will find that there is no *one* correct answer to the dilemmas or situations you face. Since one person's meat can be another's poison, the correct solution will be quite different depending upon the values of the decider.

Almost any course of action, as a manager or in daily life, will entail costs as well as benefits. In assessing alternative courses of action, the effective manager does not expect to find a choice with no costs, but seeks the choice that on balance involves the least net cost or the maximum net benefit. By identifying in advance all the likely costs, the effective decision maker can also identify steps to minimize the costs that become a reality. **There is no one best way to manage. What is best depends upon the situation and the values of the decision maker.**

The rest of the course should give you ample opportunities for practicing. The text, cases, exercises, and your instructor will try to help you clarify your own values and make better estimates of how well they will be served by what you do in a variety of human situations. While we would hardly claim that practice makes perfect, it should increase the probabilities of your being able to make sensible decisions that get you what you want and enhance your ability to learn from experience.

BASIC PREMISE: LEARNING TO LEARN ABOUT ORGANIZATIONS, EVERYWHERE

Even if you have not yet worked in a complex company you have a considerable amount of relevant experience on which to draw. Much of what you can learn about organizational behavior is quite accessible; it goes on around you all the time. You are a member of a family; may live with other people; belong to some clubs, teams, or committees; have a job involving others; eat and shop where people work; and so on. The university itself is a large organization containing many smaller organizations: the fraternity or sorority, academic departments, business and other administrative offices. Even the classroom is an organization. You are in a position to see many of the main ingredients of organizational life in your everyday contacts. All these groupings have implicit, if not explicit, goals, structures, and policies. These, in turn, seek to direct behavior in certain ways. They shape people's interactions with each other, and they are potentially a major source of an individual's productivity, satisfactions, and personal learning or development. In short, you have immediately at hand ready-made opportunities to study organizational behavior. This book will help you learn to look at an understand more of your living and working experiences, as well as prepare you for your career.

Throughout this book you will be asked to analyze your own behavior—at work, in the classroom, and in your interactions with others. Analogies will be drawn with other organizational settings, through either student experience or the use of case studies. Theories and concepts will be introduced as tools for helping you make sense out of your observations and experiences. The objectives of this book and the course for which it is designed are aimed at enhancing your ability to learn from experience, to test what you learn against new experience, and to extract new learning in a continuing fashion. In that way the organizational challenges of the 1990s and on into the 21st Century will be approachable.

Experience is a school where a man learns what a big fool he has been.
Josh Billings
1818–1885

CENTRAL THEME: LEARNING THROUGH DOING AND REFLECTING— THE MANAGER AS INVOLVED ACTOR

A central theme throughout the book is the idea of "learning through doing and reflecting." In order to learn how to *behave* effectively, rather than just *understand* behavior, it is necessary to be active and engaged, as well as reflective and thoughtful. This calls for a different educational model from what you may be used to. Most college classrooms are not organized to give practice in action and conceptualizing skills, but, rather, to enhance acquisition and understanding of material that may not have immediate direct application. In such classes the professor does most of the talking and grading; students listen, individually write notes and papers, take exams, answer some questions, and address most of their comments to the professor. But just as in a biology lab, where you have to *practice* dissecting a frog to learn the relevant skills, in a course designed to improve your organizational *effectiveness* a more active student role is necessary.

This means that you still need to master ideas, theories, and concepts; but then you practice using them in complex, unique situations, step back and observe how well you achieved your intentions, think about how to modify your ideas or your behavior, or both, then try again in new situations. Therefore, in a course in organizational behavior the classroom needs to become a kind of learning laboratory in which you, the student, have the opportunity to test out, practice, try, experiment with, and utilize the variety of concepts and ideas that are the subject matter of the book. It means that as you proceed you look for connections between what you are learning and your own behavior, as well as the behavior of individuals around you. Differences in class size and duration may limit the opportunity for such experimental learning during regular class hours. Nonetheless, when taking part in any organized activity, you can make observations and apply your conclusions to those relationships important to you in the classroom and outside. (See the learning-model questionnaire at the end of Chapter 1 to diagnose your own preferred style of learning.)

Part of what makes this course exciting—and occasionally frustrating—is that students, like managers, are highly *involved actors,* an integral component of the situations they are trying to understand and manage or change. It is like trying to run and tie your shoe at the same time. Managers cannot call time-out or say "pay no attention to me while I watch and decide what is going on"; their presence and the way people feel about bosses means that even no action or no decision has a powerful impact.

Suppose, for example, that two students in a class begin to argue over a point. No matter what the instructor says, including saying nothing, there will be an effect on the class members. The class members' reactions will depend in part on whether they perceive the instructor as approving or disapproving the open conflict between students, on which side they think the instructor believes is correct, on how well the instructor appears to handle the disagreement, and so forth. In organizations the same kinds of issues affect managers. They have nowhere to hide, and indeed they are quite often part of any problem. A manager's behavior is an inherent part of the problem, no matter how "innocent" the manager feels!

It is an inherent property of intelligence that it can jump out of the task which it is performing, and survey what it has done; it is always looking for, and often finding, patterns.

Douglas R. Hofstadter, *Gödel, Escher, Bach:*
An Eternal Golden Braid

In this course your actions, your classmates' actions, and the instructor's actions are all likely to be factors in any problem that may arise.

One dilemma you will certainly face is the struggle to remain appropriately detached or objective while you are personally involved in the learning experience. Sociologists call this role *participant-observer*; it poses a dilemma, because of the natural tendency of people to become *less* detached or objective as they become more involved in a given situation. The fine line is difficult to maintain: *Too much detachment can minimize one's appreciation and understanding of another person or a set of interactions, but too much involvement can bias (even distort) one's perspective.*

The field cannot well be seen from within the field.

Ralph Waldo Emerson

The learning process you will use—alternating between experience and conceptualization—will also provide plenty of practice in struggling with this dilemma. You will have to maintain openness to learning and a scientific attitude toward situations, some of which you are part of. What we mean by a *scientific attitude* in this respect is the process of *(a)* sorting out what is going on in one's relationships, *(b)* increasing the ability to predict likely outcomes of one's own and others' behaviors, and *(c)* thereby making more informed choices, which can *(d)* be checked for results against expectations. *It is the act of comparing the intent of any one of our actions with the effect of that action, and then learning from it.* Such an attitude requires that you constantly question, examine, and evaluate the consequences of your actions so that you learn from both your failures and your successes.

Nothing is more terrible than action without insight.

Thomas Carlyle

A word of caution is in order. Although careful and rigorous analysis is important for managers, reasoning is not a substitute for intuition. Recent research on how even scientists work has revealed the important part hunches, guesses, and wild leaps of intuition play in forming theory. Managers also require the use of this less-analytical capacity. Because most problems do not come in neat, orderly pieces, managers need to be tuned into what their instincts signal them as much as to formal deductive reasoning. Overdoing it in either direction, however, can lead to disaster.

Seat-of-the-pants decisions can be brilliant—or merely a reflection of the manager's prejudices and blind spots. Rigorous analysis can prevent stupid mistakes or freeze the manager into analysis paralysis. In their study of America's most successful companies, Peters and Waterman (1982) found repeated examples of managers and companies that analyzed things to death and thereby missed opportunities to quickly try things out and learn from experience. Mintzberg (1976) summarized research on the human brain and argued that some managerial functions, such as planning, required use of the left half of the brain (which controls logical, abstract reasoning) while the more people-oriented parts of managing require the more wholistic, intuitive right brain. In general, as a manager you will have to use all of your capacities to sort out what is going on and to formulate sensible action plans.

There is absolutely no inevitability as long as there is a willingness to contemplate what is happening.

Marshall McLuhan

The complexities involved can be demonstrated by an example. Suppose you were asked to make recommendations about a strange new sport, the rules for which you did not know. Can you imagine, for example, what the first tennis match you ever saw might be like? Some people dressed in abbreviated white costumes dash around hacking at a fuzzy sphere with a lollipop-shaped stick, shouting about "love!" Yet sometimes when the sphere comes near them, they step aside and do not wave their sticks but appear to stare intently at some white lines on the ground. The participants stop and start quite suddenly, changing positions, throwing the sphere in the air and batting at it, crouching carefully, or running rapidly toward the long, webbed object hanging between the participants. Before you could ever offer sensible advice, you would have to *watch* carefully for any *patterns* to the game, *deduce the rules* (How long would it take you to figure out the scoring rules, that "love" meant no points, a certain number of points make a "set," and so forth?), *test your assumptions* about how the game works *by predicting what will happen next* ("The first hitter aims for the opposite forecourt, so if I am correct about service rules, the second try must hit in that area or a point will be lost."), and slowly begin to *see the order in the apparent chaos*.

As you become increasingly sophisticated, you could begin to draw conclusions about the internal workings and strategy of the game, making connections between when to rush the net, when to lob over an opponent's head, and so forth. Whether you systematically dissected the components of each stroke and its relation to the opponent's weaknesses or just observed until

MANAGERIAL BULLETIN

British on NFL

The Minnesota Vikings and St. Louis Cardinals played the first NFL football game on British soil last night. . . .

All eyes were on the British contingent in the crowd to see if they liked the game. . . .

"All those people out there with big shoulders just running into each other and hiding the ball under them while they run," said Bernard Lockhurst, traffic coordinator at the game. "The clock stops, they huddle, shout out numbers, clap hands, and then they start hitting each other all over again. I mean, is that all football is about?"

SOURCE: United Press International, *Boston Globe*, August 7, 1983.

you had some hunches about what was likely to be effective, you would have to operate as a kind of scientist or detective—gathering data, asking questions of it, forming tentative conclusions based on apparent patterns, testing those by more observation, and so on. In that way you would establish an order to the buzzing confusion you first experienced.

I'm not smart. I try to observe. Millions saw the apple fall, but Newton was the one who asked why.

Bernard Baruch

Trying to make sense out of an organization can be equally confusing and even more challenging, since you are at the same time a part of what you are observing, affecting it and affected by it. People at work don't often hold still for examination by impartial, detached observers, and they seldom behave by such explicit, preagreed rules as tennis players do.

Whatever may be the context of your role in an organization now or in the future, you will need the skills of searching for patterns and connections, making predictions, testing out the consequences of an action or decision that you make, collecting information as to success, and modifying your actions accordingly. You will need to adopt and maintain an attitude of tentativeness—that is, a readiness to change your mind, to modify your views, to change your theory, to acknowledge your mistakes, and to take corrective action. Have you ever had or seen a boss who is so concerned about being right and so closed to feedback that he or she makes inappropriate decisions, saying in effect, "Don't confuse me with the facts"? Such a person is not open enough to learning to be a good manager.

MANAGERIAL BULLETIN

Charge to Graduating Seniors, 1983

The real world is not arranged for my convenience
or yours. It is rarely arranged for my knowledge or
yours. It is indeed rarely arranged.   SOURCE: G. Armour, Craig, acting president, *Amherst College.*

Propositions

As you progress through the book, examining and learning from your observations and experiences, you can build your own managerial model in the form of hypotheses and concepts—what we call *propositions*—that will help to guide your actions. An example of a **proposition** is the authors' belief that: **Experiencing and analyzing behavior is likely to produce more learning of organizational skills than merely reading or hearing about it.** A proposition can be tested and modified if necessary, then applied to other situations. The process of making propositions will aid in your development as a more effective manager and as a more competent individual. You have a chance to develop a way of looking at people in organizations that goes beyond any specific information you acquire; managers who have internalized a way of learning from experience should be able to continue learning in the changing situations facing them at work.

Throughout the book, we have used the propositional format as a way of highlighting major concepts. These propositions serve to integrate various findings from the research and experience of organizational experts. Wherever possible and useful we have identified at the end of a proposition some source in the literature keyed to selected readings at the end of each chapter, where an interested reader might find more information related to the area covered by the proposition.

In many instances the propositions were derived by the authors from their own experience and knowledge in the field. Specific sources for the propositions could not be provided in such instances, but we did include references to closely related literature for students interested in pursuing a given topic.

In summary, then, this book is concerned with the preparation of students who plan to become either managers of people or effective organizational members and who will leave a course that uses it possessing skills in the following areas: (1) identifying problems, (2) understanding their origins, (3) predicting their consequences, (4) considering gains and losses of those consequences for the short and long run, (5) possessing the willingness and capacity to choose well from among alternatives, and (6) extracting useful learning from experiences in which they are also part of the action and have an investment in the outcome. In short, this book seeks to cultivate the rare qualities of insight, analysis, and judgment. Its emphasis is on knowledge utilization, the marriage of theory to practice, and the development of managerial skills, and not just on the acquisition of knowledge for its own sake.

LEARNING STYLES

A course that demands active participation and application of concepts to actual complex situations can create some difficulties. We have already noted our assumptions about the interplay of experience and conceptualization, moving back and forth among doing, formulating conclusions, and testing them on new situations. We believe that such a process most closely replicates the process that managers (and other organizational members) go through at work.

Some individuals are not accustomed to learning in such active experimenting and conceptualizing modes. They are more used to passive learning, in which they are most distant from the phenomena being studied. While that mode of learning is valid for mastering some subject matter, it is less appropriate for studying organizational behavior, especially where there is an emphasis on developing managerial skills.

Furthermore, since the work of managers is so fundamentally intertwined with other people, it is desirable to add some collaborative modes of learning to the individual competitive modes more common in other kinds of courses. Learning from and with others is an important part of mastering skills needed for working effectively in organizations. One need not abandon the desire to do well in comparison to others in order to practice mutual teaching and learning. Your classmates will have sufficient diversity of experiences, skill, opinions, attitudes, and values to insure that someone in the course or task groups will have a different way of seeing the issues raised by the cases and concepts. Indeed, you may be shocked to find that no matter how well you prepare a case and how certain you are of your views, class discussion will reveal many angles you never thought of, along with viewpoints with which you profoundly disagree—held by students equally prepared and certain of their correctness! Learning to bend and reconsider when there is something new, yet be convincing and persuasive when you can help others gain perspective, is difficult to master.

What complicates issues of differences in learning style is the fact that individuals are at different stages in terms of their basic views of the world. Researchers have identified stages of development that individuals pass through or get stuck at, depending on their capacity to learn from making choices and experiencing new circumstances. The stage at which an individual is makes a great deal of difference in how that person approaches education and new learning (Weathersby, 1981) as well as how he or she thinks about other organizational issues, such as power, authority, work, goals, and interpersonal relationships. People at different stages tend to respond somewhat differently to leadership opportunities, and they often make different decisions about priorities based on how they understand the world (see Figure 1–2). Sometimes communication problems are the result of people genuinely trying to talk to each other from different stages. You may find it helpful to locate yourself and others you know on the chart in Figure 1–2 and also to use it to set some goals for your own learning and development.

Try to keep in mind that there is nothing inherently good or bad in any of these stages; they simply identify important issues with which we all struggle as we learn and grow. Furthermore, the issues represented at any given stage may actually be lifelong—that is, they never really disappear and in some way may always influence your perception of a given situation.

As you approach and move through this course it could be valuable for you to examine your own learning style; how the stage you are at (as best as you can assess it) affects your perceptions of the course, the instructor, and other students (especially those who are at a different stage); and, most important, your way of learning the material presented. Remember, your future skills as a manager might depend in part on your ability to understand and appreciate the differences among your employees and how these will affect their perceptions of you and how you manage.

All of this means that some students may find the book and course for which it is intended rather disconcerting at first. However, we do hold to the belief that as potential managers it is ultimately necessary to be able to use all modes of learning—active, passive, cognitive, affective, collaborative, competitive, concrete, and abstract—and that the modes inherent in using cases and treating the classroom as an organization often need reinforcement. Therefore, practicing them in and out of class even when they feel awkward is a worthwhile way of expanding your ability to learn in situations that call for active participation.

We are apt to think that our ideas are the creation of our own wisdom, but the truth is that they are the result of experiences through outside contact.

Without studying or being taught by others, we cannot formulate even a single idea. Therefore it can be said that a person who can create ideas worthy of note is a person who learned much from others.

If we are willing to learn, everything in this world can be our teacher.

With sincerity we hope to absorb wisdom from all people and all things. It is from this attitude that fresh and brilliant ideas are created. The sincere willingness to learn is the first step toward "Prosperity."

Konosuke Matsushita

▓ FIGURE 1–2   Educational Attitudes and Life Stages (Development over Time)

LIFE STAGE	EDUCATIONAL ATTITUDES
Opportunistic: Self-protective; competitive with, and ready to blame others; likely to think in only vague general terms or either/or concepts; breaks rules for personal gain; modest self-understanding.	College is a thing you do after high school; it's a drag but important. Professors are the people in charge of a course who show you what to do and keep you on track. Grades are what count; you work for the grade more than for "learning."
Socially oriented: Concerned with belonging and acceptance; typically friendly and nice toward others (except outsiders); often relies on stereotypes and clichés; concerned about rules and with what one "should" do.	College is where you get the education that helps you get a better job and prepares you for the future. Professors are the experts who provide the facts and the answers. They tell you whether or not you understand the material. Grades are important as a means to a good job and are the reward for hard work and ability.
Goal oriented: Achievement oriented, has long-term goals; focused toward mutual responsibilities in relationships; increased conceptual complexity; has self-evaluated standards; greater understanding of self and others.	The point of college is for you to grow as a person, developing your potentials, skills, and awareness for a more meaningful life. Professors' knowledge, competence, and standards of excellence give them authority. They can help one learn by exchanging ideas and modeling their way of studying issues. Grades are important to show if one has mastered the standards in a course. They don't always represent the amount one learns. In some courses I gain a lot even though I don't get a good grade.
Self-defining and relativistic: Concerned with individuality and self-fulfillment, yet also justice and humanity; desires autonomy in relationships yet is tolerant of others; thinks complexly, seeing issues from multiple points of view; lives with conflicts in personal obligations, needs, and roles while striving to resolve them.	College is a major step in a process of emotional and intellectual development that will continue throughout life. Professors are an important resource that students can draw on as makes sense. In the end, though, I'm the one who is really responsible for my learning. Grades are a measure of performance in the classroom. Their primary importance lies in giving information about how one is doing in the professor's eyes, which is only part of the story.

Table developed by Rita P. Weathersby, adapted from the work of Jane Loevinger and Rita Weathersby.

LEARNING ISSUES IN THIS COURSE

Some of the learning issues in this course are listed below. Understanding that others have encountered similar feelings may make it easier to deal with any awkwardness. For each issue we offer a possible solution; these might stimulate other options.

1. Finding it uncomfortable to speak, particularly in the full class, but also in small groups, because others appear more knowledgeable.

   Try viewing the course as an opportunity to experiment with bold behavior. There's not a lot to lose, and you'll help others who feel equally certain they are the only ones who do not know.

2. Finding others saying what you were about to say before you have had a chance to speak and, therefore, usually being silent.

   Try saying, "I'm going to reiterate what Irene said, namely; '. . .'" You'll probably find that you have added something and helped others reconsider the idea in new ways.

3. Finding it easy to learn a lot from listening and, therefore, being content to just listen.

Listening is an important skill. Try expanding on what you hear or try summarizing the thrust of the discussion.

4. Finding case discussions frustrating, because they seldom seem to arrive at a "right answer," and every alternative seems as good as another.

   Since most situations, in fact, can be handled in several ways, focus on finding an alternative that feels best to you, one that you could get behind and support.

5. Finding that an emphasis on a careful definition of the concepts and terms makes the course seem like "just a matter of semantics."

   While clearly defined concepts and terms can increase precision in expression, we suggest you practice restating concepts in your own words, so the ideas become "yours."

6. Finding that you disagree with a concept or that it is not valid in a particular situation you have experienced.

   Great! Concepts should be questioned. Share your thoughts with others and plan to utilize the concept where it does apply, or restate the concept so its limitations are clearer.

At the end of this chapter is the first of the Personal Application Exercises included to help you personalize and consolidate your mastery of the book's concepts. It is a self-scoring instrument that measures a person's learning style. Complete it, score it, and use the interpretation guide to understand and assess your own style of learning. That can help you determine what kinds of learning activities you might want to explore in this course and elsewhere. (Your instructor has additional information on this instrument if you want or need it.) We have also included a variety of ideas, set off in boxes called *Managerial Tools,* that can help you be more effective.

The learning process we are suggesting that you use in this course can serve you throughout life. The cases and exercises are all designed to put you in the position of a manager or organizational member who has to decide what is going on, what the situation calls for, what alternatives exist for resolving the problem(s) or dilemma(s) faced, and ultimately what consequences your values will permit you to accept. In the book, as in life, we do not expect easy solutions to present themselves very often; the chance to practice sorting out complexities and making informed choices can nevertheless be enjoyable if you plunge wholeheartedly into doing it.

The mind is a fire to be kindled, not a vessel to be filled.

Plutarch

KEY CONCEPTS FROM CHAPTER I

1. We live in a constantly changing world.
2. Basic premise: Much of what you can learn about organizational behavior goes on around you all the time.
3. The scientific attitude is the act of comparing the intent of actions with their effects and then learning from the process.
4. The manager, by virtue of position, has relationships that are necessary to acquire information in order to make decisions.
5. Managing requires:
   a. Awareness of multiple causality.
   b. Decisions under uncertainty.
   c. Living with consequences of decisions.
6. Central theme:
   a. Learning through doing and reflecting.
   b. The manager as involved actor.
7. Learning styles: The desirability of active, collaborative learning.

PERSONAL APPLICATION EXERCISE

The Learning-Model Instrument

Kenneth L. Murrell

Instructions: For each statement choose the response that is more nearly true for you. Place an X on the blank that corresponds to that response.

1. When meeting people, I prefer

   _____ (a) to think and speculate on what they are like.

   _____ (b) to interact directly and to ask them questions.

2. When presented with a problem, I prefer

_____ (a) to jump right in and work on a solution.

_____ (b) to think through and evaluate possible ways to solve the problem.

3. I enjoy sports more when

_____ (a) I am watching a good game.

_____ (b) I am actively participating.

4. Before taking a vacation, I prefer

_____ (a) to rush at the last minute and give little thought beforehand to what I will do while on vacation.

_____ (b) to plan early and daydream about how I will spend my vacation.

5. When enrolled in courses, I prefer

_____ (a) to plan how to do my homework before actually attacking the assignment.

_____ (b) to immediately become involved in doing the assignment.

6. When I receive information that requires action, I prefer

_____ (a) to take action immediately.

_____ (b) to organize the information and determine what type of action would be most appropriate.

7. When presented with a number of alternatives for action, I prefer

_____ (a) to determine how the alternatives relate to one another and analyze the consequences of each.

_____ (b) to select the one that looks best and implement it.

8. When I awake every morning, I prefer

_____ (a) to expect to accomplish some worthwhile work without considering what the individual tasks may entail.

_____ (b) to plan a schedule for the tasks I expect to do that day.

9. After a full day's work, I prefer

_____ (a) to reflect back on what I accomplished and think of how to make time the next day for unfinished tasks.

_____ (b) to relax with some type of recreation and not think about my job.

10. After choosing the above responses, I

_____ (a) prefer to continue and complete this instrument.

_____ (b) am curious about how my responses will be interpreted and would prefer some feedback before continuing with the instrument.

11. When I learn something, I am usually

_____ (a) thinking about it.

_____ (b) right in the middle of doing it.

12. I learn best when

_____ (a) I am dealing with real-world issues.

_____ (b) concepts are clear and well organized.

13. In order to retain something I have learned, I must

_____ (a) periodically review it in my mind.

_____ (b) practice it or try to use the information.

14. In teaching others how to do something, I first

_____ (a) demonstrate the task.

_____ (b) explain the task.

15. My favorite way to learn to do something is

_____ (a) reading a book or instructions or enrolling in a class.

_____ (b) trying to do it and learning from my mistakes.

16. When I become emotionally involved with something, I usually

_____ (a) let my feelings take the lead and then decide what to do.

_____ (b) control my feelings and try to analyze the situation.

17. If I were meeting jointly with several experts on a subject, I would prefer

_____ (a) to ask each of them for his or her opinion.

_____. (b) to interact with them and share our ideas and feelings.

18. When I am asked to relate information to a group of people, I prefer

_____ (a) not to have an outline, but to interact with them and become involved in an extemporaneous conversation.

_____ (b) to prepare notes and know exactly what I am going to say.

19. Experience is

　　———— *(a)*　a guide for building theories.

　　———— *(b)*　the best teacher.

20. People learn easier when they are

　　———— *(a)*　doing work on the job.

　　———— *(b)*　in a class taught by an expert.

The Learning-Model Instrument Scoring Sheet

Instructions: Transfer your responses by writing either "*a*" or "*b*" in the blank that corresponds to each item in the Learning Model Instrument.

	Abstract/Concrete		Cognitive/Affective	
	Column 1	Column 2	Column 3	Column 4
	1. ————	2. ————	11. ————	12. ————
	3. ————	4. ————	13. ————	14. ————
	5. ————	6. ————	15. ————	16. ————
	7. ————	8. ————	17. ————	18. ————
	9. ————	10. ————	19. ————	20. ————
Total circles	————	————	————	————
Grand Totals	————————————		————————————	

Now circle every "*a*" in Column 1 and in Column 4. Then circle every "*b*" in Column 2 and in Column 3. Next, total the circles in each of the four columns. Then add the totals of Columns 1 and 2; plot this grand total on the vertical axis of the Learning Model for Managers (see below) and draw a horizontal line through the point. Now add the totals of Columns 3 and 4; plot that grand total on the horizontal axis of the model and draw a vertical line through the point. The intersection of these two lines indicates the domain of your preferred learning style.

Interpreting the Learning-Model Instrument

The cognitive-affective axis or continuum represents the range of ways in which people learn. Cognitive learning includes learning that is structured around either rote storing of knowledge or intellectual abilities and skills, or

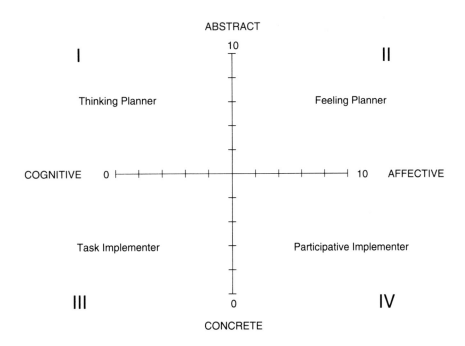

The Learning Model for Managers

both. Affective learning includes learning from experience, from feelings about the experience, and from one's own emotions.

The concrete-abstract axis or continuum represents the range of ways in which people experience life. When people experience life abstractly, they detach themselves from the immediacy of the situation and theorize about it. If they experience life concretely, they respond to the situation directly with little subsequent contemplation.

The two axes divide the model into four parts or domains. Most people experience life and learn from it in all four domains but have a preference for a particular domain. Liberal arts education has typically concentrated on abstract learning (domains I and II), whereas vocational and on-the-job training usually takes place in the lower quadrants, particularly domain III.

Occupations representative of the four styles include the following: domain I, philosopher or chief executive officer; domain II, poet or journalist; domain III, architect or engineer; domain IV, psychologist or personnel counselor.

Managerial jobs require an ability to learn in all four domains, and a manager's development depends on his or her ability to learn both cognitively and affectively. Thus, management education and development demand the opportunity for the participants to learn how to learn in each domain.

SUGGESTED READINGS

Adler, N. J. "Women Do Not Want International Careers, and Other Myths about International Management." *Organizational Dynamics,* Autumn 1984, pp. 66–79.

Bennis, W. G. "Goals and Metagoals of Laboratory Training." *Human Relations Training News,* Fall 1962, National Training Laboratories, Washington, D.C., pp. 1–4.

Berelson, B., and G. Steiner. *Human Behavior: An Inventory of Scientific Findings.* New York: Harcourt Brace Jovanovich, 1964.

Carroll, S. J., and D. J. Gillen. "Are the Classical Management Functions Useful in Describing Managerial Work?" *Academy of Management Review* 12 (1987), pp. 38–51.

Chatman, J. A. "Improving Interactional Organizational Research: A Model of Person-Organization Fit." *Academy of Management Review* 14 (1989), pp. 333–49.

Cohen, A. R. "Beyond Simulation: The Classroom as Organization." *The Teaching of Organization Behavior Journal,* Spring and Summer 1976.

Cohen, A. R., and B. A. Stein. "Task Forces in Management: A Key Development Tool." *The NABW Journal,* November–December 1980.

Cooper, E. A., and G. V. Barrett. "Equal Pay and Gender: Implications of Court Cases for Personnel Practices." *Academy of Management Review,* January 1984, pp. 84–93.

DeFrank, R. S.; M. T. Matteson; D. M. Schweiger; and J. M. Ivancevich. "The Impact of Culture on the Management Practices of American and Japanese CEOs." *Organizational Dynamics,* Spring 1985, pp. 62–76.

Ferris, G. R., and J. A. Wagner III. "Quality Circles in the United States: A Conceptual Reevaluation," *Journal of Applied Behavioral Science* 21, no. 2 (1985), pp. 155–68.

Finkelstein, J., and D. A. H. Newman. "The Third Industrial Revolution: A Special Challenge to Managers." *Organizational Dynamics* 12 (1984), pp. 53–65.

French, J. L., and A. R. Rosenstein. "Employee Ownership, Work Attitudes, and Power Relationships." *Academy of Management Journal* 27 (1984), pp. 861–69.

Gilligan, C. *In a Different Voice: Psychological Theory and Women's Development.* Cambridge, Mass.: Harvard University Press, 1982.

Goldstein, S. G. "Organizational Dualism and Quality Circles." *Academy of Management Review,* July 1985, pp. 504–17.

Gorman, A. H. *Teachers and Learners: The Interactive Process of Education.* Boston: Allyn & Bacon, 1969.

Grasha, A. F. "Observations on Relating Teaching Goals to Student Response Styles and Classroom Methods." *American Psychologist* 27 (1972), pp. 144–47.

Greenhaus, J. H., and N. J. Beutell. "Sources of Conflict between Work and Family Roles." *Academy of Management Review* 10 (1985), pp. 76–88.

Jamieson, D. W., and K. W. Thomas. "Power and Conflict in the Student-Teacher Relationship." *Journal of Applied Behavioral Science* 10 (1974), pp. 321–36.

Kohlberg, L. "Stage and Sequence: The Cognitive Developmental Approach to Socialization." In *Handbook of Socialization Theory and Research,* ed. D. Goslin. Skokie, Ill.: Rand McNally, 1969.

Kolb, D. "Toward a Typology of Learning Styles and Learning Environments: An Investigation of the Impact of Learning Styles and Discipline Demands on the Academic Performance, Social Adaption, and Career Choices of M.I.T. Seniors," a Working Paper, No. 688-73. Cambridge: Massachusetts Institute of Technology, Sloan School of Management, 1973.

_____. *The Learning Style Inventory: Technical Manual.* Boston: McBer, 1976.

Loevinger, J. *Ego Development: Conceptions and Theories.* San Francisco: Jossey-Bass, 1976.

Louis, M. R. "Surprise and Sense Making: What Newcomers Experience in Entering Unfamiliar Organization Settings." *Administrative Science Quarterly* 25 (1980), pp. 226–51.

Meyer, G. W., and R. G. Stott. "Quality Circles: Panacea or Pandora's Box?" *Organizational Dynamics,* Spring 1985, pp. 34–50.

Mintzberg, H. *The Nature of Managerial Work.* New York: Harper & Row, 1973.

_____. "The Manager's Job: Folklore and Fact." *Harvard Business Review,* July–August 1975.

_____. "Planning on the Left Side and Managing on the Right." *Harvard Business Review,* July–August 1976.

McGregor, D. *The Professional Manager.* New York: McGraw-Hill, 1967.

Munchus, G., III. "Employer–Employee-Based Quality Circles in Japan: Human Resource Policy Implications for American Firms." *Academy of Management Review,* April 1983, pp. 225–61.

Nonaka, I., and J. K. Johansson. "Japanese Management: What about the 'Hard' Skills?" *Academy of Management Review,* April 1985, pp. 181–91.

Perry, W. G., Jr. "Cognitive and Ethical Growth: The Making of Meaning." In *The Modern American College,* ed. A. W. Chickering. San Francisco: Jossey-Bass, 1981.

Peters, T., and S. Waterman. *In Search of Excellence: Lessons from America's Best-Managed Corporations.* New York: Harper & Row, 1982.

Rogers, C. R. *Freedom to Learn.* Columbus, Ohio: Charles E. Merrill Publishing, 1969.

Shamir, B., and I. Salomon. "Work-At-Home and the Quality of Working Life." *Academy of Management Review,* July 1985, pp. 455–64.

Simon, H. A. *Administrative Behavior.* 2nd ed. New York: Macmillan, 1957.

_____. *The New Science of Management Decision.* New York: Harper & Row, 1960.

Torrence, W. D. "Blending East and West: With Difficulties along the Way." *Organizational Dynamics,* Autumn 1984, pp. 23–34.

Ueno, I.; R. R. Blake; and J. S. Mouton. "The Productivity Battle; A Behavioral Science Analysis of Japan and the United States." *Journal of Applied Behavioral Science* 20, no. 1 (1984), pp. 49–58.

Weathersby, R. P. "Ego Development." In *The Modern American College,* ed. A. W. Chickering. San Francisco: Jossey-Bass, 1981.

Improving the Two-Person Work Relationship

Processes and Outcomes

"A positive relationship leads to good outcomes for both task accomplishment and member satisfaction."

In Chapter 9 we looked at the background and required factors that affect interpersonal relationships. Now we turn to an examination of what emerges from the interplay of these factors. Any two individuals are likely to have appreciable latitude to establish a type of relationship that is to their liking, and to adopt an interpersonal style that fits their preferences. Nevertheless, much can happen in a relationship that can lead to misunderstanding, disagreement, and friction. Mark Buckley and Oliver Endrunn, who you met in Chapter 9, are intelligent, high-level executives who have to work together, yet they irritate each other. Thus, what emerges takes "working at," both to develop it in a positive direction and to maintain it once it has been developed.

In discussing steps individuals can take to build and maintain positive relationships, we need to look at several *interpersonal processes* that are crucial for any relationship, namely:

- Adaptation to what is required and to one another.
- Communication.
- Reciprocity.
- Trust and other feelings.
- Dealing with blind spots (need for feedback).

In the pages that follow we shall discuss each of these processes in some detail and indicate steps the individuals can take to foster a positive relationship.

As we do this, keep in mind what we mean by a positive relationship. A positive work relationship is, first, one in which the required task gets done properly and with reasonable efficiency. Second, the relationship must at the same time be reasonably satisfying to both parties and foster, or at least not hinder, individual growth and development. What constitutes satisfaction will depend on what is desired and also on what is expected in that the situation. For example, you may be quite satisfied by a polite but distant relationship if it were with the elevator operator in your building, but quite dissatisfied if it were with your direct supervisor. Satisfaction will also depend on the relationship enhancing, or at least not disconfirming, each member's self-concept. Finally, any continuing relationship will need ways to deal with the frictions that almost inevitably arise. A positive relationship leads to outcomes good for both task accomplishment and member satisfaction, on an ongoing basis.

ADAPTATION TO REQUIREMENTS AND TO EACH OTHER

When individuals first enter into a work relationship, there may be some discrepancy between what is required and what is expected or desired by one or both individuals. For example, Buckley wants autonomy and control, while Endrunn wants information and reassurance. To the extent that each party can diagnose the situation accurately and adapt to what is required and to what the other expects and desires, relationships will develop in a positive direction. In some cases, this may mean that one party must make all of the adaptation, as in the case of the plumber's helper discussed in Chapter 9. In most cases, both must adapt, such as when two engineers of equal experience are working on a joint design project. To blindly ignore the issue or refuse to adapt is to insure the emergence of a less than positive relationship. To adapt within the range of what is at least tolerable is the way to move in a positive direction. If, however, the degree of adaptation is so great as to violate either person's self-concept, then the participants will need to openly confront the issue and find a resolution or else try to leave the situation. Finally, throughout the life of a relationship there may be times when either individual will need to adapt his or her interpersonal style to fit a particular event. Thus adaptation is usually required early in a relationship, to build in a positive direction, and also to a lesser degree throughout its existence.

One factor that can make it difficult for individuals to adapt to one another is differences in how each structures the world around them. Consider the possible difficulties individuals at different places on the four dimensions of the Myers-Briggs model discussed in Chapter 8 might have:

Introversion—Extraversion

An individual at the extraversion end of the scale, who might instinctively make it a point to touch base with many others before acting, might be seen by someone at the introversion end of the scale as indecisive, overly political, or wasting time socializing. Conversely, the former might view the latter's tendency to go it alone and avoid opportunities to interact with others as a sign of aloofness and even snobbishness.

Sensing—Intuition

Similarly, the individual who always seeks facts before acting (sensing) may easily view someone who acts more on intuitive insight as "impulsive" and as acting on mere whim without "doing proper homework." The latter, in turn, might view the former's care in getting all the facts before deciding as a case of worrying excessively about details and even as decision avoidance.

Thinking—Feeling

Thinkers are likely to see themselves as capable of making the hard decisions based on a logical analysis of a situation, and they see Feelers as tender-hearted, given to irrational judgments, and too easily swayed by emotions and compassion. By contrast, Feeling types will see themselves as sensitive, considerate and responsive to people's needs, and will see Thinking types as hardnosed, distant, and insensitive.

Judging—Perceiving

The differences here are especially interesting since they bear directly upon the problem-solving aspect of a manager's job. Perceivers see themselves as good at uncovering all the diverse implications of a problem, and they enjoy exploring these. They see Judgers as pushing too rapidly toward solutions and unwilling to spend the necessary amount of time really digging into a problem. The Judgers tend to get impatient with the Perceivers, seeing them as never able to arrive at a solution, always going off on tangents, or getting sidetracked. Judgers see themselves as decisive and capable of getting quickly to the heart of the matter and on with the business at hand.

Implications for Working Relationships

Awareness of the differences described above can be very helpful in understanding two-person work relationships. For one thing, the two people can learn to understand and even appreciate their differences. For another, it provides a way to look at *complementarity* in work relationships. Most situations call for a variety of managerial approaches, including the ability to use thoughts, feelings, intuition, judgment, and perceptions. Mutual adaptation can facilitate drawing on one another as sources of information.

COMMUNICATION

In any relationship, people must communicate; and such communication is always subject to distortion and misunderstanding. Even what may be a fairly simple and straightforward exchange of factual information in a minimal task relationship is subject to miscommunication. The likelihood of miscommunication becomes greater when the information being exchanged is more complex and emotionally charged. Misunderstanding can block the development of a relationship and create tension in an otherwise positive relationship. Unless the parties involved have the skill and the inclination to minimize miscommunication and to correct misunderstanding as it occurs, a positive relationship is not likely to develop or be maintained.

FIGURE 10–1   Four Levels of Exchange between Speaker and Listener

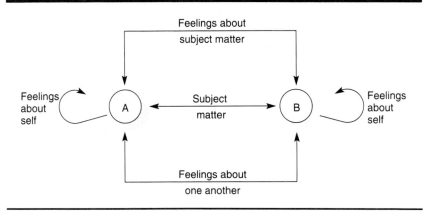

What happens when one person talks to another? The process is so complicated that it is a wonder that anyone ever understands and is understood. This section will include a description of the communication process and the factors that ease or hinder understanding.

Communication between people involves an exchange of (*a*) the content of what is being discussed, (*b*) feelings about the subject matter at hand, (*c*) feelings about the other person, and (*d*) feelings about self (see Figure 10–1).

The same exchange can be seen another way: what Speaker A says is modified by B's self-concept (which includes how B interprets A's self-concept). For example, A is B's boss. B has had many troubles in the past with people in authority—parents, teachers, bosses. He sees himself as having been misunderstood and unappreciated by them. A is in a hurry, doesn't know B's background, so calls over his shoulder on the way by, "Hey, lend a hand, will you?" B hears this as a criticism, reddens, and mutters to himself at the "attack" (see Figure 10–2).

This gets even more complicated as the self-concept of each alters the way messages are sent as compared to the actual feelings of the speaker. That is, A is feeling angry at B's apparent uncooperativeness and wants to reprimand B; but A sees himself as a kind person, so he tries to soften the blow through indirection. Instead of saying what he feels—"You infuriate me when you sit there doodling while I work hard"—he says, "Isn't it amazing how some people just can't cooperate with others?" B—who sees himself as an intelligent person, eager to be helpful when he gets an original idea, but sees A as typically aggressive and impatient—feels puzzled about where A's remarks concerning cooperation come from, misses the feeling, and replies to the content, "Well, it depends on the people involved, but I don't think

FIGURE 10–2   Other's Statements Are Modified by Receiver's Self-Concept

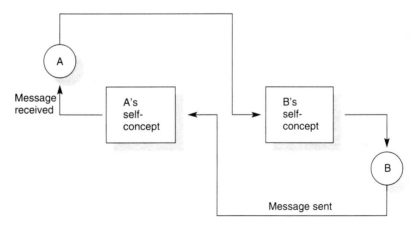

FIGURE 10–3   Self-Concepts and Perceptions of Other Filter Messages In and Out

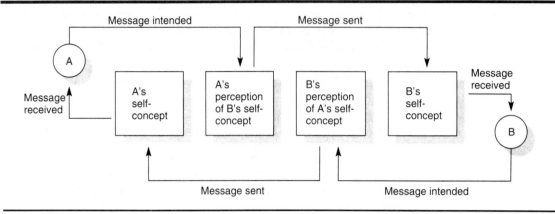

cooperation is so difficult." A starts to steam; B senses it but doesn't know why. The relationship begins to deteriorate (see Figure 10–3).

The potentials for difficulties are great. Let's take a closer look at the barriers to communication, above and beyond the perceptual ones already discussed in Chapter 7.

Barriers to Communication

Characteristics of Language

The very nature of language constitutes a barrier to communication. Many words are imprecise. The meaning of "level" to a carpenter is quite different than to a landscape contractor who is putting in a new lawn. How many is "a few?" Does "right away" mean drop the bucket with molten metal, or first pour it and then start the next job? In the sentence "Where do I begin?" is "where" a location or a procedure?

Many words have multiple meanings; miscommunication occurs when the two parties apply different interpretations. The purchasing agent who orders track spikes to repair the railroad siding may be surprised to receive a pair of running shoes. "Write," "right (correct)," "right (not left)," and "Wright" all sound the same, right? Sometimes words have different meanings to different subcultures of the country. Have you ever ordered a "milk shake" in Boston? To get ice cream in it as in other parts of the country, you must order a "frappe." Once you taste it, do you say "That's awesome" or "That's b-a-a-d" when you like it?

The fact that words are imprecise and have multiple meanings has become an ever greater threat to communication as society has become more interconnected and mobile. The possibility has increased of contact with someone of a different background or culture and, hence, a different way of using words. The fact that words are imprecise and have several meanings is also one reason why jargon develops. Jargon at its best is designed to avoid ambiguity, and, when used for this purpose, it can be helpful. On the other hand, "P. req." for purchase requisition, "M.I." for myocardial infarction (heart attack), or "social systems" for groups and organizations can be unintelligible to the outsider, even when efficient for the insider.

I'm willing to discuss it; I just don't want to talk about it.

Mr. Fairly Bear
a Shari Lewis Puppet

Finally, words have an emotional coloring that influences the communication process, because they trigger mental associations and emotional responses. Consider the following: "I want a large slab of slaughtered cow" versus "I would like the king-size cut of prime roast beef"; "let us hear the egghead's comments" versus "let us be informed by the expert intellectual." The words *slaughtered cow* conjure up many distasteful images that do not enhance people's appetites even though they may, in fact, be more precise than the term *prime roast beef*. Often the emotional color is communicated rather than the intended meaning.

Multiple Channels

Messages are transmitted by more than words; content and especially feelings are transmitted by gestures, voice intonations, facial expressions, body posture, and so forth. All these media (elements) for messages go into the same communications package. The package is clear when the messages sent are consistent with one another. This occurs when everything fits together; when the nonverbal enriches the verbal, when the "music" fits the words. When a facial expression or a gesture or a tone of voice doesn't seem to match the words, "static" is created. Have you seen someone get red in the face, pound the table, and declare, "What do you mean I'm angry?" That is giving off confusing messages; communication is incongruent. The words and music don't go together; it's like a love song sung to a march tempo. Since nonverbal messages tend to be ambiguous in meaning, thereby leaving room for interpretation by the other person, misunderstanding is likely. An embar-

MANAGERIAL TOOLS

Some Steps to Insure Effective Speaking, Listening, Understanding

If you want to communicate effectively, try some or all of the following:

Choosing Your Words

1. Talk in words that are likely to have meaning and clarity to the other person (e.g., "speak in the language of the listener").
2. Anticipate different ways your message could be interpreted, try to speak unambiguously, be alert to evidence that what you meant isn't what it meant to the other.
3. Allow yourself to be spontaneous and open. Express your feelings. Speak your mind, but consider talking *about* what you are feeling, instead of emoting, if the other person is likely to be put on the defensive by your expressiveness or is basically uncomfortable when faced with strong emotion.

Listening to Nonverbal Messages

1. Pay attention to tone of voice, facial expressions, body posture, hesitations, etc. What do they communicate in addition to the message in the words? (Listen to the music as well as the words.)
2. Pay attention to your own manner. Does your tone, pace, etc., fit your words and reflect your inner feeling?
3. If you sense something is bothering the other person besides what is being said directly, consider raising that to the surface by some such statement as:
   "Is _____ also at work here?" "Are you also concerned about _____?"
   "Is there something else beneath the surface here?"

Timing and Situation

1. Don't raise "heavy" issues when the other person is preoccupied or there isn't time to deal with them properly.
2. Consider the setting when you raise a topic for discussion. Is it too public? Will it be distracting? Will it cause misinterpretation (e.g., be seen as really unimportant or said for public consumption only)?
3. Ignore small points you may differ with and focus on the main theme. Don't digress to argue over minor errors or points of disagreement.
4. Deal with issues and tensions early. Try to handle problems while they are still small.

Testing for Understanding

1. Invite the other person to restate what you've said in his/her own words and test whether you've been clear.
2. Restate what the other said in your own words and thereby test that you have fully understood.

Preserving the Relationship

1. Don't hog the air time—give the other person an opportunity to be heard.
2. Be careful you aren't so busy preparing your response that you don't really pay full attention.
3. Don't interrupt.
4. Acknowledge that which is of worth in what someone is saying, even if you disagree with the basic message.
5. If the other person makes an especially good point, say so. Give positive feedback when you can do so sincerely.

rassed smile can easily be seen as implying agreement when it really means "I'm too embarrassed to say how ridiculous I think your idea is." Frowns of concentration may be seen as disapproval, and so forth. In Chapter 13 we discuss how communication across cultural boundaries can create serious misunderstandings.

The State of Mind of the Two People

When a person is feeling any strong emotions (anger, fear, defensiveness, and so forth), it is very difficult to *listen* to another person. *Both* parties are subject to perceptual distortions. What usually happens is that A's emotion triggers a similar emotion in B; then each has trouble listening to the other. For example, an aggressive-argumentative exchange often contains emotionally charged, defensive kinds of messages. Effective communication becomes blocked, the tensions increase, and the whole cycle escalates. Is this kind of pattern familiar to you? It is likely that everyone has faced similar problems and could benefit from learning how to change the quality of a communication process when it is blocked, defensive, and nonsupportive of the participants.

When possible differences in mental set, emotional state, channels used, words chosen, and so forth are added together, it becomes apparent how difficult it would be for the message sent to be the same as the message received. How many times have you argued about what was "really" said in a conversation? Each person *"knows* what I said" and each *"knows* what I heard," even though both are sure the other is wrong. Some degree of distortion seems inevitable in communication.

Gender Differences

Harry and Susan are driving through the downtown section of an unfamiliar city on their way to a party. It becomes obvious to Susan, after they seem to have driven in circles, that they are lost. She says, "Harry, why don't you stop and ask someone for directions?" Harry keeps driving. Susan says, "Didn't you hear me?" Harry says, "Yes, I heard you," and keeps driving around, obviously getting tense. Susan remains silent for awhile, her tension rising. The pattern repeats itself to the point where both are angry, Susan shuts up, and Harry stops listening anyway. Sound familiar? It turns out that such a pattern is not unusual and does reflect some basic differences in the way men and women tend to view and handle the same situation. Harry's need to prove that he doesn't need help and won't make himself dependent on someone else conflicts with Susan's comfort in asking for help, rather than wasting a lot of time driving in circles. The result of the differences between them is that they stop communicating, ending up feeling mutually isolated.

Since males and females are often treated differently from childhood, they tend to develop different perspectives and attitudes about life. These differences can distort communication between men and women and lead to misunderstandings. In casual conversations, it has been observed that men generally talk about impersonal topics like sports or the economy, whereas women more generally will discuss personal matters and their feelings. This can easily result in a tendency for members of the same sex to gravitate to each other and avoid attempting to hold conversations with the opposite sex. In a work setting, communication problems often occur because of this same difference; men see themselves as objective and women as too subjective, while women see themselves as direct and personally honest about their feelings, and men as cold, distant and competitive. Even though truly effective decision-making involves a blend of the so-called male and female mentalities, too often the result is a domination of one over the other, most often with the male viewpoint on top.

There are organizations where women have not been promoted beyond a certain level, in part because they were seen as not "strong" enough to handle the combative tough style that characterized the organization. While such differences are not always the case, and the situation may be improving in many organizations, be sensitive to the fact that gender differences exist and can be sources of rich interpersonal communication or barriers to it.

Some Common Problems of Commmunication

The following are some examples of common interpersonal communication problems.

Ambiguous Communications: The Mixed Message

This occurs when several channels are in operation at the same time and they are not completely in tune with each other. One channel may be sending a message that is different from or contradictory to another, making the message difficult to understand. To illustrate, the words are polite or even friendly, but the tone of voice is angry or hostile (as might be the case with sarcasm). Another example is when the words are a question, but the manner of expression is an assertion. Have you heard someone say, "Wouldn't it be a good idea to . . .?" when he or she really means, "You'd be a fool not to . . .?" Such ambiguous communication is likely to occur when a manager is trying to behave in a participative manner with subordinates but really wants to maintain absolute control over outcomes.

Incomplete Communication: The Throwaway Line

This occurs when enough of a message is sent to indicate the presence of an issue, but not enough to make clear what the issue really is or how serious it is. For example, in the middle of discussing one issue a reference is made to another problem, but it is offhand and passed over very quickly. It can be very disruptive:

> An executive had the habit of referring offhandedly to extraneous issues during important meetings, when the issues could not be discussed appropriately. On one occasion, when discussing union relations, he said to one of his managers, "Though I was pleased with the way you handled the shop steward, when he said the company is anti-union, I didn't like your interrupting me in the middle of my sentence in front of him; but never mind that now."

The target of the throwaway line was taken off guard and found it difficult to concentrate on the issue at hand; he worried about the implication of having displeased his boss.

This kind of communication tends to raise anxiety and leave the recipient in the unfortunate position of having to fill in the rest of the message with his or her own fantasies, which are often worse than the actual situation.

Nonverbal Signals: The Person's Emotional State

Watch a busy executive going about his or her business; note the speed of movement, facial expression, posture, and so forth. It doesn't take much to interpret rapid pace, furrowed brow, and thrust-out chin as, "I am harassed and under pressure; don't bother me with trivial matters." At times, such nonverbal behavior can become a part of a person's everyday style to the point of constantly appearing harassed even when not. If one is unaware of the unintended message, the reactions of others to it can be puzzling. In the example just given, the executive may wonder why people don't come around to talk over problems even when they would be welcome. Are you aware of the kinds of signals expressed in your nonverbal behavior? Does your characteristic body posture say "I like myself" or "I feel insignificant"? Does your facial expression usually suggest anger, fear, curiosity, or what? Do you sit in a way that says "don't approach me" or "I am receptive to new relationships and ideas?" This may be an area worth exploring with your fellow students or co-workers. Though you can sometimes guess at how you are seen by observing the way others react to you, asking for feedback is probably the best way to find out, though not always the most comfortable.

So don't listen to the words; just listen to what the voice tells you, what the movements tell you, what the posture tells you, what the image tells you.

F. S. Perls
Gestalt Theory Verbatim, p. 57

Nonverbal Signals: The Secret Society

While nonverbal communication goes on all the time, often two people develop "special" signals to each other, such as a knowing look, nod, or smile, a warning of threat, or a smile of support. These forms of communication can be very handy or convenient, and they also tend to confirm the solidarity of the relationship. However, they also may convey a sense of a "secret society" that walls off others. In some situations this type of communication is very important. For instance, in negotiation sessions it is important to know how others on your side feel about things as they happen without openly conferring. But even in these situations, it heightens feelings of exclusion and can have negative consequences, too.

It Takes Both People for Communication to Work

One person alone cannot establish effective communication; he or she has no means of checking out whether or not the intended message was the received one. Because of the probability that some distortion will take place, good communication requires an exchange of messages, a two-way process. For A to disclose something to B without knowing how it was received is only half the process. And the more important the disclosure is to A, the more vital it is for A to check out its reception.

   Think about the relationship between Buckley and Endrunn. If Buckley decided to tell Endrunn that he didn't want him to talk to Buckley's subordinates, what would Endrunn hear? Given his view of Buckley as political and closed, he might interpret it as a power grab, rather than a concern for the position in which this could put the subordinate. That could lead to a downward spiral in the relationship. Many exchanges, especially around work routines and the like, require a minimum amount of checking out; they are least subject to distortion. But even these communications can, if badly managed, lead to misunderstandings that may become more significant and require a great deal of clarifying. *An accumulation of little miscommunications often builds into a major source of conflict between two people.*

   We can summarize with the following working proposition: **The greater the (a) complexity of a subject, (b) importance of a subject to the parties involved, and (c) feelings aroused by the subject, the greater the possibilities for distortion, and, therefore, the greater the need for each to check with the other on what has been heard and said (Giffin & Patton, 1974).**

I only wish I could find an institute that teaches people how to listen. After all, a good manager needs to listen as much as he needs to talk . . . real communication goes in both directions.

Lee Iacocca
Iacocca: An Autobiography

This is not to suggest that every message you send to another person requires a response or acknowledgment from that person, and vice versa.

MANAGERIAL TOOLS

Guidelines for Active Listening

Objectives: To help others gain clear understanding of their situations, so they can take responsible action. To demonstrate your appreciation of meaning and feelings behind other's statements, of worth of other person, and of your willingness to listen without passing judgment.

Do	Don't
1. Create supportive atmosphere.	1. Try to change other's views.
2. Listen for feelings as well as words.	2. Solve problem for other.
3. Note cues—gestures, tone of voice, body positions, eye movements, breathing, and the like.	3. Give advice (no matter how obvious the solution is for you).
4. Occasionally test for understanding: "Is this what you meant?"	4. Pass judgment.
5. Demonstrate acceptance and understanding, verbally and nonverbally.	5. Explain or interpret other's behavior.
6. Ask exploratory, open-ended questions.	6. Give false reassurances.
	7. Attack back if the other is hostile to you—understand the source of the anger.
	8. Ask questions about "why" the feelings.

SOURCE: Cohen et al., *Effective Behavior in Organizations* (Homewood, Ill.: Richard D. Irwin, 1976). Based on Carl Rogers and Richard Farson, "Active Listening,"

Very often a simple nod of the head or observing the subsequent behavior of the other person is enough to complete the process. But: **As a task becomes more complex, as a relationship requires more avenues and frequency of communication, it calls for more attention to whatever processes insure accuracy of communication.** This principle becomes doubly important when there is some degree of tension in the situation. **The key to more effective listening is the willingness to listen and respond appropriately to the feelings being expressed as well as to the content (Rogers & Farson, 1976).** An acceptance of the existence of feelings and the legitimacy of the other person having them, even when you don't agree, usually eases the tension created when a person feels misunderstood or put down by the listener and also allows a focus on whatever is generating the original feelings.

You can probably understand by now why so many managers tend to classify human relations difficulties as "communication problems." While the phrase is often just a catchall to reduce things to their simplest possible form and can cover up the problem more than illuminate it, the observation is not too far off the mark. It is hard for people to understand one another. And while accurate understanding in no way guarantees agreement, there is little advantage in trying to sort out relationships through the additional static of unclear messages. It is worth the effort to practice listening to feelings as well as words and to check out meanings when clarity is not certain. Effective communication is a basic step in building relationships. Just be certain that when you see a problem between two people you don't automatically blame everything on communication processes when other factors may be at work, as described in Chapter 9.

☼ RECIPROCITY

Throughout this chapter we have implicitly and explicitly raised questions about the connection between what one person wants and how that affects, and is affected by, what another person wants. For a relationship to continue, there needs to be some kind of mutual accommodation of each to the other, some *reciprocity* between what each gives and gets. Just as roles develop among group members to fulfill particular group functions and are selected by individuals in line with their self-concepts, people often develop interpersonal role relationships at work.

The norm that it is obligatory to "pay back" roughly what one has "received" is almost universal and operates between individuals, groups, organizations, or even societies. Though disputes can arise about whether what one party offers is sufficient to repay the other's original "gift" (How many "thank you's" does it take to satisfy your friend of the opposite sex that you really liked the sweater?), virtually everyone accepts that everything should somehow be repaid. Gratefulness for help, dinner invitation for dinner invitation, warmth for kindnesses; whatever the currency, mutual satisfaction of debts over time is necessary to sustain an equal relationship. And failure to repay leads either to breaking off the relationship or to continued obligations and status differentials.

"Noblesse oblige," or taking care of those who are less fortunate, is a way of dealing with unequal abilities to repay, though even in that type of relationship deference, loyalty, and gratitude are expected in return for more durable goods.

This universal *norm of reciprocity* serves to stabilize relationships, to bring them into a steady state, which allows predictability and continuity. You may remember that the taking of *roles* serves much the same function. When behavior becomes patterned, meeting the expectations of others in a particular social system, everyone has a clear idea of what to expect and how to treat others. Each person develops a set pattern of behavior that provides something for the other; as long as what is provided is desired, the relationship is easy to maintain. Accepting a position will reveal that others have expecta-

---

Friendship is seldom lasting but between equals. . . . Benefits which cannot be repaid and obligations which cannot be discharged are not commonly found to increase affection; they excite gratitude indeed and heighten veneration but commonly take away that easy freedom and familiarity of intercourse without which . . . there cannot be friendship.

Samuel Johnson
The Rambler No. 64

tions about the type of relationships deemed appropriate for someone in that role. Just as the plumber had some ideas about what kind of interpersonal behavior a plumber's assistant should exhibit, and as Buckley and Endrunn had ideas about how a president and group vice president should relate, organizational members develop expectations that the role occupant cannot easily ignore despite personal preferences that might be different. It takes a while for each party to alter expectations and preferences to fit the other.

To build and maintain a relationship, one needs to fulfill the norm of reciprocity; yet the currency of "exchange" is often rather subtle. (It is not always as easy as, "You bought lunch yesterday; today I will buy.") For example, if you and another manager had occasion to assemble your teams for joint meetings sometimes in her conference room and sometimes in yours, and it had become customary for whichever one of you was on home turf to sit at the head of the conference table, it could violate expectations of reciprocity if you were to quickly move into that seat in her conference room. If the seating has come to mean a recognition of one another's status, breaking the pattern could easily be seen as an attempt to dominate and a failure to properly reciprocate her usual recognition of your status. It may not be possible to fully avoid failures of reciprocity, but you need to be alert to what is expected of you in return for what others have done for you, and to choose consciously whether or not to honor the expectations. Conversely, if you eventually want something from another person, you can utilize reciprocity by doing something useful—helping the other to meet his or her personal or organizational goals—and asking for a "return on your investment" when necessary. This need not be done in a harsh, demanding way; since most people recognize when they "owe you one," they will naturally want to pay you back.

In any ongoing relationship there are usually mutual expectations; as long as they are honored, the relationship remains stable. Often, however, the expectations are unclear or unrealistic, or one of the parties finds it difficult to live up to them. If so, it is best to discuss the issue with the other and attempt to modify the expectations in line with reality. All too often people are prone to let a situation build, perhaps because of embarrassment or a feeling that "one must always honor a commitment," until things have gotten out of control. Then, unfortunately, the relationship might end or require a major effort to rectify. If there is a lesson in this, it is that *every relationship needs nurturing, and continuing attention to mutual expectations is essential to the maintenance of reciprocity.*

In short, as needs and circumstances change, people may need to renegotiate their expectations of each other, a process that takes time and effort but pays off in mutual growth.

⁂ TRUST AND OTHER FEELINGS

Every relationship has the potential for confirming or disconfirming the participants' self-concepts. Whatever is sought in the relationship—whether it is liking, respect, or influence—a satisfying relationship confirms people's view of themselves and makes them feel good about who they believe they are. When two people agree in their goals, it makes them both feel supported; when they affirm each other's competencies, they feel a sense of adequacy; and when they reinforce each other's beliefs and values, they each feel worthy. **A relationship that makes each person feel supported, adequate, and worthy will generally lead to mutual feelings of closeness, warmth, and trust. By way of contrast, a relationship that makes each person feel unsupported, inadequate, and unworthy will generally lead to mutual feelings of distance, coldness, and suspicion (Rogers, 1961).**

The terms *closeness* (versus *distance*), *warmth* (versus *coldness*), and *trust* (versus *suspicion*) take on different meanings in different kinds of relationships. Closeness and warmth are mainly a matter of degree. For example, a minimal task relationship would certainly not draw two people as close or generate as many warm feelings as would a colleagueship; the stakes are different in each case. But even a minimal task relationship in which each person experiences self-confirmation can lead to some degree of closeness and warmth.

Trust

With respect to trust, the situation is more complex; trust is a central issue in all human relationships both within and outside of organizations. Trust can refer to several aspects of a relationship: (1) how much confidence you have in the other's competence and ability to do whatever needs doing, (2) how sound you believe the other's judgment to be, (3) your belief in the extent to which the other is willing to be helpful to you, (4) how certain you are that the other has genuine concern for your welfare rather than any desire to harm you, and (5) how confident you are that the other will deliver on any commitments made.

Since trust can refer to any or all of these areas, it is useful to be clear about which area you mean when you use the concept and helpful to check what others mean by it. "I don't trust you" is a very different statement when it means "Your lack of carpentry skills make me doubt whether you can build that chest" than it is when it means "I think you would drop it on my toes at the first opportunity." Remember Theory X and Theory Y from Chapter 8? They are sets of beliefs that express greater or lesser trust in the motives of others.

Trust is the lubrication that makes it possible for organizations to work. It's hard to imagine an organization without some semblance of trust operating somehow, somewhere.

W. Bennis and B. Nanus
Leaders **(New York: Harper & Row, 1985)**

While deep and all-encompassing trust may not be called for in a work situation, when it does emerge it can make work easier. It does this by forming the basis for greater *openness* in the relationship on all fronts. For example, two close friends probably will feel greater freedom to be open and honest in task-related areas than would two relative strangers. The two friends are more likely to be willing to take *risks* with one another, that is, to say things that may be critical or revealing in the belief that the other person will hear it accurately and not use it in a destructive way. While the level of trust in a relationship can develop gradually over time, through the course of interactions, very often it takes some kind of risky behavior in relation to the other person to build trust at the deepest levels. To deepen a relationship requires that someone take initiative in trusting the other—say, to do a really tough part of a joint task—before he or she can be certain of the consequences. If neither will take the risk of trusting at least a little, the relationship remains at the same level of caution and suspicion. Note the way Buckley and Endrunn cannot improve their relationship unless one or the other is willing to take the initiative and be more open.

On the other hand, when someone violates trust (especially when it has involved some personal risk) the relationship is usually damaged. The effect may be temporary or permanent, depending upon how deeply the violation affected the self-concept. It is easier to forgive a co-worker who goofed up some piece of the job or whose interpretation of a task was grossly in error than it is to forgive a close colleague for deliberately taking an action that puts you in a bad light with others.

In general, then: **The greater the trust one has in another's competence, judgment, helpfulness, or concern, the more open one will be about matters relating to that aspect(s) of the relationship. In turn, the more one feels trusted, the easier it is to be open** (Walton, 1969; Rogers, 1961; Egan, 1973).

But how can we go about building and maintaining trust? As just implied, in part one must act with integrity and not violate whatever trust exists. This requires meeting commitments made to the other person and maintaining such confidences as may occur. Even where you have information that was not given you "in confidence," you need to use common sense about raising issues in public that put the other person on the spot unnecessarily or unexpectedly. If the organization's culture is one where everything is open and above board, there may be very little that can't be brought up at any time, but in most cultures there are some constraints. In general, people do not like to be caught by surprise, especially high-level managers in front of their bosses or even peers. Consequently, common sense usually suggests raising issues in private or at least alerting an individual ahead of time. A person who exhibits such common sense will be seen as more trustworthy than someone who shows no sensitivity to another's feelings about not being caught off guard or embarrassed in public.

Still another way to build trust, apart from doing your own job well, is by being open about your own actions and intentions. It is not easy to trust someone who is secretive and who "plays the cards close to the vest." Keeping others informed not only avoids surprises but reduces the threat that the unknown entails. In part this means being sensitive to others' needs to know what is going on, and in part it means making yourself more vulnerable.

DEALING WITH BLIND SPOTS: THE NEED FOR FEEDBACK

The development of a relationship involves the behavior of both parties; to make it easier to look at the interconnection, see Figure 10–4. It shows the relationship from the perspective of each person and also what the combinations of their separate perspectives produce. From each person's vantage point there are aspects of the relationship that are *known* (that each is aware of) and aspects that are *not known*. What both persons are aware of (upper left box) are those things that have been shared openly; what neither person is aware of (lower right box) are those things that have not made their appearance in the relationship, the future unknowns that may or may not emerge. The other two boxes determine the direction in which the relationship is to develop, if at all. They include those aspects of the relationship that one person or the other is aware of, but not both. What person A alone is aware of (has not shared with person B) in the relationship, we call B's *blind spots* (and vice versa). The blind spots can be positive or negative in nature, but as long as they remain hidden from one person or the other, they tend to serve as obstacles to the development of a mutually enhancing relationship. **The fewer the number of blind spots one has, the greater the understanding of one's impact on others, and the greater the opportunity to choose alternative behaviors (Jourard, 1971; Luft, 1970).** It is discourag-

FIGURE 10–4   Model of a Two-Person Relationship

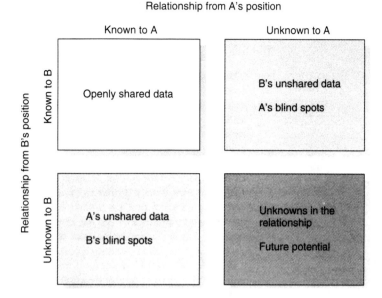

Relationship from A's position

Note: This model is a modification of the "Johari Window," a concept presented in J. Luft, *Group Processes* (Palo Alto, Calif.: National Press Books, 1970).

ing and a handicap to be misunderstood or misjudged on the basis of some behavior or mannerism of which you are not aware; you can't change what you do not know about.

In order for anyone to improve performance, please another, or change self-defeating behavior, it is necessary to be aware of the impact one is having on the other(s). Since people can best alter mistakes or unintentional consequences *with* information on the impact of their behavior, rather than without it, telling others how they are coming across is a kind of gift. It is the feedback of data, which cannot be acquired nearly so effectively, if at all, in any other way. The feedback process in which information is given on the consequences of certain actions is central to any human relationship in which learning is desired or necessary. For example, if a group member's constant jokes bother you, making it hard to take even his valuable contributions seriously, you prevent him from learning how to be more effective if you do not tell him.

But there is a dilemma in all of this. If trust is required for openness and feedback is a form of openness that can be risky (since the receiver may not welcome it as intended), how can you get others to give you the feedback you need? How can you build sufficient trust toward you to allow others to take the risk of telling you how you come across? Declaring your trustworthiness does not often work; the person who feels a risk will not easily accept testimonials! Usually it requires that you go first, taking the risk of disclosing something about yourself—your perceptions, feelings, concerns, and so forth. Self-disclosure builds trust. But self-disclosure can also be risky; it may not be received as intended, or it may be used against the discloser. Consider the following example:

> The production manager and sales manager of a record player manufacturer must write a joint report to their boss on whether or not to produce new compact disc sets. The sales manager's job will be made easier if the model is added to the line; her salespeople want to be able to meet competition with up-to-date models even though sales will not at first be too high. The production manager's job will be made more difficult if the newly designed machine is put into production, since there are already problems with the existing level of production. If the wrong decision is made, it will be costly to both of them. Do they work together to examine all aspects of the problem, or does each hold back information unfavorable to their respective positions? If the sales manager admits that she has doubts about the market potential of compact disc sets and suspects the sales staff is only using the lack of them as an excuse for poor efforts, will the production manager pounce on that and force a negative decision? Conversely, if he tells her that a special assembly line could be set up to minimize disruption to present production, will she take advantage of that to force a positive decision? Would either use the other's revelation to look good to the boss? Can they build sufficient trust to be able to share all the needed inputs and come to a sensible decision in which each does what is best for the company regardless of personal inconvenience? The degree of trust, openness, and closeness between them will have crucial ramifications for the company—and for their relationship in the future.

In general, we can say that:

1. **The greater the extent of openness in self-disclosure and feedback, the greater will be the resulting level of trust.**
2. **The greater the level of openness that is required, the greater the level of risk experienced.**
3. **The greater the level of risk required, the greater the level of trust that is needed for openness.**
4. **The closer that self-disclosure and/or feedback come to the core of the self-concept, the greater the level of risk that is experienced and the higher the level of trust necessary for openness (Rogers, 1961; Egan, 1973).**

You need trust in order to take the risk of being open. But it is hard to develop sufficient trust until you do take the risk of being open. If the risk is positively responded to, the first critical step in building trust is established; if not, then you are left only with the satisfaction of knowing that you had the courage to take the risk. Risking mistakenly can be disastrous; risking too cautiously can be isolating.

MANAGERIAL TOOLS

Guidelines for Giving Feedback

Giving feedback should be analogous to holding up a mirror where individuals can see themselves as others see them and learn how their actions have been affecting others. It is *not* telling others what is wrong with them nor telling them how they *should* change. It is offering your perceptions and describing your feelings in a nonjudgmental manner as data that recipients can use as they find appropriate.

1. Examine your own motives.

    Be sure your intention is to be helpful, not to show how perceptive and superior you are, or to hurt the other. Be on the other person's side.

2. Consider the *receiver's readiness* to hear your feedback.

    In general, feedback is most useful when it is sought, rather than when it is volunteered. When possible, wait for signs of the other wanting it; nevertheless,

3. Give feedback promptly.

    Feedback given soon after the event, except when the individual is upset or otherwise not ready to listen, is better than that given when details are no longer clear in anyone's mind.

4. Be *descriptive* rather than evaluate.

    Describe what the person did and any feelings it aroused in you, but do not label or evaluate it. ("You interrupted me and that frustrates me because I lose track" is descriptive; "You were rude" is evaluative.)

5. *Deal in specifics*, not generalities.

    Describe concrete events. ("You interrupted me when I was reviewing . . ." versus "You always try to hog all the air time.")

6. *Offer* feedback; do not try to impose it.

    Give information as something the receiver can consider and explore, not as a command that he/she change.

7. Offer feedback in a *spirit of tentativeness*.

    Offer feedback as one person's perceptions, not as "the truth." Being dogmatic usually puts people on the defensive.

8. *Be open to receiving feedback yourself.*

    Your actions may be contributing to the other's behavior; not everyone may feel the same as you do about the other, which reflects on your perceptions as well as on the other's behavior.

9. *Avoid overload.*

    Focus only on what is most important and changeable.

10. *Highlight costs of the behavior to the other.*

    If you can, help the other person see how the behavior in question costs him/her, or prevents meeting his/her objectives.

11. Watch for any behavior of the other while receiving feedback which confirms or disconfirms the feedback.

Furthermore, it is occasionally necessary to work with someone whom you do not trust; finding a way to get the job done without either making yourself vulnerable or offending the other person is a valuable skill to acquire. While open, trusting relationships are freeing and satisfying, plunging into acting as if the person will respond in kind just because you would prefer it is like diving into a new swimming place without checking for rocks beneath the surface. Conversely, assuming that *all* water is loaded with rocks can rob you of a great deal of pleasure.

Unfortunately, it is almost impossible to develop guidelines for judging when it is worth risking openness and trust. As in other human situations,

MANAGERIAL BULLETIN

What to Do When an Employee Is Talented—And a Pain in the Neck

Psychologists call them "compensators"; human resource professionals call them "abrasive." Co-workers and bosses call them a pain in the neck.

Look around your office and there's probably one lurking: the employee whose personality manages to irritate, disrupt, demoralize, or alienate.

He also may be doing his job well, thereby causing one of the more perplexing workplace issues for managers: How to cope with or change an employee's frustrating, and often ingrained, behavior. And when a star performer is the culprit, "it's as difficult a decision as any for a manager to make," says John Lenkey, a Richmond, Virginia, consultant.

Too often, consultants say, the decision is to do nothing or to fire. But neither choice is desirable: It isn't easy to justify holding onto a disruptive employee, particularly at a time of budget cuts. And firing a talented employee for personality reasons may invite a lawsuit. Moreover, firing or doing nothing often means wasting a potentially valuable employee.

Uncomfortable, but Necessary

So, more companies are urging managers to deal with troublesome employees head on, as uncomfortable as that may be. They also are teaching employees to more effectively deal with problem co-workers; as participatory management spreads, with workers more involved in management decisions, it's increasingly important that employees learn how to confront bothersome peers without damaging egos or provoking fisticuffs.

you have to decide whether the expected gains are sufficiently greater than the potential losses to be worth the possibility of a failure. Keep in mind that trust is usually built a little at a time. Pushing too hard or too fast, or both, can scare off the other person and also may be too risky for you; not pushing at all, however, is not likely to produce any change. Normally, though, your own willingness to *begin* being open will result in a reciprocal response.

Mark Buckley, for example, needs to gently initiate discussions with Oliver Endrunn about ways of effectively striking a balance between being informed and being unnecessarily interfering; blasting Endrunn for bypassing him would only make Endrunn defensive and angry. From his side, Endrunn can talk with Buckley about what information would help him relax so that he wouldn't have to seek it all the time; attacking Buckley for being too closed and political would simply lead to further guardedness.

A Recap

In summary, individuals involved in a relationship can steer it in a positive direction by being adaptable to the requirements of the job and the desires of the other person, by developing and practicing good communication skills so as to minimize and deal with misunderstanding, by honoring and utilizing the norm of reciprocity to maintain a balanced exchange, by acting with integrity in a manner that keeps the other informed about actions, intentions, and expectations, and by seeking to reduce mutual blind spots through self-disclosure and feedback. These practices will also be useful in doing the maintenance work to keep a positive relationship from falling into decline. If careful attention is given to these interpersonal processes, the result should be a good relationship leading to productivity, satisfaction, and even individual development. We close this chapter with a look at some other outcomes of a relationship that are related to productivity, satisfaction, and development.

OUTCOMES OF INTERPERSONAL RELATIONSHIPS

Liking and Respect

It's possible for two people to work together, even productively, without developing much liking or respect for one another. In a minimal task relationship this probably poses little problem, at least for getting the work done. However, as discussed in Chapter 7, most people have more needs than those that pertain only to the task; therefore, few people would find very desirable, for long, a work relationship that lacks liking and respect.

Liking is normally related to the personal and social aspects of a relationship. If the quality of communication between two people is such that feelings of closeness, warmth, and trust develop, the outcome will obviously be liking. Even when the task does not require such interpersonal communication, if the individuals themselves desire it, if their backgrounds are compatible, and if the opportunities for interaction are present, then the chances are good that their relationship will result in liking. Any one of these factors, however, can affect the outcome. For example, in one company two members of a management team had very similar styles of interacting—both were aggressive and argumentative. Their interpersonal process was terrible; neither could listen to or understand the other. Consequently, they maintained a kind of distance, coolness, and mistrust, which resulted in mutual dislike. While they did, in fact, respect each other's abilities in the job, their dislike made work unpleasant for the entire team.

It is not necessary to understand things in order to argue about them.
Beaumarchais

In a work relationship mutual respect normally occurs as a result of the recognition of one another's competencies. Can you think of people you hold in esteem because of their abilities? Are they all people you also like? As discussed in Chapter 5, feelings of respect may not be consistent with liking.

The example above illustrates this point. Furthermore, co-workers may develop a high level of task-related trust but never feel close or warm on a more personal level. And while their processes of communication may be poor when feelings are involved, the two people may be perfectly capable of exchanging needed information about the work as the situation requires it. In short, we can say that:

1. **In a minimal task relationship, liking and respect need only be minimal in order to get the task done.**
2. **The degree of liking needed in a task relationship depends upon the preferences of the individuals but also tends to be more appropriate to relationships that extend beyond the minimal task level.**
3. **The degree of respect needed in a task relationship increases as task interdependence increases and as the differentiated abilities of each person are required for satisfactory completion of the job.**
4. **To the extent that personal closeness, warmth, and trust emerge, liking will result.**
5. **To the extent that task-related trust emerges, respect will result (Bennis, Berlew, Schein, & Steele, 1973).**

While it may at times seem difficult to be both liked and respected, the two outcomes are not necessarily mutually exclusive. The assumption that they are can, in fact, result in a manager saying, "I'd rather be respected than liked; at least I'll get the job done." What is unfortunate is that this limits the range of the manger's interpersonal competence and consequently may reduce responsiveness to the needs of many employees. Insofar as a job requires more than a minimal task relationship, the development of *both* liking and respect can have important consequences for productivity, satisfaction, and development. Let's examine these consequences in the form of some propositions.

Propositions Linking Liking and Respect to Productivity, Satisfaction, and Development

While the connections are neither simple nor direct, since many other variables need to be considered, there does (except for minimal task) seem to be some very general relationship between liking and respect on the one hand and productivity, satisfaction, and development on the other. We will list the propositions without elaboration; you ought to be able to apply them to your own experience and to examples you may study.

1. **When liking and respect are both high, productivity, satisfaction, and development tend to be enhanced.**
2. **When liking and respect are both low, productivity, satisfaction, and development tend to be reduced.**

3. When liking is high and respect is low, productivity tends to be reduced, satisfaction tends to be enhanced, and development may be affected either way.
4. When liking is low and respect is high, productivity tends to be enhanced, satisfaction tends to be reduced, and development may be affected either way.

Keep in mind that these statements represent very general tendencies; that is, when all other things are equal, then the factors of liking and respect can provide predictive guidelines to productivity, satisfaction, and development. A deeper understanding of the connections, especially in regard to development in a relationship, can be obtained by examining the quality of the patterned role relationships that emerge between two people.

PATTERNED ROLE RELATIONSHIPS

In order for a work relationship to be sustained at anything more than the absolute minimum required by the task or for a nonrequired relationship to continue, a mutually satisfactory role relationship will have to emerge.

The role relationships people establish with others become important sources of stability in their lives; they count on them to help maintain personal identity, a basic sense of adequacy, and a sense of worth. Yet, once established, role relationships become very difficult to break out of even when they are no longer fully desired or are preventing needed growth and change. For example, think about the kinds of role relationships you have with members of that familiar organization, your family. How much have these changed as you have grown older? Do you find yourself being drawn into some of your "old behavior" every time you visit your parents? Well-developed role patterns are very hard to break. They tend to determine and shape a great deal of our behavior, and when they are outmoded, they serve to constrain a great many more satisfying possibilities in the relationships. Here is a 36-year-old professional person describing his relationship with his 27-year-old brother:

> When I get together with my youngest brother, I automatically fall into "older brother" behavior, giving advice (that he may or may not want), looking after him, paying the check when we eat out, and so on. Even though I try to treat him like the full-fledged adult he is, old habits are hard to break, and I slide into my most familiar and well-practiced role with him. He in turn falls into playing "kid brother," asking advice, appearing a bit unsure of himself, letting me initiate, and so forth. We have a well-established role relationship, which is convenient because it lets each of us know in advance a lot about how the other is likely to behave and react, and it saves considerable time and confusion each time we see each other.

At the same time, by definition, it also restricts each of our possible choices. Unless we are willing to make the other uncomfortable and challenge mutual expectations, he cannot really be assertative with me and I cannot easily be helpless, confused, or needy with him. So at the same time that our roles are convenient, they also constrain our behavior as long as we choose to continue them.

We tend to take for granted those to whom we are the closest. Often we get so accustomed to seeing them and hearing from them that we lose the ability to listen to what they are really saying or to appreciate the quality— good or bad—of what they are doing.

W. Bennis and B. Nanus
***Leaders* (New York: Harper & Row, 1985)**

Another example was observed at a large urban hospital:

The director of nursing, an attractive woman, had allowed the male administrators to treat her as a "dumb blonde," pleasant but not very smart. Their discomfort at the possibility that she might be beautiful *and* competent led them to treat her that way; her discomfort at upsetting their expectations and possibly being seen as an "aggressive bitch" led her to play along.

At a training session with her female assistant director, she was confronted about this behavior and began to practice using her considerable analytical abilities. Shortly after, she was at a meeting of her peers, male directors of other departments. Someone made a snide comment about something in her jurisdiction; she came back with a fast, concise, and powerful rebuttal. When all the dropped jaws were restored to the astonished faces, one of the men said, "I'm glad to see that your nice legs haven't been affected by your brains," a not very subtle attempt to get her back in role. She had to struggle hard to continue making contributions; eventually she left the hospital for a similar job where she could start fresh.

Have you ever experienced a similar dilemma? It is a problem that frequently occurs, exactly *because* the relationship is reciprocal, when you attempt to change your behavior toward another person. You can decide, "From now on I'm going to be different with so-and-so." Then when you try it, "so-and-so" either resists the change, thinks you're crazy, or simply overlooks your new behavior as a temporary phenomenon. Psychotherapists struggle with this issue when they seek to bring about change in a client's behavior and other key people in the client's life continue to cast him or her into the old roles. As a gag song put it, "I Can't Get Adjusted to the You That Got Adjusted to Me." Sometimes, even when a person changes in ways that you find desirable, it can be difficult to begin treating that person in new ways! It means building whole new role relationships, which also requires changing some of your own behavior to match the other person's. In short, to establish a new role requires stepping out of the old one. That isn't easy.

Can you see the implications of this problem for individuals who want to move upward in an organization? Every promotion or job change calls for new role relationships or altered ones with former colleagues and superiors. It can create great problems to become the supervisor of someone who formerly trained or managed you; how does one change from "promising young trainee" to "responsible executive"? Not everyone can easily let go of established patterns.

Self-Sealing Reciprocal Relationships: A Pattern of Conflict

Even more difficult than changing one person's role in a relationship is addressing the problem of mutually reinforcing limiting patterns. When two people have trouble working together, it is often because each produces in the other the very behavior that most irritates the counterpart, reinforcing the original behavior and keeping the pattern going. For example, Buckley wants autonomy and resents Endrunn's interference, so he withholds information, which induces Endrunn to poke around for information, reinforcing Buckley's conviction that he must give less information, which reinforces Endrunn's conviction that Buckley is closed and, therefore, won't voluntarily give information, and on and on. (See diagram of the self-sealing loop.)

Self-Sealing Loop

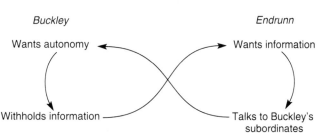

This kind of endless loop can be called a *self-sealing reciprocal relationship*. The more each tries to deal with the other in the usual way, the worse the problem gets. This is often the source of continuing interpersonal struggles. Here's another example:

Max is the cigar-smoking, aggressive vice president of manufacturing in a consumer goods company. The order entry department, where sales of the thousands of pieces sold by the sales force are recorded and transmitted to the factory, reports to manufacturing. Max is proud of his operation though he knows it isn't perfect. Shawn is the ambitious sales vice president. He can't make his bonus if manufacturing doesn't deliver. Lately there have been problems with the order entry department. Shawn raises it at an executive committee meeting. He attacks by saying, "Order entry should report to sales. Their performance stinks." Max counters, "Nothing's wrong with them, and they'd be worse if they reported to sales." Shawn can't stand being put off, so he attacks again. This gets Max to fight harder. The more Shawn makes it a battle over turf, over who "owns" order entry, the more Max insists that performance is fine. Shawn's grabbing for turf makes Max defensive; Max's denials of problems make Shawn more determined to get control. And so it goes, through many rounds.

In all of this, the actual problem with order entry is forgotten; Shawn and Max are in a self-sealing loop that makes anything but "attack and defend" impossible to discuss.

It is very difficult for one party in such a closed relationship to bring it to a halt; once inside a self-sealing loop, it is hard to see the pattern and to see how you are contributing to the problem. It's always crystal clear to each party what the *other* is doing wrong. A fellow worker, however, can often see the pattern. Once someone points it out, the involved parties can much more easily see how to break it. Max could first say, "OK, Shawn, let's actually look at the problems you're having and see how to fix them." Or Shawn could first say, "Maybe the issue isn't to whom order entry should report, but how we can get faster turnaround and more accuracy. Let's go after that, Max." Similarly, Mark Buckley could decide to supply Endrunn with much *more* information, and point out that he's willing to continue if Endrunn will stop jumping in with instructions to Buckley's subordinates. Or, Endrunn could say to Mark, "In order to be comfortable I need to feel informed. If I interfere as a result, let me know. I want you to be able to be effective."

One party's admission of what he or she is doing to perpetuate the problem is often enough to break the sealed reciprocal pattern and lead to problem solving. In general, when you're having trouble with someone else, it's useful to look for what *you* might be doing that contributes to the problem. Poor relationships are seldom caused completely by one side. And since reciprocity is likely to be the tie that links related roles together, *changing your own behavior may indeed be likely to induce changes in the behavior of another*. If you start treating your parents as if they were serious adult friends and as if you were also a mature adult, they will have to accommodate somehow to the alterations in your behavior. If the co-worker who avoids responsibility is treated responsibly and expected to come through when needed, he or she may in fact be less likely to let you down than otherwise.

Insofar as a relationship exists in which both parties feel connected to one another, there is potential leverage for affecting the other's behavior by altering your own. Though the pulls are likely to be great to get back into the old roles, it is worth exploring whether a role relationship that is giving you trouble can be redefined into a new set of reciprocal roles through your own initiative. When that works, it can be very freeing and can lead to greater influence over the work environment you are in.

▨ SUMMARY

In short, the patterned role relationships that emerge in a work environment have important consequences for productivity, satisfaction, and development. While certain kinds of fixed patterns can enhance both productivity and satisfaction, as when the various aspects of two people's jobs are reciprocal, the developmental aspects of a relationship normally pertain to learning and change. When two people learn from one another, when they are able to create new role patterns as tasks and needs demand them, then the relationship will enhance all three outcomes, especially development. While work relationships of this kind may be rare and difficult to build, they are indeed worth the effort in the long run. We hope that the concepts and examples offered in this and the previous chapter will aid you in your own quest for growth-promoting work relationships.

Figure 10–5 illustrates the total picture we have covered in Chapters 9 and 10. It should be obvious by now just how complicated a two-person relationship can be; we hope to have provided a coherent picture by following the sequence of factors shown in the chart. For your own practice, you might attempt to trace some relationships with which you are familiar through the sequence; you can go in either direction. For example, you might begin with the outcomes and try to analyze how they came about. By working your way back through processes, looking at the required relationship (if it's a work context), and considering the backgrounds and circumstances, you might be able to explain the relationship in some depth. Were the outcomes predictable from any of the factors identified in the scheme? Possibly you can use this approach in a forward direction—that is, to predict the probable outcomes of some current interpersonal relationships as you see them emerging.

By developing your diagnostic skills in this fashion, you can identify ways to alter the interpersonal processes to improve the relationship. If you can develop such interpersonal skill, you can't help but become a better manager of your own relationships and, if it's ever required of you, a better manager of other people's work relationships.

As stated earlier in this chapter, interpersonal competence is a basic ingredient of effective management; it makes a critical difference in how much *influence* you may exercise in relation to peers, superiors, and subordinates. In the next chapter, we will show just how the leadership in an organization is fundamentally a process of influence. You will be able to judge for yourself just how the interpersonal factors covered in this chapter constitute important background factors for leadership effectiveness.

FIGURE 10–5 Schema for Analyzing Two-Person Work Relationship

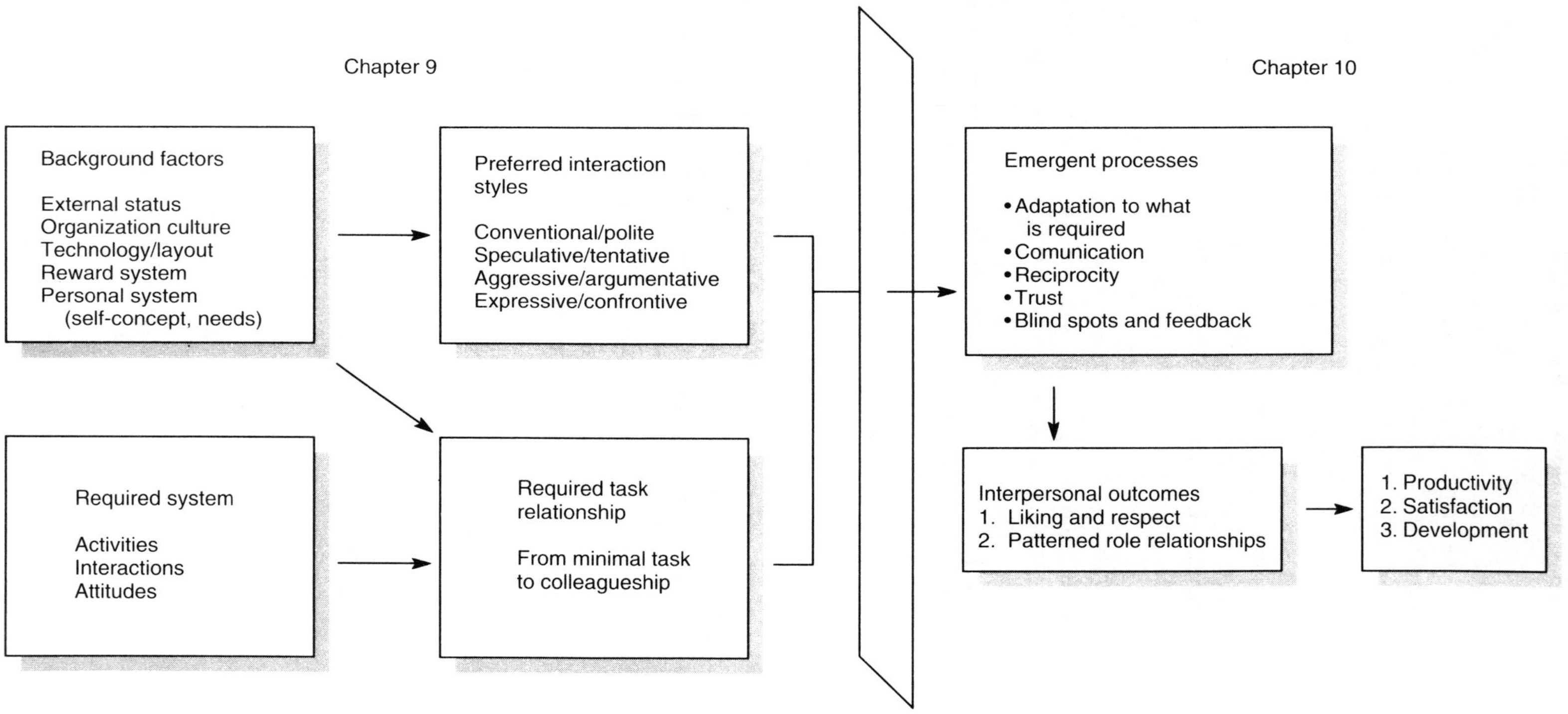

Chapter 9

Background factors

External status
Organization culture
Technology/layout
Reward system
Personal system
(self-concept, needs)

Required system

Activities
Interactions
Attitudes

Preferred interaction
styles

Conventional/polite
Speculative/tentative
Aggressive/argumentative
Expressive/confrontive

Required task
relationship

From minimal task
to colleagueship

Chapter 10

Emergent processes

•Adaptation to what
 is required
•Comunication
•Reciprocity
•Trust
•Blind spots and feedback

Interpersonal outcomes
1. Liking and respect
2. Patterned role relationships

1. Productivity
2. Satisfaction
3. Development

KEY CONCEPTS FROM CHAPTER 10

1. Interpersonal processes.
    a. Adaptation to:
       (1) What is required.
       (2) The other person's expectations and desires.
    b. Communication.
       (1) Levels of exchange between speaker and listener:
           (i)   Feelings about subject matter.
           (ii) Subject matter.
           (iii) Feelings about one another.
           (iv) Feelings about self.
       (2) Self-concepts and perceptions of other filter messages in and out.
       (3) Barriers to communication:
           (i)   Imprecision of language.
           (ii) Multiple channels (verbal and nonverbal).
           (iii) State of mind.
           (iv) Gender differences.
       (4) Common problems of communication:
           (i)   Mixed messages.
           (ii) Incomplete communication.
           (iii) Unconscious nonverbal signals.
           (iv) Conscious nonverbal signals.
           (v)   The greater the emotional involvement with a subject, the greater the likelihood of distortion.
       (5) It takes both people for communication to work.
    c. Reciprocity.
       (1) To maintain a relationship, one must fulfill the norm of reciprocity.
    d. Trust and other feelings:
       (1) Feeling supported, adequate, and worthy leads to closeness, warmth, and trust in a relationship.
       (2) Trust:
           (i)   In the other's competence and ability.
           (ii) In the other's judgment.
           (iii) In the other's willingness to be helpful.
           (iv) In the other's concern for your welfare.
           (v)   That the other will meet commitments.
       (3) Trust is easily destroyed, unless you:
           (i)   Act with integrity.
           (ii) Maintain confidentialities.
           (iii) Do your job effectively.
           (iv) Avoid inappropriate secrecy.
           (v)   Keep others informed.

  e. Dealing with blind spots (the need for feedback).
    (1) Openness and self-disclosure reduce blind spots.
    (2) Openness often means taking a risk, but can build trust.
  f. Attention to interpersonal processes is necessary to:
    (1) Build a positive relationship.
    (2) Maintain a positive relationship.

2. Outcomes of interpersonal relationships.
  a. Liking and respect.
    (1) To the extent that personal closeness, warmth, and trust emerge, liking will result.
    (2) To the extent that task-related trust emerges, respect will result.
    (3) Correlations of liking and respect with productivity, satisfaction, and development.
  b. Patterned role relationships.
    (1) A source of stability in people's lives.
    (2) Can become self-sealing.
      (*i*) To break the pattern requires both to change.

3. A positive relationship is one in which:
  a. The required task gets done properly and with reasonable efficiency (productivity).
  b. The parties involved are reasonably satisfied (satisfaction).
  c. The growth of both is fostered, or at least not hindered (development).

PERSONAL APPLICATION EXERCISE

Reducing Your Blind Spots

One of the greatest handicaps of a manager is the existence of blind spots. Unfortunately, managers often don't even know how to reduce or prevent blind spots, even if they suspect they have some. You might do well to discover your own, even before you become a manager. There are a variety of ways to do this, short of creating a potentially awkward but rewarding situation by just asking others to tell you what they think of you. The following procedure could be valuable to you, even though it may not feel comfortable at first.

  In most relationships there are things you do that people wish you would stop doing, things you don't do that they wish you would start doing, and things you are doing that they like and want you to continue. Pick someone you trust and ask that person to interview a half dozen or so of your other friends (or co-workers), using the framework described above (i.e., "stop, start, continue" categories). That person should then put together a composite of all the interviews in order to mask the sources of the comments. Any words or expressions that would identify the source should be changed or deleted. What you will receive is a fairly clear picture of the impact of your behavior on others in a form that you should find useful. Although you might expect to find a lot of negative comments, this usually does not happen. In fact, you will probably be pleasantly surprised.

Finally, in the spirit of reciprocity, you might offer to do the same thing for the other person.

SUGGESTED READINGS

Athos, A., and J. Gabarro. *Interpersonal Behavior.* Englewood Cliffs, N.J.: Prentice-Hall, 1978.

Beier, E. G. "Nonverbal Communication: How We Send Emotional Messages." *Psychology Today* 8 (1974), pp. 53–56.

Bennis, W., D. Berlew, E. Schein, and F. I. Steele. *Interpersonal Dynamics.* 3rd ed. Chicago: Dorsey Press, 1973.

Collins, E. G. C., and T. B. Blodgett. "Sexual Harassment . . . Some See It . . . Some Won't." *Harvard Business Review,* March–April 1981, pp. 76–95.

Davis, K. "Grapevine Communication among Lower and Middle Managers." *Personnel Journal,* April 1969, pp. 269–72.

Egan, G. *Face to Face.* Monterey, Calif.: Brooks/Cole Publishing, 1973.

Fidler, L. A., and J. D. Johnson. "Communication and Innovation Implementation." *Academy of Management Review* 9 (1984), pp. 704–11.

Giffin, K., and B. R. Patton. *Personal Communication in Human Relations.* Columbus, Ohio: Charles E. Merrill Publishing, 1974.

Hall, E. T. *The Silent Language.* Greenwich, Conn.: Fawcett Publications, 1959.

Halperin, K., C. R. Snyer, R. J. Shenkkel, and B. K. Houston. "Effects of Source Status and Message Favorability on Acceptance of Personality Feedback." *Journal of Applied Psychology* 61 (1976), pp. 85–88.

Haney, W. V. *Communication: Pattern and Incidence.* Homewood, Ill.: Richard D. Irwin, 1960.

Harris, T. A. *I'm OK, You're OK.* New York: Harper & Row, 1967.

Hayes, M. A. "Nonverbal Communication: Expression without Words." In *Readings in Interpersonal and Organizational Communication,* ed. R. C. Huseman, C. M. Logue, and D. L. Freshley. Boston: Holbrook Press, 1973. Jacoby, J., D. Mazursky, T. Troutman, and A. Kuss. "When Feedback is Ignored: Disutility of Outcome Feedback." *Journal of Applied Psychology* 69 (1984), pp. 531–45.

Jongeward, D. *Everybody Wins: Transactional Analysis Applied to Organizations.* Reading, Mass.: Addison-Wesley Publishing, 1973.

Jourard, S. M. *The Transparent Self.* Rev. ed. New York: Van Nostrand Reinhold, 1971.

Larson, J. R. Jr. "The Dynamic Interplay Between Employees' Feedback-Seeking Strategies and Supervisors' Delivery of Performance Feedback." *Academy of Management Review* 14, No. 3 (1989), pp. 408–22.

Luft, J. *Group Processes.* Palo Alto, Calif.: National Press Books, 1970.

Mangham, I. L. *Interactions and Interventions in Organizations.* New York: John Wiley & Sons, 1978.

Maslow, A. H. *Eupsychian Management.* Homewood, Ill.: Richard D. Irwin and Dorsey Press, 1965.

Rogers, C. "The Characteristics of a Helping Relationship." *On Becoming a Person.* Boston: Houghton Mifflin, 1961, pp. 39–58.

Rogers, C., and R. E. Farson. "Active Listening." In *Effective Behavior in Organizations.* 1st ed. Ed. Cohen et al. Homewood, Ill.: Richard D. Irwin, 1976.

Sinetar, M. "Building Trust into Corporate Relationships." *Organizational Dynamics* 16, no. 3 (Winter 1988).

Walton, R. E. "Interpersonal Confrontation and Basic Third-Party Functions: A Case Study." *Journal of Applied Behavioral Science* 4 (1968), pp. 327–44.

_____. *Interpersonal Peacemaking: Confrontations and Third-Party Consultation.* Reading, Mass.: Addison-Wesley Publishing, 1969.

Zaleznik, A., and D. Moment. *The Dynamics of Interpersonal Behavior.* New York: John Wiley & Sons, 1964.

Leadership

Exerting Influence and Power

"The core problem for leaders involves getting others to do what is necessary to accomplish the organization's goals."

The topic of leadership has fascinated people through the ages. After much discussion and research, the pursuit of a universal definition of effective leadership is still intriguing but elusive. The world awaits definitive answers to such questions as: What makes a good leader? Who can be a leader? Can anyone be a leader? Can leadership skills be taught? What makes followers follow? What are the limits to leadership?

Social science researchers for years pursued the notion that there must be some common qualities shared by all leaders. Many long lists of sterling qualities (aggressiveness, wisdom, charisma, courage, and so forth) have been generated but have not been found to apply to all leaders in all situations. To be effective a leader's qualities must relate somehow to the situation he or she is in and to the nature of the followers. This view is consistent with the situational approach taken throughout this book, yet is just barely beginning to be widely accepted. The belief does not easily fade away that General Patton, Mahatma Gandhi, Vince Lombardi, Golda Meir, and Martin Luther King—or the presidents of GM, AT&T, IBM, and John Hancock—must have had exactly the same qualities.

Throughout this and the next chapter we will be using the terms *manager* and *leader* interchangeably, even though customarily there is a distinction. A manager is usually considered to be someone who makes sure that work is carried out properly, while a leader is considered to be the person who decides on what that work ought to be (i.e., the direction to be taken). As you can imagine, the two roles are hard to separate, since most managers today do have at least some responsibility for setting direction.

As you might expect, insofar as there are common components to the manager's or leader's job, a few traits appear to be consistent requirements. In Chapter 1 we induced from Mintzberg's analysis of a manager's job some of the skills required by a manager. You will recall that a manager needs interpersonal skills to acquire information needed for decision making. For example, leaders need to have the ability to influence other people's behavior, a readiness to absorb interpersonal stress, the capacity to structure social interactions to task needs, some self-confidence, and the drive to exercise initiative in social situations, all of which are directly related to the nature of managerial work.

Effective leaders also have a strong drive for responsibility and task completion, energy and persistence for accomplishing goals, a willingness to tolerate frustration and delay (since working with and through others does not always result in immediate action!), some willingness to take risks and be original in solving problems, and, perhaps most important, a willingness to accept the consequences of making decisions and taking action (Stogdill, 1974).

In general, you can see that these traits are closely related to the kinds of situations in which virtually all leaders find themselves, having to build relationships in order to accomplish tasks and having to take responsibility for their system's performance.

MANAGERIAL BULLETIN

Can Leadership Be Taught?

Leadership is no longer seen as the exclusive preserve of the inhabitants of executive row. The nurturing of "corporate Gandhis," as one consultant terms it, has given way to a focus on developing leadership abilities among employees at all levels of our organizations. An executive, a manager, a supervisor, an hourly worker—all can learn to develop a vision for the future. All can learn to accept new responsibilities, to take risks, to build consensus and trust among subordinates and peers. Certainly not everyone has the potential of a Lee Iacocca. But everyone possesses innate leadership abilities to some degree, and those abilities can be improved.

SOURCE: Chris Lee, *Training*, July 1989, pp. 19–26.

The *particular* requirements for effective leadership in each situation, however, may well outweigh all of these traits or make only certain ones critical in importance. As we will show in Chapter 12, different kinds of tasks, different kinds of subordinates, and differing leader characteristics all affect what leader behavior will be effective. Thus, possession of the qualities listed does *not* guarantee that one will become a leader, nor does the absence of any one of them rule out the possibility of becoming an effective leader. We, therefore, must emphasize that the potential for leadership may be assumed to be widely distributed among the general population, and a wide variety of leader behaviors may be effective in particular situations (McGregor, 1960).

What, then, must be taken into account by leaders who wish to be effective in their particular organization? What behavior works best under what conditions? That is what we shall explore in this and the next chapter. We will begin in this chapter with an analysis of leadership in general as the exercise of power and influence, then continue in Chapter 12 with the roles of formally appointed managers and their leadership choices.

LEADERSHIP AS INFLUENCE

The core problem for leaders in organizations involves getting others to do what is necessary to accomplish the organization's goals. This is a complex process, since the goals as well as the means for accomplishing them are often unclear, subject to discussion or negotiation, and can change over time. A leader's boss (or bosses), peers, and subordinates all will have ideas about what should be done and how to do it, and they are likely to try to get their ideas heard. Furthermore, leaders are only human and unlikely to know everything, so they need to be able to alter their views when others make good points.

Nevertheless, once goals are determined, leaders or managers must find a way to create the conditions that will cause (or allow) subordinates to work hard and to direct that work toward organizational ends. This may call for many different kinds of influence behavior aimed in many directions; negotiating a larger budget; getting other departments to deliver accurate and timely information; providing vision, direction, or training to subordinates; simplifying or complicating work; obtaining a deserved salary increase for someone, and so forth. All these activities—up, sideways, and down—ultimately are aimed at getting others, especially subordinates, to do what is necessary to accomplish successfully the work of the system being led.

Leadership is the ability to get men to do what they don't want to do and like it.

Harry Truman

As countless leaders have discovered countless times, this is more easily said than done. Subordinates don't always know how to work well, don't always work as hard as is necessary, and don't automatically care about the unit's or organization's success, The fact is, leaders are interdependent with many others, especially their followers. They have impact on, and in turn are affected by, those with whom they must work. The key element is the *influence* the leader has on others and the *influence* they have in return. For this reason we can think of leadership as a *process* in which the involved parties *influence* one another in particular ways. *Influence is any act or potential act that affects the behavior of another person(s).* Let's look at the implications of using the concept.

First, influence cannot happen in isolation from others; it takes at least two to "tangle," just as with interpersonal relationships. The person who wants to influence must find someone to influence. Second, if you think about it carefully, you will see that only in the most extreme situations could *one* person in an influence transaction have *all* the influence—that is, affect the other's behavior without being affected in turn by the other's reaction. The machinist who leaps to attention when his boss gives an order, the secretary who bursts into tears when feeling that a request to work late is unreasonable, the student who challenges an assignment due the day after vacation, all exert influence on the person trying to influence them.

Cooperating humbly, for example, affects the person who is asking for cooperation and "pulls" more of the same from him or her. As Gandhi showed so well in India, humble, passive noncooperation can have a profound influence on those giving orders. Even the person who follows directions he or she knows are wrong out of fear of being fired or punished has influence on the behavior of the tyrant, allowing further exploitation and mistakes, since the directions were not resisted.

We must be careful, then, to remember that influence only succeeds in moving others in desired directions when the *net* influence, the amount of A's influence on B compared with B's influence on A, is greater. In the classroom or on the job, students and workers can be less *or* more influential than teachers and supervisors. *Leadership is net influence in a direction desired by the person possessing it.*

To understand this process better, we need to look at various types of influence. One important aspect of influence is whether or not it is formal or informal, part of a job's definition or acquired in some other way. *Formal influence is influence prescribed for the holder of an "office" or position in a particular social system.* It is influence *assigned* to a position. The coach of a team has formal influence in initiating practice sessions, selecting starting players and substitutes, and so forth. *Informal influence is influence not prescribed for the office holder but nevertheless affecting other members of the social system.* On the same team, for example, there may be several players whose advice other players and even the coach seek on such matters as techniques and strategy against opponents. Though by position the players have no special influence allotted or assigned to them, their knowledge or personal attractiveness, or both, and magnetism give them influence anyway. Influence based on special knowledge is *expert* influence, while influence based on personal charm is called *charisma*.

In addition to the distinction between formal and informal influence (i.e., assigned or unassigned), we need to add the concepts of legitimacy and illegitimacy. Legitimate influence is exerted by a person who is seen as having the right to do so by those influenced. In other words, legitimate influence is *accepted as proper* by the person being influenced. Conversely, illegitimate influence is exerted by a person not seen as having the right to do so by those being influenced. Illegitimate influence is *not accepted as proper* by the person being influenced. The basis for considering an influencer as legitimate may be (1) a positive assessment of his or her personal qualities, such as competence, experience, and age and (2) the acceptance of the process (such as election, appointment, or automatic succession) by which the person acquired a role calling for the exercise of influence. Legitimacy will usually be limited to areas within the scope of the system and its goals. For example, most people will believe that the boss may legitimately give orders about how to sell a machine but not about where to go on vacation. But within the scope of the organization, orders, requests, and directions will be seen as proper when they come from someone who has acquired an office by an approved process or has personal qualities considered appropriate.

To despise legitimate authority, no matter in whom it is invested, is unlawful; it is rebellion against God's will.

Leo XIII
Immortale Dei
November 1, 1885

On the other hand, even in the army—where soldiers are taught to "salute the uniform, not the man," suggesting that mere appointment to rank guarantees legitimacy—a soldier may refuse to follow direct orders under a variety of circumstances. To illustrate, if the commanding officer has disruptive personality characteristics or has acquired his office in objectionable ways, such as perceived favoritism, there may be rebellion. Furthermore, when influence is not seen as acquired legitimately, soldiers and other subordinates have many ways of subverting any orders from a person whose influence they do not accept, such as dragging their heels by following literally all rules in the books. Going passive is a common way of resisting what is seen as illegitimate influence.

Since having formal influence does not insure legitimacy nor does having informal influence insure illegitimacy, it is useful to combine the two categories into the four possible combinations, as shown in Figure 11–1.

By looking at the combinations, we can see the ways in which influence is exercised. *Formal-legitimate influence* is what is usually meant when people say "the boss has the authority" to enforce particular behaviors. It *is the influence both prescribed for the holder of an office in a social system and seen as his or her right to exert by the other members of it.* Many leadership activities in organizations involve formal-legitimate influence by someone who has been assigned a role with supervisory responsibilities and who can use organizational means to reward or punish subordinates. The right to hire, fire, promote, and adjust pay reinforces this kind of influence.

Since most people who accept jobs in an organization are reasonably willing to accept directions from their "boss" on job-related matters, legitimacy is often taken for granted and assumed to go with any formal role. During such times as the student strikes in the late 1960s and early 1970s or

FIGURE 11–1   Examples of Types of Influence

	FORMAL (ASSIGNED)	INFORMAL (NOT ASSIGNED)
LEGITIMATE (ACCEPTED AS PROPER).	Boss gives work-related orders to subordinate: "Stop making widgets and begin making frammisses." Teacher assigns an analytical paper, based on concepts in the text.	Respected colleague helps you solve a problem by showing you the proper order to make calculations. Basketball benchwarmer notices flaw in opponent's defense, convinces coach to alter offense.
ILLEGITIMATE (NOT AC- CEPTED AS PROPER).	Boss makes strong hints about subordinate's family life: "Send your son to a private school." Student put in charge of class discussion by instructor.	Co-worker threatens to beat you up if you continue to produce so much. Fellow students ridicule you for asking questions in class, despite instructor's request for questions.

the rebellions of workers in France, it becomes evident that the legitimacy of those with formal organizational positions is precarious and rests upon the attitudes of the "followers." Students challenged the rights of professors to determine subject matter, give exams and grades, hire and fire colleagues; and they exerted influence on other activities that had traditionally been seen as part of faculty prerogatives. Pressure from workers in several European countries has led to change in what were traditionally considered management's prerogatives. In several countries, workers must even be consulted for such decisions as plant location and new investments in equipment. Thus the boundaries of legitimacy for decisions is changing. Furthermore, legitimacy, even for someone in a formal position, must be earned and may occasionally need renewal. At different times a formal leader may find legitimacy slipping away, because of questions about competence or about the way in which the person is leading. Similarly, some subordinates may see the boss as legitimate while others don't. It is often the case that an appointed leader is perceived as legitimate by those with similar backgrounds and as illegitimate by those with backgrounds different from the leader's. A scientist might not, for example, accept the influence of an engineer as a project leader as readily as would another engineer. Since legitimacy is an attitude about a person by other persons, it can change just as do other attitudes. Nevertheless, much of the work of organizations is done because there is a considerable amount of legitimacy granted to those in formal positions; but that is by no means the only kind of leadership exerted.

A great deal of influence is based upon knowledge, expertise (whether perceived or real), or personal charm, rather than position (French & Raven, 1960). *This informal-legitimate influence by a member of a social system stands apart from the prescribed influence of his or her office but is accepted as within one's rights by the others in the system.* It is not predictable from organization charts but is essential to organizational functioning. Some people know things or behave in charismatic ways that others value, regardless of position, and are given influence accordingly. The most expert tax assessor in an Internal Revenue Service office may be consulted by other assessors and listened to even though he or she has no formal assignment to help others. The rewards and punishments available to this kind of influencer are more personal—that is, he or she can give or withhold important information or support in return for gratitude and respect.

Leadership in classroom groups is often of the "expert" kind, with the most knowledgeable member(s) of the group gradually becoming respected and listened to even when there is no formal leader. In fact, among many student groups, only a person with recognized expertise can take or be given leadership and then only for particular matters. There is a widespread student norm that no peer should give orders or directions to another student, so even those students put in leadership roles by a class exercise often hold back from initiating the giving of directions.

MANAGERIAL BULLETIN

A Title Is No Guarantee of Power

And these considerations . . . hamstrung LaGuardia in his dealings with [Robert] Moses: Moses' popularity; Moses' immense influence with a governor and a legislature from whom the mayor constantly needed favors; Moses' ability to ram through the great public works that the mayor desperately wanted . . . scandal-free and in time for the next election. With good reason, he doubted whether anyone else could. The powers that the mayor possessed over Moses' authorities in theory he did not possess in practice. Political realities gave him no choice but to allow Moses to remain at their head. And the mayor knew it.

Moses knew it, too. After reading the bond agreements and contracts, LaGuardia dropped all further discussion of the authorities' powers. Moses never raised the matter again. But thereafter he treated LaGuardia not as his superior but as an equal. In the areas in which he was interested—transportation and recreation—Robert Moses, who had never been elected by the people of the city to any office, was thence forward to have at least as much voice in determining the city's future as any official the people *had* elected—including the mayor.

SOURCE: Robert A. Caro, *The Power Broker: Robert Moses and The Fall Of New York* (New York: Alfred A. Knopf, ©1974).

Conversely, a fellow student making a "grab for power" will usually be resisted by other students. Sometimes such a person has quickly volunteered for a leadership role before others dare to, and is allowed to take it despite feelings that "it isn't right"; in that case, the student has *formal-illegitimate influence,* which may not last long, unless he or she is seen as helping the group reach its goals. Similarly, in organizations where members are accustomed to having considerable say in matters affecting them, the boss's decision to create a new position located between him or her and the others ("because the work load is too heavy for me") can result in resentment toward *whomever* is put in that new job and lead to only grudging cooperation. If that person, however, has the formal authorization to administer some organizational rewards and punishments, he or she may end up with considerable influence anyway.

Finally, *the person who acquires influence over others by personal access to some valued rewards or feared punishments is using informal-illegitimate influence.* Physical threats by a fellow worker can coerce compliance that would otherwise be refused, as can special relationships with higher-ups. In one school system, for example, by maintaining a close relationship with several powerful school board members, the music director forced principals to release students for weeklong band trips and to arrange schedules to suit his convenience. He thus obtained more influence over principals than was called for by his position or was seen as his right by them. Though he obtained compliance, he also created considerable resentment and was constantly criticized behind his back by the principals.

MANAGERIAL BULLETIN

Who Can Decide?

Sir Brian is well aware that the time has come for the Cavendish [Laboratory] to rethink its priorities again, but he favours developing responsibility for this. He is telling the people in his own group to think the priorities out for themselves. A dictator, he says, would cause enormous anger.

A dictator is one thing. A strong leader might be welcome in the laboratory. In 1979, Sir Brian handed over to Professor Alan Cook as head of the Cavendish. . . . Left keeping Professor Cook's job warm [while he's on sabbatical] is Sir Sam Edwards. . . . Unlike Sir Brian, he thinks the head of the Cavendish still is powerful. He reckons that Cambridge's com-

mittee structure puts power into the hands of somebody who really wants to wield it. However, as only acting head of the Cavendish, Sir Sam reckons he cannot take strategic decisions.

The lab does have an able manager, Mr. John Deakin, its secretary. . . . He takes on most of the administrative load that normally falls to heads of departments, leaving professors free to get on with teaching and research. It is an excellent arrangement. But there are some decisions only a department head can take.

SOURCE: *The Economist*, February 27, 1982, p. 83.

Taking Initiative as an Act of Leadership

Have you ever found yourself in a class that was hot and stuffy to the point that you and other students were having trouble concentrating on the lecture or discussion? What do you do? Wait and hope the instructor will recognize the problem and call a break; or raise your hand, point out the difficulty, and suggest opening some windows and taking a break? Raising your hand could be an act of leadership. To wait for the designated leader (instructor) to act can mean missing an opportunity to make it a better class. Taking initiative might have the payoff of enhancing your influence (or status) but also involves the risk of being "shot down" by the formal leader of the class.

In the next chapter we examine the obligations and choices of those who have been formally appointed to managerial positions, that is, who are in a formal role. In this chapter we have been discussing the exercise of influence by anyone and have defined *leadership as influence*. We might also define leadership as those *actions that move a group toward its goals* (such as opening a window when the room is stuffy). The distinction between formal and informal leadership is a useful reminder that as group members and as subordinates anyone can exert influence (leadership)—and often should. In small work groups it is important for all members to take initiative. Similarly, it can be important that a subordinate exert initiative in a staff meeting or a committee meeting and not just wait for all leadership to come from the designated manager or chairperson.

How People Are Influenced

There are three processes (not mutually exclusive) by which people are influenced—*compliance, identification,* and *internalization* (Kelman, 1961). The very same behavior (namely, doing what you are told to do by another person) can stem from any one or a combination of these processes.

Compliance amounts to doing something because of the costs of not doing it. You go along with the "order" on the outside, but inside you may feel resentment or resignation. Any leader's influence can rest on compliance, particularly where there is fear of punishment or a desire to gain some reward; this may be the only way in which an informal-illegitimate leader can exert influence. Where compliance is operating, leaders will be successful only as long as they have control over whatever it is followers need or want.

Identification occurs when you are influenced by someone because of the attractiveness of that person, because the person either is likable and has charisma or represents something to which you aspire (e.g., an important position). Formal, designated leaders or managers often exert influence because subordinates identify with them. They may also be legitimized by their subordinates through the same process.

Identification with a charismatic leader can dramatically affect behavior for people who want to believe in lofty goals that will somehow be ennobling. When such people see a leader as having a grand vision of what is possible and offering specific means for achieving their dreams, they identify with the leader and dedicate themselves to the cause. This can lead to extraordinary efforts by followers on behalf of the leader and, thus, unusually high organizational performance. That is why effective high-level executives spend so much time creating a vision or "story" about where they see their organization (or unit) going and then telling and retelling it to colleagues, subordinates, and outsiders (Peters, 1978).

Ironically, it has been claimed that charismatic leaders only succeed because they make followers feel weak and dependent. But research has demonstrated that some charismatic leaders can make followers feel *more* powerful, *more* confident, and *more* capable, not less (McClelland, 1975). Followers come to see themselves as achieving their *own* goals through the leader, not as

---

A statesman who too far outruns the experience of his people will fail in achieving a domestic consensus, however wise his policies. [On the other hand], a statesman who limits his policies to the experience of his people is doomed to sterility.

Henry Kissinger
***Time*, November 8, 1976**

having the leader's goals forced on them. When this happens, influence through identification with the leader can spread to another mode, internalization.

Internalization, the third kind of influence, happens when leaders have the necessary expertise and values to be credible to their followers; they come to believe that what the leader suggests is in fact the best course of action for them. The leader's opinions are seen as valid and trustworthy. The effect is that followers internalize the leader's opinions, thus giving full legitimization to the leader—formally designated or not.

. . . the ultimate paradox of social leadership and social power. To be an effective leader, one must turn all of his so-called followers into leaders.

David C. McClelland
Power: The Inner Experience

Over the long run, the most successful managers are those whose influence is based on credibility—that is, where the followers are convinced by the logic of the leader's ideas and requests, and internalize the influence.

You can see how a combination of these factors can have different effects. Compliance may be necessary under certain conditions (e.g., an emergency or when the task is minor and implementation easily enforced) but is difficult for a manager to sustain. Some people will do what you want strictly out of compliance and some because they identify with you or your position. To maximize your effectiveness as a leader, however, it is best to build credibility and reach people through internalization, so that they will do what is necessary because they want to.

Generating Employee Commitment

The important outcome of both identification and internalization is *commitment*, which is an attitude driven from within the person. You know when you are committed to something—a person, an activity, a belief—when your behavior is motivated by forces inside yourself and not from outside pressures, as with compliance. In the past, organizations have depended heavily on compliance and control to accomplish their goals; today more and more organizations are attempting to build employee commitment, which obviously has more long-lasting benefits. Leadership efforts have been directed to three major areas: the work itself, the relations among people, and the organization as a whole.

Approaches to building commitment to the work itself include both formal methods, like work redesign, and informal ones, like permitting em-

MANAGERIAL BULLETIN

What the Leaders of Tomorrow See

Forget your old, tired ideas about leadership. The most successful corporation of the 1990s will be something called a *learning organization,* a consummately adaptive enterprise with workers freed to think for themselves, to identify problems and opportunities, and to go after them. In such an organization, the leader will ensure that everyone has the resources and power to make swift day-to-day deci-

sions. Faced with challenges we can only guess at now, he or she will set the overall direction for the enterprise, after listening to a thousand voices from within the company and without. In this sense, the leader will have to be the best learner of them all.

SOURCE: Brian Dumaine, *Fortune,* July 3, 1989.

ployees a high degree of freedom to manage their own work procedures. Approaches to generating interpersonal commitment also have included formal and informal methods. Planned team-building is an example of the former, while the encouragement of collaborative norms typifies the latter. Similarly, organizational commitment is developed in both formal and informal ways. The "transformational" leader, who inspires people to excel and articulates a meaningful vision for the organization, acts in both formal and informal ways to build employee commitment (B. M. Bass, 1985). In Chapter 12 we will introduce you to the concept of "developmental leadership," which is similar to that of transformational leadership, but which goes beyond it by spelling out practical applications in the workplace.[1]

Finally, it is important to recognize that, while commitment in the three areas discussed above tend to be related, they also exist independently of each other. Many workers are committed to their work and not to their colleagues or to the organization as a whole. And many employees are committed to their "team" and even to the organization and feel a very low level of identification with the work they are doing. Since there are a variety of combinations of the three dimensions, it is important for a manager to develop a diagnostic profile of the three as they fit his or her part of the organization. Such a diagnosis allows for a focused approach to actions that will address problems of commitment where they exist. In the Managerial Tools box on page 323, we have listed some of the key issues that pertain to employee commitment as they affect the individual, interpersonal relationships, group behavior, and the organization as a whole.

---

[1] It might interest you to know that the traits of the transformational or developmental leader are claimed to be more typically characteristic of women than of men. The implications of this for future organizational needs and for personal learning and opportunity are extremely important. See "Ways Women Lead" by Judith Rosener in the *Harvard Business Review,* November–December 1990, pp. 119–25, and the responses in the following issue, January–February, 1991.

MANAGERIAL TOOLS

Gaining Commitment from Your Employees: Some Key Points

- For the *individual*, it depends upon:
  1. Involvement.
  2. Choice.
  3. Meeting positive expectations.
  4. Feeling supported and valued.
  5. Need fulfillment.
  6. Feedback that facilitates improvement.
  7. Intrinsic satisfactions.
  8. Challenge and opportunities to grow.
  9. Being treated fairly.
  10. Affirmation of self-concept.
- In *interpersonal relationships*, it depends upon:
  1. Mutual support, acceptance and reinforcement of self.
  2. Openness where needed and appropriate.
  3. Trust and confidence (mutual).
  4. Compatible styles:
     a. Similar or
     b. Complementary.
  5. Acceptance or appreciation of differences, or both.
  6. Opportunities to problem solve jointly.
  7. Willingness to manage conflicts.

- For a *group*, it depends upon:
  1. Norms that support organizational goals.
  2. Cohesiveness around those norms.
  3. Rewards at a group level.
  4. Group being valued by organization.
  5. Acceptance of individual differences in abilities, preferences, and values.
  6. Ability to match member resources to any given task.
- For the *total system*, it depends upon:
  1. The parts being aware of the whole.
  2. Groups being willing to accept each other's legitimacy and importance.
  3. Willingness of people to interact across group boundaries.
  4. Recognition of the importance of reciprocity.
  5. Appreciating the importance of diversity with respect to:
     a. Ideas and
     b. People.

SOURCE: Stephen L. Fink, *Building Employee Commitment* (forthcoming).

POWER

The capacity to exert influence is power. (Often "power" and "influence" are used interchangeably.) People who have the ability to exert one or more of the four types of influence have power, which can be used toward the organization's ends or toward subgroup or individual goals, including those in direct opposition to organizational goals. As suggested earlier, no one is completely without influence, but some people have more net influence than others and hence more power.

Power is often perceived to be a bit "dirty," at least in the United States, though in the past few years the idea of acquiring power has begun to become more respectable. A few best-selling books on power[2] have helped

---

[2] Examples: *Power: How to Get It and How to Use It*, by Michael Korda; *Winning through Intimidation*, by Robert Ringer; *The Power Broker*, by Robert Caro.

MANAGERIAL BULLETIN

Tyrants Beware

Nobody minds being subjected to the power of somebody who's genuinely interested in getting the job done and making more money and exacting maximum performance. But nobody wants to be told that they have to have their pencils sharpened and the erasers all facing in the same direction before they leave the office at night.

SOURCE: Michael Korda. "Psychodynamics of Power," *Mainliner,* March 1977.

bring power tactics out of the closet (or at least out of the corporation suite) and made power discussable. But power is more than a set of sneaky tactics for grinding others into the dirt; *power in organizations is the ability to make things happen* (Kanter, 1977). Organizational work cannot be done without that ability, and managers need to understand it in order to bring together the people and resources to accomplish what must be done.

Sources of Power in Organization

How, then, is power obtained by individuals in organizations? In general: **The more legitimate one is perceived to be, the greater the likelihood of acceptance of one's attempts to influence, and the less resentment at going along (Simon, 1957).** Power goes to those who are seen as having a right to it. Conversely, the less legitimate forms of influence breed resistance and resentment, though they will probably enhance the power of someone who already possesses other kinds of legitimate influence.

Additionally, informal influence is often necessary for those with formal influence if they want more than grudging cooperation; when a formally designated leader does not have some knowledge seen as helpful by subordinates, it will be difficult to secure more than token compliance. As organizations become more complex and technically demanding, more people in leadership positions do *not* have the technical expertise necessary to gain influence beyond that of their own job description, making it hard for them to get full cooperation from those who know more than they do about some other aspects of the job. They must then find ways of gaining informal influence through their own personal attractiveness and their ability to make friendly relationships—or they must settle for a low-power position relative to their subordinates.

Perhaps the primary source of power is the ability to enhance the organization positively in relation to its "environment" or key problems (Pfeffer, 1977; Pfeffer & Salancik, 1977). Those who can help the organization achieve its goals by overcoming the most difficult, pressing, and dan-

MANAGERIAL BULLETIN

Rep. Bolling Takes His Leave of Power

It took me 32 years to realize that it's sometimes more important to have the trappings of power than power itself. If you've got a good-looking room with a nice chandelier, your colleagues may think you've got power. Actually, all you've got is a chandelier and room. Washington is full of illusions like that.

SOURCE: Dennis Farney, *The Wall Street Journal,* January 1, 1982.

gerous problems are likely to acquire power. A marketing expert in a company that can sell everything it can make but cannot solve its production problems is less likely to gain power than the production engineer who can eliminate the bottlenecks. So it helps either to acquire skills that are (and will be) critical to the organization or to seek employment where the skills one has are most likely to be needed.

Furthermore, it helps to do things that are not routine, that are unusual or extraordinary in the organization. **A person who performs critical tasks in a way that is already established and routinized will receive less power than a person who develops new methods or procedures, starts a new unit or task, creates a new project or product (Kanter, 1977).** That is why those who are organizationally ambitious do not like to be the second or third person in a job; they would prefer to be the first to do a job, so they can most easily leave their mark. And in any job they move into, they often seek early changes in something, even office layout or decor, to show that they intend to do things differently.

That suggests a third important aspect of power acquisition: It is not enough to be doing extraordinary, critical activities; one's efforts must be visible and recognized. **Power goes not just to those who do well, but to those who are also *seen* to do well (Kanter, 1977).** (In fact, some cynics claim that appearance is all, though it is hard to sustain power when one does not actually produce.) Those who want power must find ways to achieve recognition. Among other things, it is a political process.

This can happen in many ways. A well-written and well-timed report can help promote visibility, as can a well-presented oral report at a meeting. The opportunity to make a presentation to higher-ups creates a natural chance for "showing one's stuff" and for demonstrating the importance and relevance of the work done. Similarly, serving on committees, often seen as a nuisance, is a chance to show others besides one's boss what one can do. "Doing one's homework" before meetings often helps both to make a good impression and to lead to more responsibility and thus power within the committee. Those who want power look for responsibility, for chances to demonstrate ability to get things done.

MANAGERIAL BULLETIN

Labor Letter

Firing rights are eroded by courts, forcing employers to revise methods.

The long-held right to fire employees "at will" has been limited by state court decisions. As a result, "you can still fire people," says a New York apparel concern executive, but if companies aren't careful,

"you can have some very expensive consequences" if employees sue. Corporate personnel manuals "are getting very detailed" as protection against legal action, says Columbia University professor David Lewin.

SOURCE: *The Wall Street Journal*, October 1, 1985.

Through committee work or social contacts, power seekers make connections with one or more people higher in the organization. A higher-up who thinks a person shows promise might become a kind of "sponsor" who will look after the aspirant's career, help create opportunities, and build reputation. Also, when people are perceived as "having a friend or friends in high places," then others may defer to them or seek them out even without direct intervention on the powerful person's part.

Since power is a social process of influencing others to act, it comes in part from being able to do things for others that obligate them to be helpful in return by fulfilling the norm of reciprocity (Gouldner, 1960; Kotter, 1979). Thus, the person seeking power needs to find ways to be helpful to others in the organization. Volunteering to handle unpleasant tasks, finding ways to make others' jobs easier, and doing favors whenever possible are all ways of creating obligations, which can be collected on when needed. That is exactly how politicians, who have to be interested in power, build it.

Another way of looking at this is in terms of control of key rewards and punishments in the organization. Power reflects the ability to give rewards or punishments in order to get others to do what one believes needs to be done (Kotter, 1979). **The more a person has access to controlling rewards and punishments, the greater his or her power (French & Raven, 1960).** Thus, a person who can give the formal rewards or use the formula punishments of an organization—hiring, firing, promoting, adjusting salary, allocating choice assignments or space, giving recommendations, and so forth—*and* give informal rewards or punishments, such as help, information, and liking, will have the most power. Just what the rewards and punishments are depends on the organization and the perceptions of those in it; but whatever it is that people value or fear, those who control it will have power to influence behavior. Attention to what the rewards are to those in the organization, who manages them, and which departments or units currently get them in greatest proportion, can aid in determining how to get control of

MANAGERIAL BULLETIN

Want Office Status? Remove All Papers from Top of Desk and Then Remove the Desk; Very-Top Bosses Favor Living Room Atmosphere

The next time you're in an executive's office, ask yourself the following questions:

- Is the desk big and imposing with lots of drawers?
- Is there an expensive desktop pen-and-pencil set in evidence?
- Are important-looking documents stacked about?

To keen observers of the corporate scene, an affirmative answer to any of those questions has but one indication: Almost as surely as if he wore a short-sleeved shirt and a clip-on bow tie, the occupant of the office can be stamped as lower echelon. At the very top, "Everybody wants an office that doesn't look like an office. . . ." [T]he offices of today's really powerful executives show few if any signs that any work is performed there. Those at the top . . . want a relaxed, living room–library feeling. . . . Today the idea is to be accessible. "Executives don't want offices anymore that give the feeling you're entering the Vatican."

Edward E. Elson, the president of a privately owned Atlanta news distribution agency, achieves the "home, sweet home" look with an 18th-century Chinese rug, six club chairs, a pony-skin lounge chair, and no desk at all. Whenever he needs to write, he settles down with a lap pad.

"Visitors are disarmed," Mr. Elson says. "My office gives the impression that there is more to this guy than just business."

Working Fireplaces

Elsewhere the living room–library atmosphere is imparted by a working fireplace. . . . Sanford Weill, [when] chairman of Shearson/American Express, Inc., had one installed in his office. . . . ([T]he touch of warmth wasn't attained without . . . "a considerable amount" of money; the chairman's office is on the 106th floor of a 110-story building, and it was necessary to channel a chimney through four floors to reach the roof.)

This home away from home for the truly powerful is generally set off from the rest of the herd. (If the carpeting that runs through the hallways of the executive floor continues into an office . . . , it's a dead giveaway that the occupant lacks status; for top people, Oriental rugs are de rigueur.) . . .

And if you're really powerful, you have your own private dining room adjacent to your living room–library. That is a room distinct from the "executive dining room" used by the masses of lesser-titled folk. . . .

Private Bathroom

Of course, home at the top of the heap isn't complete without a private bathroom—a convenience and a sanctuary that many corporate observers regard as the ultimate power symbol. True, sometimes the symbol is diluted; at Minnesota Mining & Manufacturing Company in St. Paul, Minnesota, for example, one executive building houses no fewer than 37 private bathrooms. But the truly powerful at some companies go beyond mere bathrooms of the tile-and-porcelain, closet-sized variety; at Johnson Publishing Company in Chicago, publisher John Johnson's bathroom has marble trimmings, an adjacent dressing area, and even a sauna. . . .

them. At the very least, power seekers figure out what rewards they already control so that they can more wisely use them to create obligations or induce cooperation when needed. One common accessible reward (even at lower levels of the organization) is finishing, on time, work that someone else needs and is waiting for. That builds gratitude—or, as it is called in some organizations, *chits*—which can be "cashed in" when needed.

One interesting aspect of the kind of power that is associated with rewards is the power obtained by helping to relieve people's anxieties (reduce their tensions). "Got a problem? Go see Joe. He'll help you work it out." In fact, when this kind of power is carried to an extreme, unusually high expectations can be imposed on the holder and may even put a strain on that person's ability to retain that power.

Pfeffer (1977) points out the power one obtains by being seen as someone who can reduce uncertainty in an otherwise chaotic situation. Given the nature of organizations today, this source of power is undoubtedly on the increase. Most people have a limited tolerance for uncertainty (or ambiguity); the person who can help to reduce that uncertainty is likely to attract a following. It is not unlike the following of any person who is viewed as "having the answers."

None of the methods described provide for easy access to power; in fact, sheer willingness to work hard is almost always a requisite for acquiring power. As should be clear by now, hard work alone may not be sufficient—it is necessary to work at critical unusual tasks with or for people who recognize what you are doing—but without hard work it is extremely difficult to acquire power. Furthermore, **a desire for power with little genuine concern for the well-being of the organization and for other members can be very destructive to the organization—and even to the power seeker.**

Consequences of Possessing Power

Regardless of the source of power, its possession tends to lead toward certain consequences. These can be stated in the following propositions (Berelson & Steiner, 1964):

1. **The more power attributed to a person, the more he or she is the recipient of:**
   a. **Communication.**
   b. **Solicitous behavior.**
   c. **Deference by others seeking power.**

This proposition suggests that those with power will be deferred to and that, when those with less power are in the presence of powerful persons, they will address comments to them more than to one another. Large discrepancies in power between individuals, however, can interfere with successful work. If subordinates do not have sufficient power, they often will not be able to get their work done, because they can't get the resources or responses they need. This in turn reduces the leader's power. Furthermore, large power gaps often lead to avoidance of the high-power person by the low-power person and to distorted communications—telling the powerful person what

---

MANAGERIAL BULLETIN

"That Report Is on My Coffee Table"

Many of your readers . . . have aspirations of becoming wealthy and powerful. If they succeed, however, I hope their egos will not require offices with private saunas and push-button controls. If one is important and powerful, the right people know it. If not, handpainted china will not change it.

With the economy in a depression, dividends being omitted, and millions unemployed, it is embarrassing to read about the conspicuous consumption and crystalline egos of America's top executives. What we need is offices that look like offices, not living rooms.

SOURCE: From a letter to the editor of *The Wall Street Journal* by Sam Bosch, January 28, 1982.

---

one thinks that person wants to hear. Any powerful person will have to be keenly aware of this problem and work hard to find ways to make less-powerful people feel comfortable enough to tell the truth. Without accurate communications (and probably multiple sources), a powerful person will lose touch with actual feelings and is likely to make mistakes.

2. **The more a person is treated as though he or she has power, the greater will be his or her self-esteem.**

Feeling deferred to, powerful people have a tendency to begin to view themselves as important, which enhances how they feel about themselves. Rosabeth Kanter (1977) points out the change in Gerald Ford's appearance after he—much to his own surprise—became President when Nixon resigned. Ford began to walk taller, speak more confidently, and in general demonstrate that having acquired power, even by default, made him feel better about himself.

Not surprisingly, then, people who are powerful tend to seek one another out. Power breeds more power. Thus:

3. **The more power attributed to a person, the more that person will tend to identify with others who also have power.**
4. **Those with high-attributed power are attracted to and communicate more with others with high-attributed power than with those who have low-attributed power.**

Many political leaders have been known to shift their attention and allegiance from their constituencies to their fellow politicians. The same thing can happen in an organization, especially as people climb increasingly higher in the hierarchy. Are you familiar with instances in which an emergent social leader in a group was appointed formal leader by the system, thus enhancing his or her degree of influence? Very often the individual is then seen to "change"; he or she is seen as less friendly to "us mere workers" and as

---

MANAGERIAL BULLETIN

"CEO Disease: Egotism Can Breed Corporate Disaster—and the Malady Is Spreading

Pampered, protected, and perked, the American CEO can know every indulgence. The executive who finally reaches the top of a major corporation enters an exclusive fraternity. The CEO's judgment and presence are eagerly sought by other captains of industry and policymakers. CEOs zip around the world in private jets and cash the heftiest personal paychecks in industry. They take home 85 times what the average blue-collar worker makes, unlike their counterparts in Japan, where the ratio is closer to 10 to 1.

It is a job that can easily go to one's head—and often does. . . .

SOURCE: *Business Week*, April 1, 1991.

---

playing up to the powers that be. This frequently happens as people find themselves in new leadership roles, having influence over people in areas never before experienced.

In fact, one of the dangers of superiors having great power differentials over subordinates is that they begin to perceive any successes as due to their own skills and to discount the capacities of the subordinates. **Great power differentials lead to overestimates by the powerful of their own contributions and to blindness to the contributions of others (Kipnis, 1976).**

By examining these propositions, you can see why it is often said that power corrupts. The entire constellation of behavior and relationships that follow from the possession of influence generates a cycle in which people with high power tend to become more and more differentiated from those with low power, even though each is dependent upon the other. The person with power has it only because it is given by others; it ends the moment those who are doing the giving choose not to do so. A leader is a leader only so long as there are followers. It certainly raises the question of who really possesses the power, the one who leads or those being led.

There go my people. I must find out where they are going so I can lead them.

Anonymous

Another consequence of power for someone new to a position is the likelihood of being closely observed by subordinates about where the leader's loyalties and priorities will be, how open they can be, how friendly and close the leader will allow them to be, and the like. Such early "testing" is often symbolic: The test is not direct, and the leader's reactions are carefully scrutinized for favorable and unfavorable signs of what is to come. A leader who is

MANAGERIAL BULLETIN

The Bureaucrat Gets the Last Word

Ed Garvey was scheduled to make a business trip and needed a cash advance. He went to the controller's office to get the necessary signature on a form in order to receive the cash. Mr. Pomeroy, an administrative assistant, was the person whose signature Ed needed. But first Ed had to get past Mrs. Arnold, the secretary and receptionist in the controller's office. The conversation went like this:

Ed: I'd like to see Mr. Pomeroy for just one minute. I need his signature for a cash advance.

Mrs. Arnold: Mr. Pomeroy is very busy, so you'll just have to wait. Please sit over there.

Ed: Mrs. Arnold, I really have to get back to my office. Could you ask Mr. Pomeroy if he could take a minute to sign this?

Mrs. Arnold: Well, I hate to interrupt him, but I'll see if he can take a moment. (Goes into Pomeroy's office and returns after about two minutes.) He'll see you, but you may have to leave the form here.

Ed goes into Pomeroy's office and explains that this trip was a last-minute thing and he was under time pressure. The conversation went like this:

Pomeroy: You know that at least 24 hours is required for approval of a cash advance.

Ed: I know, but I don't have 24 hours before I have to leave. I need the cash advance today.

Pomeroy: Well, I don't know if I can take it upon myself to sign this. If I break the rules for you I could end up with endless requests like this from others.

Ed: Look, this is an exceptional situation. The rules don't cover every situation.

Pomeroy: I know, but I do have a job to perform.

Ed: Would you get into trouble if you signed it?

Pomeroy: No, but I believe in following proper procedure, Mr. Garvey.

Ed: I do too, but sometimes other things are more important than rules. Is there someone over you I can go to?

Pomeroy: I don't think that will be necessary. I'll make the exception this time, Mr. Garvey, but please try to give me the proper notice in the future.

Ed: That's very nice of you, Mr. Pomeroy. Thank you.

When Ed walked out, he had the signature, but he felt like he bought it with his soul.

unaware that such testing is inevitable can make inadvertent mistakes that are hard to live down.

For example, one of five senior vice presidents of an insurance company was appointed president. Having been there a long time, he had many friends in the company. Two key events made problems for him. First, delighted and rather surprised at being named president, he decided to have a small party at his house to celebrate. Immediately, another senior vice president who had also wanted the job decided that the new president was "rubbing it in" and that the president was no longer going to be as easily influenced as he had been! A few days later, the president met with a group of middle managers. Two of his friends in that group (one a bright young woman whose career he had greatly helped), thinking that now that he was president some problems could at last be straightened out, raised questions about the way the problem was being handled. The president, feeling surprised at the questions and betrayed by his friends, snapped back an answer. Though he did not mean his answer to be more than an instant reaction to what was for him a sensitive issue, others at the meeting spread the word that the new president was going to be "very tough" and could not be disagreed with! The president had not been aware of the symbolic impact of his spontaneous and, to him, harmless reaction.

Consequences of Not Possessing Power

Although too much power can indeed be corrupting, so can too little. Since power is needed to make things happen in organizations—being without it means insufficient resources, information, and support—managers who lack it have difficulty being effective, The manager who does not know what is going on, can't get the needed budget, and is not backed by higher-ups will inevitably be resisted by subordinates. Why should they cooperate with someone who can't deliver?

As a result, managers who are in positions that yield too little power (or who fill their positions ineptly and lose what power they had) tend to:

1. **Overcontrol subordinates, try to make them cooperate.**
2. **Become petty tyrants, taking out their frustration on anyone they can dominate.**
3. **Become turf-minded and rules-oriented, carving out a fiefdom where they can reign supreme (Kanter, 1977).**

In this way, powerlessness also corrupts, since managers who become so dominating are seldom effective. Their attempts to find someone on whom to exercise power only increase the resentment of their victims, causing even stronger attempts at domination, more resistance, and so on. Without the proper tools, few managers can be successful.

Some Currencies of Influence

Often people see themselves as having little power, because they do not occupy some formal position of power. But, "People also underestimate their power, because they aren't creative in seeing connections between what they have and what someone else wants" (Cohen & Bradford, 1990). They point out that these connections are like "currencies," which serve as a basis of exchange: "I give you my time, and you give me appreciation." "I generate ideas and you feel empowered to act in ways that I, in turn, value." Managers have a vast array of currencies to influence their subordinates, their peers, and their bosses. Students don't even begin to recognize the currencies they have to influence their instructors, ranging from nods of the head during a lecture to high levels of performance on papers or exams. The chart below (Management Tools), shows a variety of currencies that are valued in organizations.

MANAGERIAL TOOLS

Currencies Frequently Valued in Organizations

Inspiration-Related Currencies

Vision	Being involved in a task that has larger significance for unit, organization, customers, or society.
Excellence	Having a chance to do important things really well.
Moral/ethical correctness	Doing what is "right" by a higher standard than efficiency.

Task-Related Currencies

New resources	Obtaining money, budget increases, personnel, space, and so forth.
Challenge/learning	Doing tasks that increase skills and abilities.
Assistance	Getting help with existing projects or unwanted tasks.
Task support	Receiving overt or subtle backing or actual assistance with implementation.
Rapid response	Quicker response time.
Information	Access to organizational as well as technical knowledge.

Position-Related Currencies

Recognition	Acknowledgment of effort, accomplishment, or abilities.
Visibility	The chance to be known by higher-ups or significant others in the organization.
Reputation	Being seen as competent, committed.
Insiderness/importance	A sense of centrality, of "belonging."
Contacts	Opportunities for linking with others.

Relationship-Related Currencies

Understanding	Having concerns and issues listened to.
Acceptance/inclusion	Closeness and friendship.
Personal support	Personal and emotional backing.

Personal-Related Currencies

Gratitude	Appreciation or expression of indebtedness.
Ownership/involvement	Ownership of and influence over important tasks.
Self-concept	Affirmation of one's values, self-esteem, and identity.
Comfort	Avoidance of hassles.

SOURCE: Cohen and Bradford, *Influence without Authority* (New York: John Wiley & Sons, 1990).

Although many are not likely to fit your present circumstances, you might explore the chart and possibly discover some influence currencies you do in fact possess and never realized you have. Also, try using the Personal Application Exercise at the end of the chapter.

MANAGERIAL TOOLS

Guide to Managing Your Boss—Or Anyone Else You Don't Control

- Understand your boss and the forces surrounding him or her:
  - Boss's goals and objectives.
  - How boss is rewarded.
  - Pressures on boss:
    - Form his or her boss.
    - From the organization.
    - From the environment.
  - Boss's power (capacity to mobilize resources).
  - Boss's strengths, weaknesses, blind spots, and hot buttons.
  - Boss's managerial style—preferred degree of:
    - Control.
    - Information received and shared.
    - Formality.
    - Openness.
- Work to make your boss's life easier:
  - Aid in accomplishing boss's goals.
  - Increase boss's visibility and reputation.
  - Pick up tasks boss doesn't like or isn't good at.
- Tie your requests/preferences to boss's/organization's goals; show how giving you what you want will help achieve the goals.

- Ask boss for evaluation of how you can perform better:
  - If boss is uncomfortable, offer self-appraisal to ease discussion.
- Keep boss informed:
  - With frequency preferred by boss.
  - With level of detail preferred by boss.
  - In form preferred by boss:
    - Oral?
    - Brief reports?
    - Extensive reports?
    - Executive summary?
- Work to demonstrate dependability; keep your word.
- Reward boss whenever he or she manages in way you prefer:
  - Many bosses feel underappreciated.
  - Public praise increases boss's reputation, aiding obtaining of resources.

SOURCE: Based on J. J. Gabarro and J. P. Kotter, "Managing Your Boss," *Harvard Business Review*, January–February 1980; and Allan R. Cohen, "How to Manage Your Boss," *Ms. Magazine*, February 1981.

Liking versus Respect

It is not uncommon for those who have power to be less well liked; as noted in the group chapters, the group members who contribute most to getting tasks accomplished are usually most respected but seldom most liked. Informal task leaders often have to trade liking for respect; while occasionally someone can get both, most often: **The more a leader strives for popularity, the less effective he or she becomes as task leader. Also, the more the leader strives to maintain task leadership, the more he or she will lose popularity (Slater, 1965).** Can you think of any conditions where these propositions would not be true? How important each factor is in comparison with the other depends upon the nature of the situation and the person involved in the leadership role, When a strong task leader brings a group through a very difficult situation, popularity may soar, at least for awhile.

MANAGERIAL BULLETIN

The Pentagon "Club" Closed Ranks to Shut out Resor

Some defense officials sympathetic to Mr. Resor do feel, however, that he contributed to his own troubles by an unwillingness or inability to deal with the petty intrigues that are, after all, a cornerstone of any self-respecting bureaucracy.

"There was no major conspiracy to undermine Stan; it just happened, and he helped," said one. "You needed someone who could go to these little empires that have been built up and say, 'What are your priorities, what are the major issues, what are you doing?' Stan just waited for people to come to him, and very few did."

A top defense official said in exasperation: "This is a very tough place. There's a lot of power; a lot of money at stake. In comes Stanley Resor—a very decent gentleman, somewhat old-school, not a self-serving type in any way.

He was entirely wrong for the job."

SOURCE: Bernard Weinraub. *The New York Times*, March 18, 1979, copyright © 1979 by the New York Times Company. Reprinted by permission.

All leaders have to struggle with the question of how close they can be with their followers. Can a leader also be a friend? If so, does this still allow him or her to push them into working harder? Or, if the leader remains distant, will the followers still feel the loyalty and commitment necessary to put forth sufficient effort?

For some situations and people, the task maintenance function must take priority over social maintenance; in other situations and for other individuals, the opposite might be true. The important thing to keep in mind is that there is more than one option and that there may be some trade-offs in each.

But *why* does this dilemma occur? Why is it so difficult to mix these functions? For one thing, not many people are really good at both; as a result, the task leader is likely to be someone who has the best skills or abilities related to the task (as it should be), and the social leader is often the most outgoing person in the group. If that's the case, then other group members tend to become dependent upon the task leader and may even see him or her as superior to the rest of the group. While this may generate respect for that individual, it also tends to breed resentment.

Furthermore, since people are social beings and usually have other interests in addition to interest in working well—or will retreat into socializing when tasks become unpleasant or might lead to conflict—task leaders occasionally have to refocus attention back to getting the task done. As a result, when the task leader pressures others into working, they may feel grateful for the direction but also may feel resentful, annoyed, and resistant to the task (Zaleznik, 1963). This sequence of events is not inevitable and may be overcome when it leads to group success, but it occurs frequently enough to warrant particular attention. We have also found it to be characteristic of a great many work groups in our classes. Does it apply to your own experience?

MANAGERIAL BULLETIN

Happy Meal

Golden State Coach Don Nelson recently had his rookie players over to his house for dinner. "I wanted them to know I can be their friend," Nelson said. "I don't really hate rookies. I just wish they were smarter."

SOURCE: "NBA Update," *USA Today,* February 1, 1991.

There is yet another problem. With a few exceptions, most people have the greatest difficulty being totally honest or giving directions to those to whom they feel closest. When someone else is emotionally close, people feel the risk is great that the relationship will be harmed by saying negative things or giving directions. Thus they find themselves unable to ask much of close friends. A few people, however, find that when they build close, supportive relationships, they can be both demanding and caring—and be cared for and receive demands in return. This kind of openness allows closeness with subordinates without harming productivity, but it requires high skill and mutual commitment and probably only works where both boss and subordinate have roughly equal expertise.

THE USE AND ABUSE OF POWER

In general, it should be apparent by now that leadership can be an exciting opportunity to use power or influence for getting work done; but it can be abused. You have undoubtedly known or heard about people in power primarily to serve their own ends, and usually at the expense of others.

David McClelland distinguishes between *personal* power and *socialized* power, the former referring to self-serving uses (or abuses) and the latter to uses that consider the effects (usually benefits) on others.[3] Sometimes it's difficult to make a clear distinction between the two, especially when a leader claims to be acting for the benefit of others yet engages in behavior that reflects anything but the best of motives. The actions of the Bagwan Bajneesh on "behalf" of his followers—who, incidentally, seemed to feel that 90 Rolls–Royces were a deserved part of his benefits package—is a good case in point, as is the wealth, including an air-conditioned dog house, accumulated by Jim and Tammy Bakker.

---

[3] David C. McClelland, *Power: The Inner Experience* (New York: Irvington, 1975).

An example closer to home is the manner in which some professors treat their students. Actions that intimidate or harass students represent a gross abuse of a faculty member's power. Whether intended or not, such behavior violates the ethical responsibilities of the role and certainly does little to enhance student learning. Have you ever heard an instructor say things like, "If you can't grasp this concept you probably don't belong in college!"? The intent *might* be to stimulate effort, but usually the effect is demoralizing.

Any act by a person in power that pressures another person to behave in ways that violate that person's sense of personal worth is a form of manipulation. At best, it's insensitive; at worst, it's a form of violence. Today's organizations are paying increasing attention to these kinds of issues, including the specific problem of sexual harassment in the workplace. Laws and policies are being developed, in part because of pressures from the courts, that are designed to protect individuals from sexual harassment in their jobs. What was once looked on as harmless teasing has come to be recognized as a humiliating abuse of power. Such behavior is now being seen as unacceptable and unprofessional, as well as illegal. How long it will take to educate organizational leaders and managers, university professors, and the general public to understand such abuses and take action to prevent them remains to be seen. However, it is important for *you*—as a future manager and as someone who will possess power—to appreciate the ethical burdens of your job and the kinds of actions you might be required to take in living up to those ethics.

The Opportunity to Empower Others

In the coming years the effectiveness of leaders/managers will be measured as much by the performance of their subordinates as by their own performance. It will be the job of the leader—of a team, a department, or a company—to *empower* others to perform at their best. Simple rewards and punishments won't do the job, at least over the long run; it will take efforts at employee involvement, shared purposes or vision, and, in general, a spirit of collaboration heretofore known in few organizations. Even as you consider the situational options available to the leader, keep in mind that, in most cases, any choice that fails to empower others is likely to be a poor one. Coercive approaches, while seemingly effective for the short run, rarely sustain positive effects for the long run.

KEY CONCEPTS FROM CHAPTER II

1. Leadership is mostly situational, rather than determined by personality traits.
2. Leadership is an influence process with subordinates, peers, and colleagues. Even subordinates are not totally without influence; thus, leadership is net influence.

3. Influence is an act or potential act that affects the behavior of another person(s). Types of influence:
   a. Formal: prescribed by office or position.
   b. Informal: based on expertise or charisma.
   c. Legitimate: influencer seen by influenced as having the right to do so.
   d. Illegitimate: influencer seen by influenced as not having the right to do so.
   e. Types *a* and *b* can each combine with *c* or *d* when examining influence.

4. People can be influenced through:
   a. Compliance: fear of influencer.
   b. Identification: attraction to influencer.
   c. Internalization: belief in influencer's beliefs.

5. Importance of employee commitment to:
   a. The work itself.
   b. The relationships with others.
   c. The organization as a whole.

6. Power is the capacity to exert influence, to make things happen.

7. Power is based on:
   a. Greater legitimacy.
   b. Ability to enhance organization in relation to key problems.
   c. Doing new activities rather than routine.
   d. Visibility, recognition.
   e. Creating obligations through helpful acts.
   f. Controlling rewards and punishments.
   g. Reducing uncertainty.

8. The greater one's power, the more one receives:
   a. Communication.
   b. Solicitous behavior.
   c. Deference.
   d. Self-esteem.
   e. Close observation in new situations.

9. Powerlessness often leads to:
   a. Overcontrol.
   b. Petty tyranny.
   c. Rule orientation and turf-mindedness.

10. Currencies of influence.

11. It is difficult for those with power to gain both respect and liking:
    a. Task orientation often breeds resentment.
    b. Closeness to followers may constrain task orientation.

12. The use and abuse of power.

13. Empowerment of others

PERSONAL APPLICATION EXERCISE

Assessing Your Influence Currencies

As we pointed out in the chapter, you probably have more influence on others than you realize. In other words, you may not fully appreciate the "currencies" you have that are valued by friends, family members, instructors, and others. The following exercise is designed to help you assess your currencies and, thereby, develop a picture of the ways in which you influence others and how you might even increase that influence.

We want you to start by identifying *two* people in each of *three* categories: (1) friends, (2) family members, and (3) instructors. (Refer to the example below as a guide). Then list the currencies you can offer that are valued by *both* individuals in each category and assign a value on a scale of 1 to 10 indicating the importance of that currency to each person, with the higher numbers reflecting greater importance.

You should find similarities (closer numbers) and differences (numbers further apart) between the individuals in a category, and you certainly should find some major differences in the currencies of the different categories. In the example, the numbers reflect a closer friendship with B than with A, since the currencies of "caring" and "support" are more highly valued by B. In the family category the currency that counts more with the father than the mother is "success," while the opposite is true for the "dependency" currency. In the instructor example, "listening quietly" will work better in accounting class than in organizational behavior, while the opposite will be true for "offering opinions."

If the example were you, can you see how your behavior could be different in the different situations and in relation to the different individuals? This kind of diagnostic process could be a valuable way for you to strengthen your interpersonal power. It could be especially useful in a work environment, where the career stakes are high.

Example

Friends	A	B	Family	Mother	Father	Instructors	Acctg.	O.B.
Caring	5	8	Love	10	8	Listening		
Support	5	10	Pride	6	7	quietly	9	4
Feedback	6	6	Dependency	8	3	Asking		
Help	8	6	Success	5	10	questions	7	6
Knowledge of			Doing chores	9	9	Good work	10	10
sports	2	9				Offering		
Humor	10	7				opinions	3	9

SUGGESTED READINGS

Agor, W. H. "The Logic of Intuition: How Top Executives Make Important Decisions." *Organizational Dynamics*, Winter 1986, pp. 5–18.

Bass, B. M. "Leadership: Good, Better, Best." *Organizational Dynamics,* Winter 1985, pp. 26–40.

_____. *Leadership and Performance Beyond Expectations.* New York: Free Press, 1985.

Bennis, W., and B. Nanus. *Leaders; The Strategies for Taking Charge.* New York: Harper & Row, 1985.

Berelson, B., and G. Steiner. *Human Behavior: An Inventory of Scientific Findings.* New York: Harcourt Brace Jovanovich, 1964.

Beyer, J. M. "Ideologies, Values, and Decision Making in Organizations." In *Handbook of Organizational Design*, vol. 2, ed. P. Nystrom and W. Starbuck. New York: Oxford University Press, 1981, pp. 166–97.

Caro, R. *The Power Broker.* New York: Alfred A. Knopf, 1974.

Cobb, A. T. "An Episodic Model of Power: Toward an Integration of Theory and Research." *Academy of Management Review,* July 1984, pp. 482–93.

Cohen, A. R. and D. L. Bradford. *Influence without Authority,* New York: John Wiley & Sons, 1990.

Conger, J. A. and R. N. Kanungo. "Toward a Behavioral Theory of Charismatic Leadership in Organizational Settings." *Academy of Management Review* 12, no. 4 (1987), pp. 637–47.

Deaux, K. "Authority, Gender, Power, and Tokenism." *Journal of Applied Behavioral Science,* January–February–March 1978, pp. 22–26.

Dobbins, G. H., and S. J. Platz. "Sex Differences in Leadership: How Real Are They?" *Academy of Management Review,* January 1986, pp. 118–27.

French, J. R. P., Jr., and B. Raven. "The Bases of Social Power." In *Group Dynamics: Research and Theory,* ed. D. Cartwright and Z. Zander. New York: Harper & Row, 1960, pp. 607–23.

Gabarro, J. J., and J. P. Kotter. "Managing Your Boss." *Harvard Business Review,* January–February 1980, pp. 97–100.

Gouldner, A. "The Norm of Reciprocity: A Preliminary Statement." *American Sociological Review,* April 1960, pp. 161–78.

Heller, T. "Changing Authority Patterns: A Cultural Perspective." *Academy of Management Review,* July 1985, pp. 488–95.

Howell, J. P., and P. W. Dorfman. "Leadership and Substitutes for Leadership among Professional and Nonprofessional Workers." *Journal of Applied Behavioral Science* 22, no. 1 (1986), pp. 29–46.

Jay, A. *Management and Machiavelli.* New York: Holt, Rinehart & Winston, 1967.

Kanter, R. M. *Men and Women of the Corporation.* New York: Basic Books, 1977.

Kelman, H. C. "Processes of Opinion Change." *Public Opinion Quarterly,* Spring 1961, pp. 57–78.

King, D., and B. Bass. *Leadership, Power, and Influence.* Lafayette, Ind.: Herman C. Krannert Graduate School of Industrial Administration, Purdue University, 1970.

Kipnis, D. *The Powerholders.* Chicago: University of Chicago Press, 1976.

Korda, M. *Power: How to Get It and How to Use It.* New York: Simon & Schuster, 1977.

Kotter, J. P. *Power in Management.* New York: AMACOM, 1979.

_____. *The General Managers.* New York: Free Press, 1982.

_____. *Power and Influence.* New York: Free Press, 1985.

Liden, R. C. and T. R. Mitchell. "Ingratiatory Behaviors in Organizational Settings." *Academy of Management Review* 13, no. 4 (1988), pp. 572–87.

McClelland, D. C. *Power: The Inner Experience.* New York: Irvington, 1975.

McGregor, D. *The Human Side of Enterprise.* New York: McGraw-Hill, 1960.

_____. *Leadership and Motivation.* Cambridge, Mass.: MIT Press, 1966.

_____. *The Professional Manager.* New York: McGraw-Hill, 1967.

Peters, T. J. "Symbols, Patterns, and Settings: An Optimistic Case for Getting Things Done." *Organizational Dynamics,* Autumn 1978.

Pfeffer, J. "Power and Resource Allocation in Organizations." In *Psychological Foundations of Organizational Behavior,* ed. B. Staw. Santa Monica, Calif.: Goodyear Publishing, 1977.

_____. *Power in Organizations.* Marshfield, Mass.: Pitman Publishing, 1981.

Pfeffer, J., and G. Salancik. "Who Gets Power and How They Hold on to It." *Organizational Dynamics,* Winter 1977.

Ringer, R. *Winning through Intimidation.* Los Angeles: Los Angeles Publishing, 1974.

Rosenbach, W. E., and R. L. Taylor, *ed. Contemporary Issues in Leadership.* Boulder: Westview, 1984.

Rosener, J. "Ways Women Lead." *Harvard Business Review,* November–December 1990, pp 119–25.

Sayles, L. *Leadership: What Effective Managers Do and How They Do It.* New York: McGraw-Hill, 1979.

Schlesinger, L. A., and B. Oshry. "Quality of Work Life and the Manager: Muddle in the Middle." *Organizational Dynamics,* Summer 1984, pp. 4–19.

Simon, H. A. *Administrative Behavior.* New York: Free Press, 1957.

Slater, P. E. "Role Differentiation in Small Groups." *American Sociological Review* 20, 1965.

Stogdill, R. M. *Handbook of Leadership.* New York: Free Press, 1974.

Trevino, L. K. "Ethical Decision Making in Organizations: A Person-Situation Interactionist Model." *Academy of Management Review,* July 1986, pp. 601–17.

Tichy N., and M. A. Devanna. *The Transformational Leader.* New York: John Wiley & Sons, 1986.

Zaleznik, A. "The Human Dilemmas of Leadership." *Harvard Business Review,* July–August 1963.

13

Relations among Groups in the Organization

"The more differentiated the tasks necessary to accomplish the organization's work, the more appropriate it is to create separate subsystems for doing each task."

Since virtually every large organization requires some division of labor, it is usually necessary to have departments, branches, divisions, units, teams, and so forth to accomplish the various tasks. Helping the individual subsystems do their parts and insuring that their work is integrated toward the goals of the organization as a whole is a key way in which a manager determines the system's overall effectiveness. When the organization has groups doing tasks that differ in terms of complexity, rate of change of the technology used, skills needed, length of time it takes to complete the task, and so forth, then the job of coordinating the subunits becomes a major managerial undertaking.

In general: **The more differentiated the tasks necessary to accomplish the organization's work, the more appropriate it is to create separate subsystems for doing each task.** And as you might expect: **Each subunit works best when organized in a way that fits the demands of its task (Lawrence & Lorsch, 1967).** The subunit's structure, personnel, operating style, reward system, and leadership should be matched to its particular tasks. In other words: **When the background factors and required system "fit" the unit's goals, it is most likely to be effective; when the emergent system also fits, it is even more likely to be effective.** Even when subunit organization is not perfectly matched to task, there is a tendency for the group to acquire an identity that is at least partly reflective of the type of work it does, the skills needed to do it, who the members are, the technology involved, the rate of change in the group's environment, and what behavior the organization rewards.

An increasing number of manufacturing companies are using small teams on the shop floor to solve problems and maintain quality standards. These teams have been known to develop their own distinctive ways of working, reflecting the particular combination of people, tasks, and interaction patterns that occur. In some cases, they have even given themselves names, made up group T-shirts, and generally made it known to other teams that they see themselves as different and special. This is not really surprising. **Work groups tend to develop a group concept, which they strive to maintain and enhance (Blake, Shepard, & Mouton, 1964).**

Part of the basis of the concept that develops is that people naturally gravitate into groups that reinforce their values. Most voluntary groups form on that basis, and their cohesiveness can be directly attributed to the fact that membership serves to reinforce basic personal values. While work groups in most organizations do not form on a voluntary basis, it is safe to say that, **the more differentiated a work group's task, the more likely will members be recruited who share *common background factors*.** These may include education, professional identity, ethnic grouping, race, religion, common interests, and so forth. **The more similar are members' background factors, the clearer the group's emergent identity will tend to be.** Since in most organizations the division of labor is based upon specialized task and skill areas, work groups at all levels of the system will tend to be composed of people with similar backgrounds, at least in regard to a given skill area.

Rewards can have an especially potent effect on group identity. Different units responsible for different tasks are often rewarded for different behavior. For example, employees responsible for quality control are rewarded for making sure that products *do not deviate* from prescribed standards, whereas those in a research and development function are often rewarded for *experimenting* with *deviations* from previously established standards. Rewards that differentially reinforce behavior serve also to reinforce distinct group identities. Consequently, without strong organizational rewards for cooperation among such differentiated groups, it becomes difficult to achieve satisfactory integration of functions where needed.

Interviewer: *Did you have national anthems?*

2,000-Year-Old Man: *It was very fragmented. It wasn't nations; it was caves. Each cave had a national anthem.*

Interviewer: *Do you remember the national anthem of your cave?*

2,000-Year-Old Man: *I certainly do; I'll never forget it. You don't forget a national anthem in a minute.*

Interviewer: *Let me hear it, sir.*

2,000-Year-Old Man: [Singing]: *Let them all go to hell except cave 76.*

The 2,000-Year-Old Man
Album by Carl Reiner & Mel Brooks

Furthermore: **The more cohesive the group, the clearer and more strongly felt the identity is likely to be to group members** (Blake & Mouton, 1961). As you may recall, in Chapter 4 we offered a number of propositions on the factors that increase a group's cohesiveness, including common values and goals, a common enemy, high required interactions, and low interactions required outside the group.

And we also postulated that the more cohesive the group, the more closely members would conform to the group's norms. Thus, when a group emergent system that is attractive to members develops out of what is required to get the work done, the group's way of doing things is likely to be seen by members not only as appropriate but also as extremely desirable and valuable. The *group's* "self-concept" becomes worth protecting.

VARIATIONS IN GROUP IDENTITY

What are some of the ways in which group identities may differ? How do differing emergent systems compare with one another? You will already have observed many groups in cases, in class, and at work, and have seen that they have different ways of doing things. In order to examine the reasons why groups sometimes have difficulty working together, we need to suggest a few important dimensions on which work groups often differ, to add to those discussed in Chapter 6 on group effectiveness.

Time Horizon

One important way group members in organizations may differ is in their view of time. Certain kinds of tasks tend to call for a relatively short-term time horizon, and others call for a long-term time horizon. These task "demands" transcend the fact that we all have different preferences for work pace. Basic research, for example, is not a process that can easily be hurried along, and it tends to require a rather distant time horizon. Competitive sales, on the other hand, normally calls for rapid decisions and a series of short-term checkpoints on the way to long-range objectives. **The time horizon tends to be shortest for those tasks that require immediate feedback and have outcomes that can provide such feedback; the time horizon tends to be longest for those tasks whose relevant outcomes and, consequently, sources of feedback are more delayed (Lawrence & Lorsch, 1967; Rice, 1969).** You can see how people in a sales division of a company can measure their successes in terms of immediate sales and how inevitable it is that they would operate out of a relatively short time horizon. If, however, such sales commit other divisions of the system to delivery times that are incompatible with their own time horizons, some degree of conflict is bound to ensue. Research and development people, for example, may find such commitments impossible to meet and foreign to their concepts of how their work should be carried out. Each group is likely to deal with time issues in its own way and believe in the "correctness" of its procedures and assumptions. Since time is so much a part of everything in organizational life, it is often taken for granted. Groups with different time horizons frequently have difficulty understanding one another.

Are you a person who gets to meetings on time or even early? Or, perhaps, a person who is habitually late? Groups' and departments' attitudes toward time also differ in this respect, with some likely to start and stop meetings right on time while others are much more casual about how rigidly people are expected to stick to schedules. Since attitudes toward time often take on a connotation of good and bad, such differences can create tension. Imagine five researchers strolling into a meeting at 4, 6, and even 12 minutes after 2 P.M., with production personnel, who all arrived at 3 minutes before 2!

Different countries also have differing attitudes toward time, a point which we discuss further in the last section of this chapter.

Perspective on the Task

Some units have jobs that keep members narrowly focused upon one aspect of the work. An extreme example would be on an assembly line, where the workers put the same kind of bolt in the same kind of hole all day long, never getting to see the end product or even some of the subassemblies. Contrast that task to one involving a quality check on the final product; the perspective of each is very different with respect to the scope of the task.

The broader the perspective on the task, the greater will be member awareness of task group interdependencies and the greater will be concern for the total effort (Blake et al., 1964). Normally, the higher a unit is in the hierarchy, the greater the likelihood of members seeing the "big picture"—that is, the overall relation of subunits and their connections to organizational goals. Members of lower-level units often focus only on their particular set of tasks, with less sense of the context in which they are operating. But this difference in perspective is not limited to differences in hierarchical level. It can vary with the unit's required interactions with outside subsystems. **The greater the number of interactions required with other subsystems, the broader is a subsystem's task perspective likely to be (Lorsch & Lawrence, 1972).**

Because breadth of perspective can vary, different units can place different priorities on organizational goals. And subunit goals can seem more important than overall goals to a group with limited perspective. Thus, there can be distinct differences among groups in perspective on tasks.

In order to broaden employees' perspectives, more and more companies are redesigning tasks in ways that expand worker responsibilities for carrying through several stages of a job. In addition, workers are being given increasing responsibility for managing and coordinating work activities individually and in groups. Some of these approaches are discussed in Chapter 14, but at this point we wanted to introduce you to the idea that many problems associated with a narrow task perspective are solvable through direct modification of the way in which the work is carried out.

Professional Identity

If you ever get the chance, talk to a quality control engineer about his or her priorities; do the same with people in sales, people in financial operations, and people in the human resources area of a company. Ask each group about their perceptions of the other groups. What you are likely to discover are some very fundamental differences in how each profession sees itself, its priorities, its importance to the total organization, and the qualities of the other groups. The very nature of the sales activity places a high premium on being able to make commitments to customers that the company can honor. This usually places heavy time pressures on the production end of the process. The very nature of the quality control function places a high premium on making sure that only the best gets delivered to the customer, even if it takes more time to get the product out. When these two sets of priorities collide, we have what is called an *inherent conflict*—that is, one that is a reflection of the background factors of the parties involved. Ironically, such conflicts are not all that undesirable, since the conflicting views are both usually legitimate. It is a manager's job to balance those views in ways that

MANAGERIAL BULLETIN

Whose Takeover? Some GM Data Processing People Feel the Auto Firm, Not EDS, Was the One Acquired

Almost everyone agrees that the two companies have very different work environments. That of GM's white-collar work force, for example, reflects the omnipresent blue-collar unions, even though they represent fewer than 200 salaried workers. Strict job rules, restrictions, and guidelines make it difficult to reward strong performers in GM's lower ranks, managers say. White-collar workers ride the coattails of UAW members, usually getting any salary and benefit increases won in new union contracts. "Now we've got everything they've got, except one thing," a GM veteran says. "We don't have protection."

In contrast, successful EDS employees describe a brutally competitive atmosphere: low pay, strict personal discipline, and hard work. "EDS is very up-front about how to get on the fast track," a former EDS executive says. "Work hard, keep your nose clean, and keep that nose to the grindstone." . . . One result: Its employees are hard-charging, extremely loyal, and devoted to EDS and its leaders.

Upright personal conduct is demanded. The company outlaws drinking at lunch and frowns on extramarital affairs and abortions. But clothes are the most visible symbol of the difference between the two groups. EDS insists on a conservative dress code outlawing loud ties, short skirts, and even men's shoes with buckles or tassels.

"All the EDS people dress alike," a GM data processor says. "I swear they all have brown hair, medium build, and medium height." Because the issue is so sensitive, EDS modified its stand so that only GM employees working with EDS's outside customers must comply with the dress code. But one GM data processor notes that a co-worker who never used to dress up for work has begun wearing sport jackets every day.

benefit the total organization and not to allow one side to dominate the other at the expense of the organization. In the example given, it is important to deliver a quality product to a customer, but also important to do so within a reasonable time. In a healthy organization, these differences are managed and do not become occasions for internally destructive consequences. But they do require attention and some skill on the part of a manager to keep things from deteriorating into win-lose or lose-lose battles. Unfortunately, the history of some interprofessional relations has been less than collaborative, union–management relations being a good example.

Attitudes toward Authority and Internal Structure

As you may recall from the chapters on leadership (11 and 12) and group effectiveness (6), the amount of control and participation in a group should be related to the group's needs in accomplishing its tasks. Groups where expertise is widely distributed and needed for the solution of complex, changing problems require a more participative, free-wheeling, noncontrolling style of operation than those where task requirements are clear and expertise strongly differentiated.

Furthermore, over time groups develop quite different notions about the proper style of leadership, the appropriate amount of latitude for individual decision-making and involvement, and for allowable amounts of initiative. Can you see how groups that differ along these dimensions might view one another with less than full approval?

In many high-tech companies today there is a growing problem around the management of computer experts. Similar to research and development people, the computer engineers and scientists tend to be so heavily involved in their work that they often ignore the usual organizational rules about specific hours, reporting relationships, and general work habits. The dilemma for top management is how to allow these employees the freedom and latitude that suits them and fosters their productivity without incurring the resentment of other groups whose work style is more in line with traditional management practices. Is it possible to have two (or even more) different sets of rules for employees in the same organization? Here is where the emergent norms of a subpart of the total organization may be highly functional for that group's work, but be dysfunctional for total system harmony. As you will see a little further on, this problem can proliferate into intergroup stereotyping and rivalries, which are potentially damaging if they are not managed constructively.

Interpersonal Orientation

One further way in which group identities differ is in their orientation to interpersonal relations. Groups vary in terms of whether they value closeness or distance, openness or politeness, seriousness or kidding, and so forth. Members who have arrived at some agreement on how people should relate to one another often think that members of other groups with different orientations are strange or unlikable. Others are "too pushy and effusive" or "too cold," "too blunt" or "too indirect," "too pompous" or "too frivolous," depending on the group to which one belongs. Whatever the emergent orientation, "the way our group relates to people" comes to be seen as the best or only way for sensible people to deal with one another.

In one company a department made up of highly educated people with similar outside interests tended to socialize a great deal during nonworking hours and were demonstrably friendly even during working hours. Individuals who were not a part of that group developed a very distorted picture of the group, seeing it as a bunch of goof-offs who did not care about their work or the company. The fact that the department was one of the most productive in the company didn't seem to change the perception. Obviously, the perceivers were finding the behavior of this department to be a threat to some aspect of their self-concepts. Furthermore, it reflected a frequently observed tendency for members of one group to interpret the behavior of another group

THE STRANGER

The Stranger within my gate,
He may be true or kind,
But he does not talk my talk—
I cannot feel his mind.
I see the face and the eyes and the mouth,
But not the soul behind.

The men of my own stock,
They may do ill or well,
But they tell the lies I am wonted to,
They are used to the lies I tell;
And we do not need interpreters
When we go to buy and sell.

The men of my own stock,
Bitter bad they may be,
But, at least, they hear the things I hear,
And see the things I see;
And whatever I think of them and their likes
They think of the likes of me.

Rudyard Kipling

according to their own norms and values, which, unfortunately, leads to further misperceptions (Hall & Whyte, 1973).

This matter is even more complicated when there are intercultural differences. Globalization is accompanied by inevitable misunderstandings and misinterpretations stemming from fundamental differences in beliefs, values, ethical considerations, and overall ways of doing business. The negotiation style of a Saudi businessman is governed by different ground rules from that of the typical American business leader. As a result, the American is likely to misjudge and mistrust the Saudi, unless he or she is sensitive to these differences. Doing business in Latin America has posed many problems for Americans, who typically want to "get down to business," while the Latin prefers to spend some time (often more than the American can tolerate) building a more social relationship (talking about family, personal interests, and so on). Over time these differences can be a source of enrichment to the workplace, but all too often they tend to create barriers to cooperation across organizational boundaries. We will explore these issues further in the latter part of this chapter.

Summary

Thus, in terms of attitudes toward *(a)* time, *(b)* authority, and *(c)* structure, *(d)* perspective on tasks, and *(e)* interpersonal orientation, organizational subsystems can and do differ. Each develops its own identity in coping with the tasks assigned to it. That identity is the group equivalent of individual self-concept; the more cohesive the group, the greater the members' commitment is to preserving and enhancing its identity and the more likely members are to see the group's way of doing things as correct, valuable, and superior to other groups' ways. Finally, insofar as group organization should follow from and be appropriate to the group's tasks: **The more differentiated a subsystem's tasks, the more effective it will be when its identity (or way of operating) is also differentiated from the identities of other subsystems.** (See Figure 13–1.).

FIGURE 13–1　　How Group Identity Develops

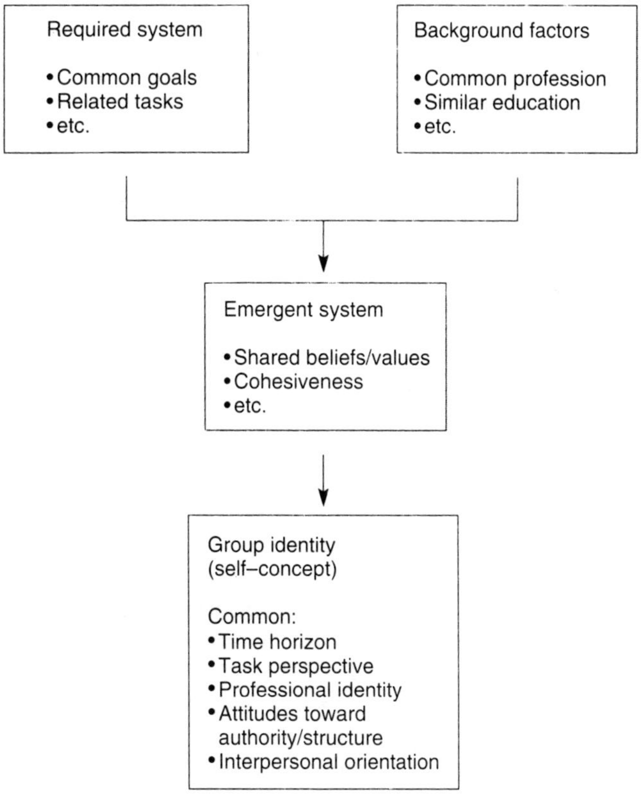

THE PRICE OF APPROPRIATE DIFFERENTIATION: PROBLEMS ARISING FROM STRONG GROUP IDENTITY

Unfortunately, however, as you by now may have anticipated: **The clearer and more distinct a subsystem's identity, the greater the difficulty in coordination with other subsystems when their tasks are interdependent** (Blake & Mouton, 1961). Insofar as differentiated groups carry on interdependent tasks, there is a need for coordination among them. And the greater the degree of interdependence, the more important is the coordination. In order for there to be effective intergroup coordination:

1. Each group must be aware of its own functions in relation to those of other groups.
2. Each group must be willing to maintain communication links with the other groups.
3. Each group must be willing to accept the legitimacy of the needs of the other groups.
4. Each group must be willing to meet its own needs within the framework of the total system.

But a group with a sharply differentiated identity is likely to resist any form of coordination that conflicts with its identity. **The extent of a group's resistance to coordination with other groups will be directly related to the degree to which the required interactions conflict with the group's basic norms, ideals, and values.**

Just as with individuals and relationships: **To the extent that a group perceives a relationship with another group as enhancing its own identity, it will strive to develop and maintain that relationship. To the extent that a group perceives a relationship with another group as in some way threatening its own identity, it will strive to resist or avoid that relationship.** In those instances in an organization where the nature of the task *requires* a working relationship between any two groups, these propositions become extremely important. **The more an intergroup relationship requires activities and interactions that are compatible with the identities of the groups involved, the more effective will that relationship be; the more it requires activities and interactions that are contradictory to the identities of either or both groups, the more that relationship will be a source of conflict.**

Once a group has developed a strong identity, there is a tendency to see any rival (or potential rival) group in predictably distorted ways. **Members of a differentiated cohesive group with a strong sense of its own identity will show the following tendencies** (Blake & Mouton, 1961, 1964):

1. Perception of their own group as "better" than the other group.
2. An upgrading of their own ideas and a downgrading of the other group's ideas.
3. An overestimation of their own competence and an underestimation of the competence of the other group.
4. Overvaluation of their own leader(s) and undervaluation of the other group's leaders(s).
5. Avoidance or limiting of interactions and communications with the other group.
6. Distortion of information about the other group in ways that cast the other group in an unfavorable light.
7. Mistrust of the members of the other group.

Perhaps you can recognize some or all of these tendencies from your own experience. Intergroup rivalries in school, competing gangs in the neighborhood, and organized team sports are all familiar examples. More troublesome, of course, are situations involving race relations, political and military conflicts, and the like. Prejudice feeds on limited and distorted information, strengthening the intensity with which the prejudiced beliefs are held and making the possibilities of misunderstanding and escalated conflict even greater.

Even when contradictory data are present, people tend to maintain stereotyped perceptions. The individual member of that group who behaves differently from what the stereotype suggests is always the "exception to the rule"; the individual who happens to behave according to the stereotype simply confirms its "validity." In our current era of social change, in which minorities and women are moving into more positions heretofore inaccessible to them, they face this kind of problem. Kanter (1977) calls this "double jeopardy" and finds that it places incredible stress on those who experience it. In short, the consequences of intergroup stereotyping include damaging effects on both group relations and individuals in the organization. We comment further on this issue later when we discuss the management of diversity.

Prejudice and war are more dramatic and dangerous manifestations of the tendency to misperceive other groups. But even within formal organizations these tendencies occur whenever two working units find themselves interdependent and in conflict. The conflict creates uncertainty and anxiety; often rumors develop about what one or another group is doing or plotting, which heightens the antagonism, causes "retaliation" in advance ("preemptive strikes" in military jargon), which in turn further angers the other group and "confirms" their worst suspicions. The more either or both groups see the conflict as a threat to group identity, the more evident these tendencies become and the more difficult it is to achieve resolution.

MANAGERIAL BULLETIN

Costly Lesson: GE Finds Running Kidder, Peabody & Co. Isn't All That Easy

. . . GE . . . knew there were big cultural differences between its own organization men, proud of their in-house management school and generous pension plan, and the entrepreneurial prima donnas of Kidder, who chafed at any management controls and who made so much money they didn't *need* a pension plan. But these differences didn't seem to pose insurmountable problems either. GE had been running a highly successful commercial lending and leasing business for years, and finance guys are finance guys, right?

. . . Just about everything that could go wrong with the Kidder merger has. The cultures have clashed, and GE financial units and Kidder at times have competed with each other when they should have been cooperating. GE and Kidder leaders developed widely disparate views of what Kidder should be. Thus, there was confusion among Kidder executives and the impression among subordinates that the firm was rudderless.

Relations between the two organizations have been so awkward that when Kidder submitted a strategic plan to GE in October 1987, GE executives blessed the plan only because they thought an honest appraisal would devastate Kidder's morale. "It's kind of like when your kid builds his first model airplane," says GE vice chairman Lawrence Bossidy. "You don't say its awful."

. . . GE had entered the relationship with grand visions of cooperative efforts between Kidder and GE Capital, the cornerstone of GE's financial services empire.

. . . But differences in culture and business philosophy sharply handicapped those efforts. Employees of the two units didn't like each other. Kidder investment bankers generally make a lot more money than their GE Capital counterparts, yet GE Capital, which earns hundreds of millions of dollars a year, is far more profitable.

Kidder officials derisively referred to their GE counterparts as "credit clerks." And Kidder officials say GE Capital staffers would deliberately treat them as competitors.

GE Capital officials thought Kidder people were overly sensitive, overpaid and arrogant, and not nearly as talented as their counterparts at certain other investment banks. Sometimes Kidder would bid competitively for GE Capital business against other investment bankers and lose.

SOURCE: By Steve Swartz, with Janet Guyon contributing to the article. Reprinted by permission of *THE WALL STREET JOURNAL,* © January 27, 1989. Dow Jones & Company, Inc. All Rights Reserved Worldwide.

GROUP STATUS

We have been examining the sources of group identity as they follow from task differentiation and showing how the differentiation can lead to difficulties. But another aspect of a group's identity is important for understanding coordination problems.

It is inevitable that, in assigning jobs to various subsystems, an organization will confer differing amounts of legitimate influence to groups. Some subsystems will be expected to give orders to and initiate interaction with others; other subsystems will be expected to wait for initiatives from subsystems doing different jobs. This allocation of influence will usually be based on the flow of work, though it may not have a very explicit rationale. Whatever the reasoning behind the particular way power is allocated: **The more *legitimate power* a group has within the system, the more freedom it has to initiate actions and the more that other less-powerful groups are dependent upon it to initiate actions (Seiler, 1963).** The marketing department in one firm might have the right to decide what products will be tested and sold, while the production department has to go along despite its reservations. In another organization, the financial group might be given the power to exert control over operating departments to insure adequate returns. But the formal-legitimate power of groups is not the only determinant of influence. The informal social system, as usual, has an important part to play.

Informal Group Status in the System

We have already pointed out in Chapter 11 about leadership, that influence in an organization is based upon both formal position and informal status, the latter being determined by a variety of factors, including education, social status of a given profession or occupation, special abilities, "whom you know," how important the work is to the overall organization, and seniority. Just as some individuals in an organization seem to carry more informal influence than they have been formally assigned, because they have been around for a long time or do a very special kind of work, it is not unusual for a particular subsystem to possess informal influence and status that far exceed what is formally designated to it.

A common example of this is the case of technical staff in industry. While they do not normally possess the designated formal authority of line people who are responsible for the operations of the firm, their special expertise and advanced degrees often give them an informal status that carries a great deal of influence with top management. Or, it may lead them to *see* themselves as higher status, and, therefore, as having more influence than they are formally assigned. It becomes an intergroup problem when line people and staff people compete for influence and control because legitimacy is in dispute. Take the case of efficiency experts coming into a department to study its operations and make recommendations for improving that department. It doesn't take much imagination to see how the outside experts can be seen as the "enemy," since they pose the threat of carrying more influence than the organizational chart indicates. Similarly, within a university, power is delegated from the board of trustees to the administration; but informal status is attributed to the faculty, who are seen as the backbone of the educational process. Who carries the most weight and with whom? Struggles around this kind of issue can generate great tension and serious questions about what outcomes are functional for the *total* system as opposed to any one of the competing subsystems.

Groups that possess expertise crucial to the success of an organization often have considerable power attributed to them by other groups whose status in the power hierarchy is lower. Consequently, one of the interesting paradoxes of organizational life is that groups with special power (especially when it is not related to the structural hierarchy) tend to be envied, resented, and yet paid extra deference by other, less-powerful groups. It is typical of the tension between "haves" and "have nots" (Brown, 1978).

The more *informal status* a group has within the system, the more freedom it has to initiate actions and the more other lower-status groups are dependent upon it to initiate actions (Seiler, 1963). With the exception of the *source* (formal versus informal) of influence, this proposition is a repeat of the previous one. When a group has both legitimate power and informal status (e.g., a medical staff running a hospital, engineers with advanced degrees managing a manufacturing company), one major source of intergroup conflict is eliminated. But most large organizations tend to promote people on the basis of demonstrated managerial competence, which may or may not have anything to do with technical expertise. High-status *professionals* often tend to view "mere administrators" as having less status and, therefore, as not legitimately able to control the professionals, even though the organization chart assigns the administrators formal authority.

In short, the existence of the two important sources of influence frequently results in incongruencies in intergroup relations. These incongruencies exist when a group possesses higher legitimate power than other groups but lower informal status, or vice versa. **An incongruency between legitimate power and status tends to result in confusion about which group can exercise the greater freedom to take actions that affect the other and which group "has the right" to initiate interactions with the other (Seiler, 1963).** Can the university faculty decide to limit class sizes without considering the registration, cost, and facility problems that such an action poses? Can the administration decide to expand the university for financial reasons without obtaining faculty consent? Can the quality control expert stop production over the protests of the production manager? And when serious conflicts occur, how can one group initiate action without in some way affecting the identity of the other group?

Social Diversity and Intergroup Relations

The management of diverse professions and varied educational backgrounds of employees has long been known to practicing managers. Similarly, most managers today are becoming increasingly conscious of the impact of employee social backgrounds on behavior and attitudes in the workplace. Differences in race, sex, age, and ethnicity are now becoming challenges for creative

MANAGERIAL BULLETIN

Pinpointing the Source of Air-Traffic Disputes

Potential FAA supervisors are not screened for their ability to oversee subordinates, nor are they trained in employee relations. Moreover . . . superfluous layers of management tend to alienate regional FAA managers and leave top officials of the agency with little sense of the rigors of a controller's job. As a result, "although the dissatisfactions of controllers and managers arose for different reasons, the poor attitudes of each group reinforced each other."

[There is an] age gap between supervisors and the well-educated, restless generation of controllers hired during the 1960s.

SOURCE: Business Week, April 5, 1982

management, management that successfully *integrates* the work activities carried out by employees with such widely diverse backgrounds.

This diversity often gets played out in the relations among groups of employees in the same organization. The attitudes, perceptions, and problems that exist among groups in society are frequently carried into the work setting and create barriers to cooperation among groups that need to work together. Many nurses (mostly women) react to doctors (mostly men) in part from their perceptions as women reacting to men; young high-tech engineers often discount the opinions of older engineering managers because of the age difference; many white professional managers find it difficult to defer to the opinion of a black counterpart even when that person is obviously competent. These are all background attitudes that people bring into their organizations; they add to some of the already present intergroup problems. A competent manager needs to be sensitive to the *sources* of intergroup attitudes, especially when they are totally outside management's sphere of control.

CHOOSING BETWEEN CONFLICT AND COOPERATION

For the manager, whether or not to attempt to do something about subsystems in conflict depends on an assessment of the functionality of the dispute for the total organization. While conflict can be costly, as in the above example, in some cases it is a necessary part of achieving full consideration of legitimately differing viewpoints. Without conflict among subsystems, the total needs of the organization might be ignored in favor of the highest-status subsystem's needs or be pushed aside by the more powerful subgroups. Allowing or even encouraging conflict by greater differentiation of group ways of working may be the only way to achieve some balance among subsystems, each of which would like to maximize its own effectiveness, regardless of the consequences for the whole organization. Remember the rationale for the matrix organization in Chapter 2? Balanced decisions often require conflicts over issues.

For example, while the survival of a company might depend upon rapid sales pricing decisions, it may also be crucial for the company to maintain a reputation for quality products and service. If the quality control, engineering, and service departments all took the same short-term view as the sales department and exercised very little control over their individual employees in order to speed up decisions, they might get along better with sales but shortchange long-term quality. Only if the respective subgroups are properly differentiated, encouraged to fully express their respective points of view, and allowed to struggle with the trade-offs between keeping prices down and quality up will a proper balance be achieved.

Where intergroup problems surface as wasteful conflict, they need to be approached in terms of reducing conflict and building cooperation; where problems are created by disproportionate dominance of one subsystem, they need to be treated with measures to further differentiate subgroups and/or increase open conflict among the groups (Seiler, 1963; Blake et al., 1964; Kelly, 1970; Pascale, 1991). In short, conflict can be a result of genuine differences in group values, which are reflected in disputes about desired system goals, in which case they may be functional and necessary for the total system. Without thorough discussion, the total system may be harmed. On the other hand, when conflict is a result of the group identification that often occurs with differentiated groups and goes beyond legitimate disagreements into stereotyping, sniping, and sabotaging, it can be very dysfunctional for the total system. Energy is used that could be better focused on the actual tasks.

Similarly, cooperation can be functional or dysfunctional for the total system, depending on whether it reflects genuine integration of efforts or covering up of disagreements that need to be aired to arrive at balanced decisions. And as noted in Chapter 2, there are times when it is not possible to produce functional consequences for all subsystems as well as for the total system. Imperfection is a price that must often be lived with in a complex organization.

TYPES OF INTERDEPENDENCE

The importance of intergroup cooperation versus conflict depends upon the degree and kind of interdependence of the work groups involved (Thompson, 1967). If, for example, the work of each subsystem contributes to the productivity or welfare of the total system, but is not directly related to that of the other, there are very few, if any, coordination issues. This is called

MANAGERIAL TOOL

Sports Illustrations of Group Interdependencies

Pooled

Baseball companies . . . loosely coupled . . . include the classic sales organization, made up of high-performing soloists. Also . . . aggregations of basic researchers, in which each individual independently pursues his or her own line of inquiry—as happens with university professors.

Serial

Football companies . . . "long-linked" technologies; . . . production processes involve a complex of discrete steps, tightly coupled in serial (and sometimes parallel) order . . . example is . . . mass assembly line.

Reciprocal

Basketball companies . . . tightly coupled but less than tightly hierarchical . . . depend more on member interaction than on managerial direction. Examples . . . [are] think-tank consulting firms . . . creative advertising agencies, . . . state-of-the-art computer manufacturers. . . . [They] resemble (sets of) autonomous work teams: . . . self-organizing and highly flexible.

SOURCE: From Robert Keidel, "Baseball, Football, and Basketball: Models for Business," *Organizational Dynamics*, Winter 1984, pp. 15–18.

pooled interdependence. The various subdivisions of a large department store (housewares, sporting goods, clothing, and so forth) might be a familiar example of pooled interdependence. Each can try to maximize its own sales effectiveness without hurting other units.

However, if the work is carried out in such a way that one group cannot begin its task until another has completed its work, then you can see the critical nature of interdependence. This type is called *serial interdependence;* it is typical of assembly line operations, construction companies, printing firms, and even health services where treatment at one point in the system depends upon diagnostic tests at an earlier point in the system.

The most complex kind of interdependence occurs when work groups need to exchange information on a continuing basis. This is called *reciprocal interdependence.* In the development of plans for a new car model, for example, it is necessary for designers, engineers, market researchers, and production experts to exchange information and ideas over and over so the final product is both innovative and sound.

You can probably see for yourself how the manager's job will vary with each of the three kinds of situations described above. In the case of pooled interdependence, a manager needs to make sure that each of the various groups maintains a satisfactory level of output but not worry that one group is holding up the work of any other. With serial interdependence and reciprocal interdependence, the task is more complex and difficult. In fact, very few modern-day work patterns have the simplicity of pooled interdependence alone; a great many have elements of all three types. Take, for example, a research and development firm in which scientists, engineers, designers, production specialists, and so forth all need to coordinate their efforts. The later stages of product manufacturing and testing are dependent upon the earlier stages of invention and development; the research chemists need to be aware of the manufacturing constraints, and the manufacturing people must understand the time it takes to develop new ideas. The overall process requires ongoing information exchange among the various groups, and it is all oriented toward the goals of the total system.

You can appreciate by now just how important it is for a manager to understand and develop competence in dealing with intergroup relations. Whether the fostering of conflict or cooperation is called for, it is important that the manager understand the need for differentiated subsystems, the likelihood of their developing diverse identities or cultures, and the need for methods to resolve wasteful conflict when greater coordination is needed to achieve serial or reciprocal interdependence. Similarly, managers should know some methods to achieve greater differentiation when too much harmony is creating imbalances.

> For example, one of the major international oil companies established foreign regional divisions, each of which was to attempt capture of a significant portion of a regional market. At the same time, the company headquarters insisted upon having final say on prices of products to new customers. Problems occurred when regional salespeople needed rapid decisions in order to make a sale and were delayed by the policy of checking back with headquarters. The regional people felt that they were in the best position to know the local scene and ought to be able to take action as that scene demanded; the headquarters people insisted that their perspective was more worldwide and that they were in a better position to evaluate the going price on the world market. Both groups were right, but neither could acknowledge the legitimacy of the other's viewpoint. The longer the conflict went on, the more it got complicated with stereotypes, sabotage, miscommunications, and the like.

We'll describe how the issue was resolved later in this chapter when we discuss approaches to intergroup problems. Do you think you could come up with some approaches of your own? It could be useful to then try to compare your approach with the one used in the actual situation.

FOUNDATIONS OF INTERGROUP COOPERATION

How, then, can cooperation be built when it is necessary? As you study the following propositions on the foundation of intergroup cooperation, see if you can recognize their parallel from the chapters on group behavior. In fact, the fundamental proposition is almost identical in both cases.

The more frequent the interaction between any two groups, the greater the tendency to cooperate with each other. However, as in the case of interactions among members of a group, it is important to qualify the above proposition. **To the extent that there is frequent and open information flow among groups in a system, common goals are more likely to develop (Gouldner, 1960).** And add to this proposition the following one: **The more that groups recognize and accept common goals, the more likely they are to cooperate (Walton & Dutton, 1969).**

These propositions are basic to the effective management of all intergroup relations in an organization. To the extent that managers use a "divide and rule" approach by preventing open exchanges of information among working units, they risk intergroup competition and conflict, possibly to the serious detriment of the total system. Where task interdependence necessitates cooperation, bringing key managers together frequently and encouraging constant flow of communications among various interdependent work units increase the likelihood of ongoing cooperation and goal achievement.

Since we also know that: **The more groups share a common source of threat, the more likely they are to cooperate,** it becomes crucial for manager to avoid becoming that "common source of threat." In competitive fields, the common source of threat obviously must be the outside competition. Here is where an effective manager can mobilize cooperative effort by making certain that any source of threat serving to bind groups together lies *outside* the system and does not have divisive effects inside the system.

There are three additional propositions that help to complete the foundation for intergroup cooperation:

1. **The more groups share common responsibility for problem solving and for decision making, the more likely they are to cooperate.**
2. **The more groups are able to establish joint memberships, the more likely they are to cooperate.**
3. **The more groups are willing to share and discuss their perceptions of each other, the more likely they are to cooperate (Blake et al., 1964).**

The Norm of Reciprocity

For the propositions stated above to be translated into effective strategies for managing intergroup operations, the various groups involved need to recognize the significance of their interrelationships. Each needs to recognize that its own identity can be enhanced by its contribution to another group, and each needs to recognize the obligations for a return contribution. This kind of "fair exchange" principle increases *mutual* functionality and also is functional to the system. This is part of the "norm of reciprocity" discussed in Chapter 10, and it is often considered to be a critical factor in maximizing interdependence (Gouldner, 1960).

An example of this norm in operation occurs in many business schools where several groupings of faculty, each from a different discipline, make decisions on curriculum content. With respect to each group's sense of its own importance it might be functional for it to dominate the decisions, but that would lead to an imbalanced program. The finance people would push for more finance courses, the marketing people for more marketing courses, the behavioral scientists for more organizational behavior courses, and so forth. If the faculty can establish a norm of reciprocity, then it is possible for each group to enhance the other, with the net result being a broad and balanced set of courses and a program that is functional for the school and the students.

On the other hand, if the groups are too understanding of the others, they may not demand the proper time for their own subject! Reciprocity can also become a form of "you scratch my back and I'll scratch yours," or "live and let live," which avoids tough priority decisions by giving everyone a bit of the goodies, deserved or not. It can be as dysfunctional to a total system to secure false peace as to fight endless battles.

METHODS FOR MAXIMIZING INTERGROUP COOPERATION

When greater cooperation is called for, several techniques can help foster it. Listed below are six basic strategies for maximizing intergroup cooperation. These approaches are both preventive and curative—that is, each may serve as a means of establishing intergroup cooperation from the start or as a means of resolving intergroup problems or conflicts that have already developed. Obviously, the more these strategies are in operation, the fewer problems are likely to develop; but few, if any, organizations are free from intergroup problems no matter how well they implement these approaches.

The six strategies are as follows:

1. Overlapping or multiple group membership.
2. Liaison or linkage people.
3. Joint task forces.
4. Joint group meetings.
5. Job exchanges across groups.
6. Physical proximity.

Let's examine each of these approaches and see the advantages and disadvantages of each. Keep in mind that different situations call for different strategies and also that combinations of two or more of the approaches are often appropriate. Each of the six strategies is directly or indirectly derivable from the propositions stated in the previous section.

Overlapping or Multiple Group Memberships

In most organizations, it is not unusual to be a member of more than one work group at any given time. A department manager, for example, is a member of both his or her own department and that group of people identifiable as department heads. (In a linking-pin organization, this is formalized in its structure.) Managers also may be assigned to a committee or task force to represent the interests of their own department on some matter of planning, policy, budget decisions, and so forth, This type of multiple group membership has the obvious advantages of keeping the several groups in contact with one another, helping the manager to coordinate efforts of the different groups, helping him or her to see various perspectives, time horizons, and styles of operating, as well as facilitating a total system perspective. In all these respects, such an approach is functional.

One of the problems, however, is the fact that multiple group membership can trap a person between the norms or goals of conflicting groups. For example, a committee or task force will tend to develop its own identity as it continues to meet. All members become subject to the emergent norms and pressures of the "new group" and may, at times, be faced with the dilemma of choosing between the interests of their "home group" and those of the "new group." To the extent that they maintain absolute loyalty to the interests of the home group ("We'll get every dollar we can for our department no matter how hard we have to fight"), they may hang up the new group; insofar as they succumb to the pressures and influence of the new group ("We have to cut our budget for the sake of the other departments"), the home group can accuse the manager of forsaking the department.

This dilemma may be further complicated by the fact that, the more frequently the individual meets and interacts with the members of both groups, the more difficult the loyalty bind becomes. Remember, this often tends to occur in the absence of other sources of interaction between members of the two groups, in which case the individual (manager, in our example) is the principal link between the groups. As a manager becomes more aware, via committee membership, of the legitimacy of the views and needs of other groups and interacts more frequently with the members of the committee, greater mutual liking and respect will develop. The individual becomes most acutely aware of this loyalty bind when: (*a*) attempting to explain and defend each group's position to the other group and (*b*) each group increases pressure on the individual to hold firm and maintain loyalty.

In addition, the more the individual representing a group embodies the norms and values of that group, the greater will be the bind in the face of conflicting pressures. And the more *cohesive* that group is, the more pressure it will exert to take an unyielding position.

In short, the multiple group memberships generally experienced by managers in large organizations can serve important functions in maintaining intergroup interdependence, but they also have built into them some serious obstacles related to conflicting pressures from the different groups. Some of the difficulties, however, can be offset by implementing additional approaches for intergroup interactions, as you will see in the next few pages.

Liaison or Linkage People

Over the years as organizations have faced increasing complexities and uncertainties, it has become more important for them to be able to process information and make decisions rapidly. The classical chain of command has become obsolete in many areas of work. It simply cannot manage the demand for flexibility and responsiveness to change and uncertainty. It has become more imperative than ever for groups in a system to maintain a fairly constant and open flow of important information. As a result, heavy demands are made upon managers to serve as the critical information links for the various subunits of the system, But managers have their limits and, in modern society, can easily suffer from overload problems.

One important development that has occurred in response to this problem is the creation of liaison or linkage people for the groups in the organization. These individuals, or sometimes groups of individuals, are not normally identified with any one operational unit nor do they carry any specific task responsibilities. Their role is simply (and it may not be so simple) to coordinate the efforts of various work groups, to facilitate the necessary exchanges of information, and to help keep each unit apprised of the related activities of other units.

The advantages of utilizing liaisons who are not identified with existing work groups lie in their relative neutrality with respect to group pressures, their immunity from the sanctions of any single group, and their relative freedom to move back and forth in the system as the task demands it. One disadvantage, of course, lies in their lack of legitimate "clout" to make things happen. However, through demonstrated competence, they can develop a great deal of informal influence.

Linking people and groups works best when their emergent norms and attitudes toward time, structure, authority, and so forth fall approximately halfway between those of the groups being linked. If either group sees the linking people as too similar to the other group, the rejected group members are likely to feel ganged up on or misunderstood.

Joint Task Forces

The creation of a joint task force composed of members of different work groups, even groups that have experienced some conflicts, tends to be a very powerful and effective way of breaking down sharp lines between groups (see Chapter 3 for notes on task forces). Each member of the task force enters the new group with the security and support of members of the old group, but it generally follows that the interactions among the members across old group lines tend to generate liking and respect that eventually supersedes old group differences. Certainly some loyalty binds will be experienced, and certainly the old group will never quite be the same. But the payoff in terms of greater productivity, mutual group enhancement, and a wider perspective for all individuals can more than compensate for the loss of "the way it used to be."

Joint Group Meetings

Meetings of total groups with one another go even further than joint task forces to break down barriers. Obviously, a small task force can get more work done, but there are times when it is appropriate for all the members of two or more work groups to meet together in a face-to-face situation. If there has been a history of conflicts between the groups, for example, it is likely that each has built up stereotypes of the other. Since stereotypes tend to be maintained in the absence of real data and direct contact, the logical step is to bring the groups together in a setting that will facilitate interaction. Under such circumstances, groups normally find it difficult to maintain the stereotypes and the related conflicts.

> Remember the oil company situation described earlier? The regional people who wanted decision-making authority over prices had developed very negative stereotypes of the headquarters people who wanted final say, and vice versa. Since they were several thousand miles apart and had never even met each other, with the exception of a few top level managers, it was inevitable that their differences and their stereotypes would become fixed.
>
> The strategy that was employed as a first step to resolving the conflict was for each group to state explicitly its perceptions of the other and then to begin sharing these perceptions in a series of meetings designed to force a great deal of direct interaction. As you might guess, the stereotypes did not hold up for very long; the members of both groups began to perceive each other as individuals and to both like and respect one another. The joint meeting provided the necessary vehicle for the groups to recognize and accept their interdependence.
>
> Since meetings of all the members were too expensive and time-consuming to hold very often, they created several joint task forces whose purpose it was to stay on top of problems and decisions affecting both groups. They also agreed to have certain individuals serve as liaison persons whose job it was to maintain a constant and rapid flow of information from the region to headquarters and back.
>
> Whereas previously the managers were carrying the burden of all the problems and complaints and were consequently caught in the middle, the use of the above strategies for promoting intergroup cooperation ultimately removed a very dysfunctional load from the managers' backs.

Job Exchanges across Groups

Some organizations increase cooperation by having people from different departments exchange jobs. It is difficult to appreciate another person's position until you've had a chance to walk in his or her shoes. Judgments about the behavior of other people are usually made from outside the situation. If that situation happens to involve the other person's membership in another group, judgment can be colored by previous perceptions of that group. Also, it may be difficult to understand how it feels to be a member of that other group. By exchanging members, chances are increased that members of each group can appreciate the needs and operations of the other. It has the same kind of benefits as a cultural exchange.

> In one large physical rehabilitation hospital, the chief of occupational therapy exchanged jobs with the chief of physical therapy for two weeks. This action established a pattern for cooperation between the two departments that had never before existed. Members of the two departments increased their contacts and began to learn many skills from each other. Whereas the relationship between the two departments had been built upon rivalry, with each trying to demonstrate its greater value to the patients, the outcome of the job exchange was each group's recognition of its own and the other's unique but interrelated contributions to the welfare of the patient.

Physical Proximity

Perhaps all too obvious but certainly not to be overlooked is the importance of physical distance in the relations between groups. If two work groups are in different buildings, the chances for interaction are minimal during the normal working hours. The best that can be hoped for is linkage people, joint task forces, occasional joint meetings, and the like. Given what we have already stated in regard to these strategies, we certainly do not underestimate their effect. But sometimes there is simply no substitute for frequent ongoing exchanges, both task related and of a social nature. None of the previous approaches allows much room for emergent social interactions among the members of the different groups. Each strategy is task related and normally has limited time boundaries. **To the extent that two working groups are co-located, interactions are likely to develop that will enhance intergroup cooperation and minimize intergroup conflict.** Perhaps each of the other approaches is a poor approximation of this one, but necessary because of the great variety of organizational constraints that dictate physical separation (e.g., job specialization and the technology of the work). However, all too often managers overlook the obvious: The physical placement of people at work can have a major effect upon their performance. The physical proximity of working groups can be a significant factor in establishing their cooperation.

CREATING INTERGROUP COOPERATION ACROSS INTERNATIONAL AND REGIONAL CULTURES

With all economies becoming increasingly global, managers must deal with identity differences, not only among groups within their organization, but also among organizations, among regions of their home country, and throughout the world (Adler, 1986). Managers must deal with groups and individuals from other countries who operate from a different cultural framework, and must travel to or live in different countries all around the world. We turn next to an exploration of some of the ways cultures differ, describing how they differ and the implications of those differences for management.

An understanding of cultural differences and skill in adapting to various cultures can be crucial for personal and organizational effectiveness. Consider the following experience of one of the authors while teaching managers who were candidates for the MBA degree in the Southwest Asian country of Sri Lanka:

> I grew up at a time when it was common for middle-aged females to be referred to as "girls," especially by men, but also by other women. However, given more recent developments in the United States I had come to appreciate the disrespect that calling adult females "girls" entails and as I approached teaching in a rather traditional Southwest Asian culture I was careful to refer to the females in the MBA program as "women." Feeling good about my own awareness and sensitivity, I was taken aback when after the third class, several of the male students came to me asking why I was "insulting our ladies" in the class by referring to them as "women"! Discussion brought out the fact that in their culture the word "woman" was used in reference to the servant women employed in the households of university-educated professionals. The females of the class were "ladies."

Such are the potential pitfalls of working in another culture where words can take on different meanings. Fortunately, the men, apparently driven by their culturally dictated obligation to defend and protect women, were able to go against another strongly held cultural instinct—deference to authority—and confront the visiting professor, despite his presumed higher status.

This experience reflects at least three dimensions which often differ among cultures: connotations of words, relationships between men and women, and directness of expression or confrontation of differences. We turn now to a discussion of these and other cultural dimensions.

Some Dimensions of Culture

1. The Connotations of Words

In the previous anecdote, the MBA class attached a connotation to the word "woman" that never crossed the professor's mind. As we explained in Chapter 10, such unexpected misunderstandings are always possible among people of different cultures. Even the English language, widely used by businesses throughout the world, receives different connotations in different cultures.

In some cultures (especially in the Orient), it is considered impolite to say "no" directly. Consequently, a "yes" may not mean "yes" the way it might in North America. It may mean "maybe," or "I'll try," or even "I wish I could." The failure to do what a "yes" promised does not evidence a lack of responsibility or dishonesty; it is probably evidence of that person's politeness and the underlying cultural standard.

2. Directness of Expression and Confrontation of Differences and Conflict

In the United States people often pride themselves on "calling a spade a spade" or "telling it like it is." In contrast, many other cultures take pride in being considerate of others' feelings by being much less direct. Japanese management has a reputation for never directly saying "no" to a subordinate's proposal. Instead, the supervisor raises questions which indicate how to reshape the proposal to gain approval. This saves the proposer from losing face and eventually can lead to acceptance of a modified proposal.

Imagine the reaction of someone from a more direct culture, ignorant of the Japanese way, when he or she doesn't get a direct answer. The questions and the lack of a definite yes or no might easily be interpreted as indecisiveness when the Japanese are merely behaving appropriately within their culture.

Fortunately for the author in Sri Lanka, the MBA students were ready to confront more openly than was characteristic of their culture. Otherwise he might easily have continued to "insult" the ladies, especially if he failed to notice the class members' subtle reactions to his behavior.

3. The Relationship between Men and Women

In the anecdote, the behavior of the men reflected a culture in which men have higher status than women, are expected to protect and defend them, and are more assertive than women; as a result, they feel possessive of women.

Such a patriarchal relationship has been characteristic of many cultures throughout the world, including North America. However, differences exist even among patriarchal cultures. Thus, in Muslim cultures and the Japanese culture women are outwardly more subservient than are women in Western cultures even though all the cultures are patriarchal.

A Western businessman visiting Saudi Arabia risks making a social faux pas if he inquires about his host's wife's health.[1] A Western businesswoman

---

[1] From the training film series *Going International*, Copeland Griggs Production, San Francisco, CA.

visiting a Buddhist temple in Sri Lanka, or even meeting a monk elsewhere, should not offer her hand. A Buddhist monk is not supposed to touch a woman at all. In extending her hand, the businesswoman could create an embarrassing situation for the monk and for herself.

4. Orientation toward Time

North Americans and many Northern Europeans think of the clock as running and speak of time as flying. A literal translation of the same phrase in Spanish suggests that time walks. This reflects the difference between the orientation to time common in the United States and that of Mexican people and many other cultures of the world, including Native Americans. Generally, North Americans and Northern Europeans value time, seek to save it, and are concerned about wasting it by not being punctual. Other cultures take time as it comes.

How would you feel as a customer if you had an appointment with a supplier and the supplier kept you waiting for 10 minutes? You'd probably be a bit surprised, but not upset. How about 20 minutes? Certainly irritated? And if 30 minutes? Take your business elsewhere? In many places in the world such a lack of punctuality would not stir up negative feelings. To be late for an appointment by 30 minutes would be viewed in some cultures as a North American might view being 5 minutes late. But 5 minutes late might be seen by a punctual German or Dutch businessperson as very rude. You can see what kind of misunderstanding could occur when individuals who count time by the minute interact with individuals from cultures for whom time is relatively unimportant (Hall, 1980).

5. Distribution of Power/Emphasis on Rank

Cultures differ significantly in their attitudes toward others with power. Some expect directive, even autocratic, leadership patterns while others prefer more participative, egalitarian patterns, or industrial democracy.

In many cultures, managers dare not offer suggestions to their superior lest he (and it is likely to be a he in most countries) feel insulted by their apparent disrespect for his position and his personal competency. This reflects a strong cultural emphasis on respect for authority, position, and even age. Participation in decisions by individuals from many levels, departments, and ranks is seen as disrespectful and even morally wrong. To base influence on expertise and logical persuasion, as team and matrix structures require, rather than on position and rank, would smack of the manager abdicating his or her role.

During World War II a number of United States soldiers, captured by the Japanese, received additional punishment and even torture because they refused to bow to their captors and in other ways failed to fulfill Japanese cultural expectations that the less powerful show respect and deference for those in power.

Not so many years ago a lower-ranking individual in a U.S. corporation would put on a suit coat before entering the department manager's office, address the manager by last name and even remain standing throughout the conversation unless explicitly invited to take a chair. While such outward expression of respect for position and age is not common today in the United States, it would be found in many British organizations and elsewhere in the world.

6. Emphasis on Individualism versus Group Orientation

Another way that cultures differ is in the relative emphasis on individual rights versus group needs. United States managers often value self-reliance, individual achievement, and competitiveness. Many cultures will emphasize much greater concern for the group, and will expect the individual to subordinate his or her personal gain to the well-being of the family, the work group, the organization and the wider society. An arranged marriage for the purpose of developing a political or economic alliance perhaps epitomizes, in Western eyes, the placing of collective interests ahead of individual interests.

The Japanese have an expression, "The nail that sticks up gets hammered down." This expression captures the social disapproval attached to someone who personally seeks the limelight, or is inappropriately given it by a supervisor.[2] Thus, a manager from a country where individualism is prized could easily make a mistake by publicly praising an individual's performance in Japan. In a group-oriented culture, praise should go to the group rather than to the individual, or possibly to the senior member as representing the group, but certainly not to a younger member, however competent and effective he or she may be.

Also, management is likely to find that group pay incentives will be more suitable in a group-oriented culture than piece work or other incentive systems based on individual performance.

7. The Relative Importance of People and Relationships, and Quality of Work-Life

In some cultures, such as Denmark, concern for people and relationships, and for the quality of life, weigh more heavily than the acquisition of material things, i.e., "the bottom line" in the United States. (Hofstede, 1980). While these values orientations are not either/or categories, but instead a matter of emphasis and importance attached to each cluster of values, the implications for doing business in one culture or another are significant.

For example, in many cultures, managers as well as employees expect to have their weekends free. While they expect to work hard for the scheduled 40 hours of the work week, they do not find it reasonable to take time away from family life by working 60–70 hours per week, as is common in many U.S. companies. A manager from the United States, working in such a culture, needs to redefine what constitutes a hardworking, loyal employee

---
[2] Ibid.

from that which may apply in the United States and the rest of North America. This can be difficult for a manager who is strongly committed to business-first attitudes. A manager from the United States stationed in Mexico felt very critical of a Mexican subordinate manager who failed to keep an afternoon appointment with him. At lunch the Mexican ran into a friend he had not seen in a long time, and instead of keeping his business appointment the Mexican spent time with his friend. By his values, he was putting first things first, namely putting the relationship ahead of mere business (Fayerweather, 1959).

These are seven dimensions on which cultures can differ. There are others, including the use of personal space; uncertainty avoidance; attire, including degree of physical exposure (nudity); forms of address; and public expressions of affection (movies from the United States showing couples kissing are shocking, even disgusting, for some cultures).

Consequences of Cultural Unawareness

Anyone who has been a member of a group for a long time will tend to take the group's ways of doing things for granted. Since culturally determined customs and norms are typically behavioral patterns with which members of a culture have grown up, awareness of these dimensions is often quite limited. Actions are typically undertaken without a lot of conscious attention. The possibilities of violating the customs, mores, and values of another, not well-understood culture are great. Furthermore, because a particular culture's position on any dimension becomes, for that culture, the "right" way to do things—the way things "ought" to be done—personal insult, uncomfortable misunderstandings, and damage to interpersonal relationships can happen all too easily. Yet, if work is to get done effectively, such consequences must be minimized, and this requires developing cross-cultural skills.

Developing Cross-Cultural Skills for Working in Another Country

Learning how to handle yourself in a new and different culture is a long-term process. It starts with developing an awareness of cultural differences. It means learning about another perspective on life, other ways of thinking and acting, and an appreciation for different beliefs and values. Reading about culture, in general, as you have just been doing, is one step to that end. Seeking to identify attributes of your own culture is another. Talking to international students on campus to learn what struck them about your country when they first arrived, and even now, would give you insight into your culture as well as theirs.

A second step is to learn about the culture of the country you are traveling to, or think you may want to travel to someday, before you go. Reading about a country's history is valuable for understanding its culture. Exhibiting some knowledge of a country's history and exhibiting a genuine interest in its traditions, art, and historically important sites can endear you to the citizens of that country. Talking to visitors from what country and to citizens of your own country who have visited that country can also be very valuable. Seek to learn what they found different when coming here or going there. Inquire about important social customs and traditions of the country. Ask questions directly about the cultural dimensions discussed above and others that you encounter in your reading.

As you learn about a culture before you go, a third step is to decide how you might adapt your own behavior. Would you be particularly punctual, as you'd need to be if you went to Switzerland? Would you need to modify your attire in any way, such as wearing only conservative suits if you were going to a very proper country or wearing only ankle-length skirts if going to a Muslim country? While thinking along these lines, you may also consider behaviors which you would not be comfortable adopting because they would force you to violate your personal values.

In preparing to teach Organizational Behavior in Sri Lanka, the author mentioned above decided to lecture more than he does at home, since lecture is the established pedagogy in South Asia. However, sticking only to lectures would have violated an important part of his educational philosophy. Consequently, he also decided to employ small group discussions and experimental learning exercises even though their use would probably feel strange and even inappropriate to the manager-students. Similarly, a manager may decide that group pay incentives rather than individual incentives would be appropriate for a given culture, but would feel a need to take steps to encourage greater individual initiative on the part of employees than might be common in that country.

Fourth, observe how things are done locally and try to be a "participant observer," paying attention to how your behavior is being received. The cues may be subtle and nonverbal, but they can reveal a violation of some cultural norm, and thereby suggest possible further adaptation.

It is hard to be both culturally sensitive and true to one's own values. For example, in a culture that emphasizes deferring to authority and seniority how would you deal with a much older boss you think is making a big mistake? Do you speak up to pursue efficiency, or keep quite to be adaptive? Generally, it is probably better to be oneself, yet alert to learning from one's mistakes, than to be so on guard against making a mistake that one is stiff, unnatural, and lacking spontaneity. You can decide how best and how much to adapt before reaching the country, but you should continue to consider your decisions after you arrive.

A useful fifth step is to find someone from the culture to act as cultural advisor—someone from whom you can learn about the culture and who will give you feedback when you unknowingly step on cultural toes.

Finally, remember that you are a guest in the country and approach the experience with an attitude of inquisitiveness and a desire to learn about the country and its culture, rather than being judgmental because their ways differ from what you are used to. However different, their ways probably work for that country, even if they might be viewed as less effective than the pattern at home. Stay observant, openminded, flexible, and courteous.

Dealing with Regional Cultures within Your Own Country

What we have said about cultures of different countries applies to a degree to different regions of most countries. Each can have its distinct regional culture. If you are from North America you may have heard Californians described as laid back, New Englanders as reserved, and Southerners as gracious and hospitable. Historically, New York City has had a reputation for being very businesslike, with individuals getting right down to business without wasting much time on social amenities. In contrast, in Texas historically it was seen as necessary to develop a relationship before doing business. As you travel around the United States or do business with individuals from other parts of the country some use of your awareness of cultural differences and some application of the cross-cultural skills discussed above will be appropriate.

Diversity within Organizations

Groups, regions, and countries all exhibit their own identities or cultures. Individuals do also, due to their racial background, ethnic heritage, socioeconomic class, and gender. Consequently, within a single organization in North America, one can be working cross-culturally.

Although it is important to avoid stereotyping and thereby fail to notice individuals who are different from the group(s) they have been part of, when joining an organization each person brings some cultural background experienced at home and growing up. While we will have been influenced by the regions of the country in which we grew up, we will have also been influenced by our racial and ethnic origins (Native American, African American, Spanish-speaking American, Asian American, and Euro-American with roots in Poland, Germany, England, France, Italy, Scandinavia, Ireland, Greece, etc.).

Furthermore, we differ as to gender. Females experience a different culture than do males whatever their racial and ethnic origins, because throughout the modern world the role of men and women differ and female and male children are raised in subtly different ways. As we have mentioned throughout this book, women and men tend to differ in interpersonal style, in managerial style, in thought processes (relative emphasis on intuition versus analytical/rational processes), and in values (particularly in terms of the importance attached to relationships versus status and power) (Tannen, 1990). Diversity within organizations is increasing. The world of management in North America is no longer inhabited only by white, Euro-American males. The ability to respect, know, and work with a wide range of diverse individuals has become an important skill for effectiveness in working in one's own country as well as working internationally.

IMPLICATIONS FOR ORGANIZATIONAL CHANGE

As you will see in Chapter 14, groups can be important leverage points for bringing about change in an organization. The need for change often is related to the general issue of system interdependence and specifically to problems of intergroup cooperation and cooperation among individuals from diverse social groupings. Any of the strategies for increasing coopera-tion represents a significant intervention into the system, whether utilized to resolve an existing conflict or as a means of minimizing the potential for future conflict. Even organizational change efforts that are not directly in-tended to affect the relationships among work groups more often than not do have some important impact on them. As you read through the chapter on organizational change, it would be useful to keep in mind the basic proposi-tions related to intergroup cooperation and see how they relate to the basic concepts and strategies for change.

KEY CONCEPTS FROM CHAPTER 13

1. The more differentiated the tasks necessary to accomplish the work, the more appropriate it is to create subsystems.
2. Variations in group identity.
   a. Attitudes toward time, authority, and structure.
   b. Perspective on the task, including professional identity.
   c. Interpersonal orientation.
3. Intergroup coordination depends on:
   a. Awareness of own function in relation to others.
   b. Maintenance of communication links with others.
   c. Acceptance of legitimacy of the needs of others.
   d. Willingness to meet own needs within the framework of the total structure.
4. The degree of resistance to the above is related to resulting conflict with the group's basic norms, ideals, values.
5. Problems with strong group identity.
   a. Seeing one's group as better than other(s).
   b. Seeing one's ideas as better than other(s).
   c. Overestimation of own competence.

      d. Overvaluation of one's leader(s).

      e. Avoidance of interaction with other group.

      f. Distortion of information about other group.

      g. Mistrust of the members of the other group.

6. Groups may have formal or informal status.

7. Groups may have legitimate or illegitimate power.

8. Diversity of backgrounds contributes to intergroup conflict.

9. Cooperation and conflict may be either functional or dysfunctional to the total system.

10. Types of interdependence:
    a. Pooled.
    b. Serial.
    c. Reciprocal.

11. The foundation of intergroup cooperation.
    a. Frequent interactions.
    b. Frequent and open information flow.
    c. Development and acceptance of common goals.
    d. Sharing a common source of threat.
    e. Shared common responsibility.
    f. Ability to establish joint memberships.
    g. Willingness to share and discuss perceptions of each other.

12. The norm of reciprocity maximizes interdependence.

13. Methods for maximizing intergroup cooperation:
    a. Overlapping or multiple group membership.
    b. Liaison people.
    c. Joint task forces.
    d. Joint group meetings.
    e. Job exchanges.
    f. Physical proximity.

14. Creating intergroup cooperation across cultures; dimensions of culture
    a. Connotations of words in same langugage.
    b. Directness of expression/confrontation of differences.
    c. Relationship between men and women.
    d. Orientation toward time.
    e. Distribution of power/emphasis on rank.
    f. Individualism vs. group orientation.
    g. Relative importance of people, relationships, quality of work life.
    h. Other.

15. Developing cross-cultural skills for working in other countries, regions, even within own organization.
    a. Develop awareness of differences.
    b. Learn the specific culture.

   c. Decide how you plan to adapt.
   d. Be participant-observer; note cues to your impact.
   e. Find a local to be your cultural advisor.
   f. As a guest, stay open to learning.

PERSONAL APPLICATION EXERCISE

Taking a Look at Gender Stereotyping

Although your instructor might use this exercise in class, you can still try it out on your own. All it takes is a group of men and a group of women, about a half dozen in each group, and enough space for the two groups to spend some of the time in separate groups and some of it in a total group. It also would be helpful to have a large flip-chart available for each group, but you can also manage with ordinary-size pads of paper.

Begin by having the men and women separate. Each group has the assignment of making up a list of all the traits that it can think of that typify the other. Males make a list of typical female traits (attitudes, behavior, and so on) and females make a list of typical male traits. After completing the list, each group then makes up a list of what it *thinks* the other group is writing down. These two steps might take 20 to 30 minutes.

The two groups then exchange their lists, remaining in their separate groups to discuss them. It is important for each group to check out its expectations about what it *thought* the other was writing, as well as to see what the other group actually did identify as typical gender characteristics. Although a great deal of what gets listed is not surprising, usually some things are. Furthermore, many positive traits get listed by both groups, despite the fact that each usually expects mostly negative.

Each group then should identify the traits on the lists that it would like to discuss, perhaps for clarification, for a deeper understanding, or out of confusion or disagreement. Now the groups join together and share their reactions, with the purpose of achieving a better mutual understanding and appreciation of differences. In addition, it is important to discuss the extent to which the traits are overgeneralized stereotypes that, in actual fact, are not even characteristic of any of the people in the room. Then the discussion can focus on the traits that do fit some or many of the people present, explore why this is the case, what are some of the roots of these traits, and so on. What impact do these traits have on productivity, satisfaction and individual development? Where do they help or hinder group understanding and collaboration? Finally, it is important for the total group to identify the *value* of the so-called male and female traits as these might fit the demands of a work setting, especially for carrying out the managerial role. How should managers deal with gender issues?

SUGGESTED READINGS

Adler, N. J., *International Dimensions of Organizational Behavior*. Belmont, Calif.: Kent Publishing, 1986.

Alderfer, C. P. "Group and Intergroup Relations." In *Improving Life at Work*, ed. J. R. Hackman and J. L. Suttle. Santa Monica, Calif.: Goodyear Publishing, 1977.

Blake, R. R., and J. S. Mouton. "Reactions to Intergroup Competition under Win-Lose Competition." *Management Science*, July 1961, pp. 420–25.

_____. "Overevaluation of Own Group's Product in Intergroup Competition." *Journal of Abnormal and Social Psychology* 64, no. 3 (1962), pp. 237–38.

Blake, R. R.; H. A. Shepard; and J. Mouton. *Managing Intergroup Conflict in Industry*. Houston: Gulf Publishing, 1964.

Brown, L. D. "Toward a Theory of Power and Intergroup Relations." In *Advances in Experiential Social Processes*, Vol. 1. Ed. C. L. Cooper and C. P. Alderfer. New York: John Wiley & Sons, 1978.

Copeland, L. and L. Griggs, *Going International*. New York: Random House, 1985.

Dalton, D. R., and W. D. Todor. "Unanticipated Consequences of Union-Management Cooperation: An Interrupted Time Series Analysis." *Journal of Applied Behavioral Science* 20, no. 3 (1984), pp. 253–64.

Fayerweather, J., *The Executive Overseas: Administrative Attitudes and Relationships in a Foreign Culture*. Syracuse, N.Y.: Syracuse University Press, 1959.

Fisher, R., and W. Ury. *Getting to Yes: Negotiating Agreement without Giving In*. Boston: Houghton Mifflin, 1981.

Gercik, P. E., *On Track with the Japanese*. New York: Kodansha International, 1992 (in press).

Gouldner, A. "The Role of the Norm of Reciprocity in Social Stabilization." *American Sociological Review* 25 (1960), pp. 161–78.

Hall, E. T., *The Hidden Dimension*. Garden City, N.Y.: Doubleday & Company, 1966.

_____. *The Silent Language*. Garden City, N.Y.: Doubleday & Company, 1959.

Hall, E. T., and W. F. Whyte. "Intercultural Communication: A Guide to Men of Action." In *Readings in Managerial Psychology*, 2nd ed. Ed. H. J. Leavitt and L. R. Pondy. Chicago: University of Chicago Press, 1973.

Harris, P. R. and R. T. Moran, *Managing Cultural Differences*, 2nd ed. Houston, Tx.: Gulf Publishing, 1987.

Hofstede, G., "Motivation, Leadership, and Organization: Do American Theories Apply Abroad?" *Organizational Dynamics*, Summer 1980.

Kanter, R. M. *Men and Women of the Corporation*. New York: Alfred A. Knopf, 1977.

Kelly, J. "Make Conflict Work for You." *Harvard Business Review*, July–August 1970, pp. 103–13.

Lawrence, P. R., and J. W. Lorsch. *Organization and Environment: Managing Differentiation and Integration*. Cambridge, Mass.: Division of Research, Graduate School of Business, Harvard University, 1967.

Leavitt, H. J., and J. Lipman-Blumen. "A Case for the Relational Managers." *Organizational Dynamics*, Summer 1980, pp. 27–41.

Lentz, S. S. "The Labor Model for Mediation and Its Application to the Resolution of Environmental Disputes." *Journal of Applied Behavioral Science* 22, no. 2 (1986), pp. 127–40.

Lewicki, R. J., and J. A. Litterer. *Negotiation*. Homewood, Ill.: Richard D. Irwin, 1985.

Lorsch, J. W., and P. R. Lawrence. *Managing Group and Intergroup Relations.* Homewood, Ill.: Richard D. Irwin and Dorsey Press, 1972, pp. 285–304.

McCann, J. E., and D. Ferry. "An Approach for Assessing and Managing Interunit Interdependence." *Academy of Management Review,* January 1979, pp. 113–20.

Pascale, R. T., *Managing on the Edge.* New York: Simon & Schuster, 1991.

Phatak, A. V., *International Dimensions of Management.* Belmont, Calif.: Kent Publishing, 1983.

Rice, A. K. "Individual, Group, and Intergroup Behavior." *Human Relations* 22 (1969), pp. 565–84.

Schelling, T. C. *The Strategy of Conflict.* New York: Oxford University Press, 1960.

Schopler, J. H. "Interorganizational Groups: Origins, Structure, and Outcomes." *Academy of Management Review* 12, no. 4 (1987), pp. 702–13.

Seiler, J. A. "Diagnosing Interdepartmental Conflict." *Harvard Business Review,* September–October 1963.

Smith, K. K. "An Intergroup Perspective on Individual Behavior.'" In *Perspectives on Behavior in Organizations,* ed. J. R. Hackman, E. E. Lawler, and L. W. Porter. New York: McGraw-Hill, 1977.

Tannen, D., *You Just Don't Understand.* New York: William Morrow & Company, 1990.

Thomas, J. M., and W. G. Bennis, eds. *Management of Change and Conflict.* New York: Penguin Books, 1972.

Thompson, J. D. *Organizations in Action.* New York: McGraw-Hill, 1967.

Walton, R. E. "Third-Party Roles in Interdepartmental Conflict." *Industrial Relations* 7 (1967), pp. 24–43.

Walton, R. E., and J. M. Dutton. "The Management of Interdepartmental Conflict." *Administrative Science Quarterly* 14 (1969), pp. 73–84.

Von Laue, T. H. "Transubstantiation in the Study of African Reality." *African Affairs* 4, no. 10 (1975), pp. 401–19.

3

The Work Group

"Technology sets limits on what social interactions and emergent behavior are possible and causes interactions to occur. Even noise level affects the likelihood of social discourse."

One of the most important subsystems in any organization is the work group. Though many students and managers think of organizations as consisting of a collection of individuals, each doing a separate and distinct job, much of the world's work is actually done in some kind of group. Even when the individual employee is not formally assigned to a clearly defined group of people, much of his or her work will likely be carried out in conjunction with a particular set of other people, and feelings of "being part of a group" will emerge. Even executives who often like to think of themselves as rugged individualists seldom work alone or in isolation; they are members of a top management team, committees, task forces, study groups, and so forth, which directly affect their success or failure in the organization.

Yet it is not easy to work effectively in a group. Anyone who has ever had to coordinate activities and come to decisions in conjunction with other people will remember at times having felt something like, "If only I could get rid of the others, I could do this job much better myself and save a lot of time, too!" Working together, at least in most Western individualistic cultures, is not easily or automatically accomplished.

God created the world in 6 days—but had the advantage of working alone.

**C. Roland Christenson
commencement speech,
Babson College, 1987**

WHY GROUPS?

Why then is group work so recurrent? Perhaps the most important reason is that few jobs can be done alone. Only when it is clear that one person has much greater expertise than the combined efforts of others could yield, the task requires a creative synthesis and individual intuition, or when solo work will be good training, is work best done by lone individuals. It takes more than one person's energy, knowledge, skills, and time to get most complicated jobs done. That is increasingly the case as organizations become more technologically complex and require ever greater numbers of experts. Furthermore, when tasks are even the least bit complex, a division of labor makes it possible to use individual efforts more systematically and to take advantage of different talents and skills. A committee studying ways to cut fuel consumption in a company, for example, could have all members engage in the same research and discussion activities, but the complexities of the task make it desirable to divide up the work. One member might review technical literature, another survey the existing heating/cooling system, a third investigate what other companies have done, another check costs of conversion to alternate fuels, and so forth.

Yet in such a committee, as in other group activities where participants have different assignments from one another, activities must somehow be coordinated in order to not duplicate efforts, leave something undone, or work at cross purposes. Thus, a group must find a way to allocate work, coordinate activities, define and agree upon goals, and then gain the commitment of members to carry out the group's work in a manner consistent with its objectives.

Groups also exist for another, more personal, set of reasons. Even where a task does not call for coordinated effort, people working near one another often form relationships to fill social needs for conversation, companionship, or friendship. Human beings are social animals and seem to need human association as much as they need food and drink. So groups often form for reasons above and beyond needs for task coordination. Indeed, for many members of work groups, individual needs for social relationship may be even more powerful in affecting behavior than organizational objectives.

Long before getting jobs, everyone has developed considerable experience with groups; they are the primary units of all social systems. Most people are born into a group—the family—and spend the greater part of their lives living, working, and playing in a wide variety of groups. When young, they belong to cliques, gangs, or clubs. As they grow up, they tend to move into social settings where group belonging gives support and provides avenues to do things they could not do by themselves. Thus, it is not surprising that, in the work world, people continue to find groups to be a principal vehicle for carrying out tasks, not solely to seek superior organization goals through collective effort, but to meet individual needs as well.

What is more surprising is how difficult it is for groups in organizations to be effective and satisfying to their members. Occasionally this is caused by groups being utilized to do what could better be executed by one individual, as implied in the old joke: "A camel is a horse designed by a committee." More often, however, groups are just not run effectively; members do not know how to help the group take fullest advantage of its potential. We will address this issue in depth in Chapter 6, because we believe that the ability to help make a group function effectively can be learned and is worth learning. Thus, we aim to help you improve both your *understanding* of how task groups work and your *skills* at getting what you want from the work groups of which you become a member.

Though many of the concepts we will introduce apply equally well to nonorganizational groups, we will focus on those that are task oriented, because at least half of an adult's waking life is spent at work and most education does not give emphasis to this important area of concern. Non-work applications of what is learned can be a personal bonus for mastering the course materials.

We can call upon your past experiences to bring to life the several concepts we need to build on. For example, you probably remember groups in which you played a dominant part and others in which you were more on the sidelines, times when you were part of the "in group" and times when you were on the "outs." Think about some of the groups of which you currently are or have recently been a member. How are they organized? What is your place in them? Who controls them? Is there equality among members or a "pecking order"? These are the kinds of questions we will be addressing throughout the next few chapters.

The answers to these questions, among others, will help to give you a better understanding of how groups function and what determines the effectiveness of a group in meeting its goals. As we go along, we encourage you to use your own immediate and past experiences to validate the theories and concepts that will be introduced. Most of these concepts will also be directly applicable to the classroom setting and will help you to understand various aspects of your own experiences as the course unfolds. You should come out with a better sense of the consequences of your own membership in various groups, how your sense of individuality is affected, and how you can strike a balance among (1) your needs, (2) those of other individual members, and (3) the needs of the group as an entity.

HOW DO YOU KNOW WHEN A GROUP *IS*?

What exactly do we mean by a "group"? Is it any collection of individuals, like strangers at a bus stop, or is it something more? As explained in Chapter 2, any social system is defined by the relative number of interactions among its components. Though the boundary can be drawn anywhere, depending on one's purpose, work groups often are clearly identifiable to others and to their own members. From now on we will use the word *group* to mean small face-to-face groups, consisting of more than 2 people and usually no more than 12 to 15. Such a group has an existence over an extended period of time, tends to see itself as separate and distinguishable from others around it, and has members who are mutually aware of their membership. As noted in the beginning of this chapter, some organizational groups are not formally defined as such but function nevertheless as distinguishable units.

If a group appears to its members as a useful vehicle for meeting individual needs, then keeping relationships going among members of any group becomes an end in itself. This is why the size of the group is an important factor. If a group becomes too large, it is difficult for the members to maintain direct personal relations, and there is an increasing chance of fragmentation into subgroups.

In summary then, we can determine the existence of a group by noting its *size,* its *degree of differentiation from other groups,* the *existence of personal relations that have some duration, identification of the members with the group,* and often some *common goals.*

Thus, a small collection of people waiting at a bus stop would not be a group by the definition we use in this book. While every individual presumably has the same goal, namely to catch a bus, it is not a common goal in the sense of being a goal that will result from joint effort. While a few individuals might be friends, most would be strangers or, at best, "nodding acquaintances" from the same neighborhood. Furthermore, individually they would not think of themselves as an identifiable group.

By defining groups as stated above we include the following types:

1. Groups that are ongoing parts of an organization, like departments or work teams.
2. Temporary task groups, like a committee or special problem-solving group whose life is compressed into a defined span of time. (Note the differences from ongoing groups in the next Managerial Tools box.)
3. Groups that are voluntarily formed purely for friendship or other social needs as noted earlier; these will not be our focus but must be considered since they exist within and across types (1) and (2) above and directly influence these formal system groups.

You might like to note the characteristics of any groups of which you are a member and to share these with other students both within and outside of the groups in question. This process should give you a clearer sense of the existence of each group. It might also provide you with some perspective on the degree to which your memberships in a number of different groups at one time influence the pattern of your own life.

MANAGERIAL TOOLS

Differences between Ongoing Work Groups and Temporary Groups

Ongoing Groups	Temporary Groups
Conduct most organization work that is predictable, continuing, regular.	Used for unusual projects or problems when diversity of opinion, talent, or expertise needed. Task forces, committees, project teams.
Job surrounded with a sense of permanence; a presumption that, with satisfactory performance and the absence of unforeseen catastrophe, the group will continue indefinitely.	Job is temporary, to be worked on until done; then members are expected to disperse to some other task(s) with some other group(s).
Existence of a common identity (as a member of this department or work group) and the sense of a common purpose. Can result in too little diversity of opinion or in forced conformity, or in both.	Member primary loyalty is elsewhere to ongoing "home" group; often act as "representatives," not independent problem solvers. Difficult to achieve common purpose. Can result in maneuvering for advantage, defensiveness about home group, hidden agendas to settle old scores. Members less committed to temporary group, may withhold their time, energy, expertise.
History of working together often results in considerable knowledge about one another and patterned role relationships; makes working together comfortable. Danger of freezing others into existing behavior roles.	Sense of working with "strangers"; need to develop skills of building effective relationships rapidly and being effective in dealing with emergent process problems promptly.
A recognized boss: focal point for resolving issues and making decisions when all else fails. Also a recognized source of organizational rewards.	Likely to be self-governing or led by a chairperson with less clearly defined authority and less power; rewards for effort unclear, while home-group work piles up; individual members may see opportunity of contact with people from other parts of the organization (sometimes in higher positions) as way to make good impression. Can lead to "grandstanding"; focus on audience, not problems.

THE NEED FOR SOME CONCEPTS

Students have often asked us why it is necessary to have a fancy conceptual scheme for analyzing groups. Isn't common sense enough? Unfortunately, common sense can carry you just so far—and usually not far enough. Social science has given us some valuable organizing principles that fortunately help to sort out what otherwise might be an undifferentiated mass. Everything that one sees can appear equally important—and there are many things one is not likely to notice without some kind of guideposts. The ultimate object of analysis is action: doing something to solve problems or to sustain good results. But action is too risky without good analysis of *why* things are as they are. We all need ways of figuring out just what factors have led to the particular behaviors we find in groups of which we're a part or which we somehow have to manage.

Though in actuality no social system sits still while you hold different parts constant, for analytical purposes we will take the liberty of talking as if various components of a work group can be separately examined. Only then can you begin to improve your ability to understand and affect the behavior of the groups of which you are a member.

We will start by introducing a basic social system conceptual scheme, which will help you to organize the pieces and put together the puzzle that explains why a group has developed in its particular way and what might be done to alter its development.

The scheme we have chosen identifies four essential factors: (1) everything that individuals and the organization bring to a group, (2) what the job itself requires, (3) what behavior and feelings result from (1) and (2), and (4) the consequences of what is actually happening. The scheme is a systematic way of identifying what is going on, why it is going on, and what difference it makes.

A CLOSER LOOK AT SOCIAL SYSTEM CONCEPTS

In Chapter 2 you were introduced to the concept of a social system consisting of two mutually interdependent elements: *behavior* and *attitudes*.[1] We will now look at groups in depth, expanding on the concepts to heighten their analytical usefulness.

Behavior

The most directly observable aspect of a social system is the *behavior* of its members—that is, their *interactions* and *activities. Interactions—exchanges of words or objects among two or more members*—are particularly crucial types of behavior, since their frequency helps determine system boundaries, friendships, and other feelings. Other types of behavior can be categorized as *activities—that which members do while they are in the group except for their interactions with other people*—such as operating a machine, writing on paper, and issuing a license. In addition to these kinds of work-related activities, there are likely to be a variety of nonwork activities, such as drinking coffee, listening to music, or tapping a pipe on the table.

---

[1] The balance of this chapter is our adaptation of the work of George C. Homans in *The Human Group* (New York: Harcourt Brace Jovanovich, 1950) and in *Social Behavior: Its Elementary Forms* (New York: Harcourt Brace Jovanovich, 1961).

Attitudes

Attitudes constitute the other category used for sorting out the parts of a social system. These can include neutral *perceptions* ("Whenever I help Charley, he smiles"), *feelings* ("I like my job"), or *values* ("Nothing is more important than being honest in my dealings with the people I work with"). When all three are combined, the result is reflected in the unique way in which each individual perceives a given situation or reacts to others. We will look at such issues in depth in Chapters 8 and 10 when we discuss the importance of the self-concept and the complexities for interpersonal communication. For now, keep in mind that these are important elements of any social system.

Norms

Perhaps the most important type of attitude is that which members of any group inevitably develop about how members in good standing *ought* to behave in that group. These attitudes we call *norms;* they are the cement that holds a group together, because they tell members exactly what behavior is believed desirable to foster the group's goals and maintain its existence. *Norms are unwritten rules, shared beliefs of most group members about what behavior is appropriate and attainable to be a member in good standing.* Behind every norm is the implicit statement: "Follow this norm because, if you don't, the group will be harmed somehow." For example, some common norms in student groups are: "Don't act as if you're trying to impress the person with authority" (as in, "Don't brownnose the teacher"), "Don't act like a big deal," "Participate at least a little, but don't dominate the conversation," "Try not to say anything that will hurt other members' feelings." Can you see what members of a student group might perceive as the dangers if these norms were not followed? Here are a few norms of an executive group at the head office of a national company: "Executives do not bring their lunches," "Eat or take coffee only with your own group, unless you have specific business with others," "Always wear your suit jacket when going in or out of the building, no matter how hot it is," "Carry only a thin zipper briefcase, not the three- or five-inch one the company gives out."

Norms such as these are not always explicit; often they are understood implicitly (or assumed to be understood). Frequently, the only way a norm is observable is by inadvertently breaking it and seeing others' reactions. If a norm has been broken, members will usually react in some kind of negative way—with a dirty look, a sarcastic comment, a "joke" that has a cutting edge, even a physical punishment, such as a "friendly" punch on the arm, or some other negative response. Those who consistently violate norms and cannot be pushed into going along will usually be given the worst punishment of all: They will be ignored and considered inferior. Norms are not written on all members' foreheads; they can only be inferred from watching actual behavior, since they are not the behavior itself but the *beliefs* in most members' minds about what behavior should be.[2] While behavior common to all members of a group usually indicates existence of a norm, it may also just be coincidental or customary. Some checking out of what members believe, or observing whether a nonconformer is punished, may be necessary to establish a norm's existence.

Since norms are not universal—in some executive groups, for example, it may be considered phony *not* to try to impress the boss or weak *not* to dominate conversations—each group develops its own norms, which give the group its particular character. And very often groups feel not only that their norms are useful ways of guiding members' behavior but are inevitable, correct, and better than any possible alternatives. Thus, violation of the norms by current members or even members of other groups is judged quite harshly even though an outside observer might be puzzled at the intensity of the group members' beliefs in its own ways.

The longer I was in the world of managers, the more I missed my union buddies, their ribald spirit, our singing together, their sensuousness, their sexuality. By comparison, managers were a deadhead lot who had traded humor and sensuality for the role-playing Kabuki world of the corporate headquarters. I have met more people having fun as clowns on one plant floor than in all of the many corporate headquarters I have gone in and out of.

[from an interview of a manager, Bob Schrank]
Bob Sales
Boston Globe

Have you ever entered a new group and found, quite accidentally, that you have violated members' notions of "proper" behavior? Here is an example of a new employee discovering a powerful norm:

A young business student got a summer job working at a bank as a credit trainee. He arrived on a hot Monday morning in a suit and tie and reported for work on the 16th floor. As the air conditioning had been off during the weekend, the open office where all trainees sat was quite warm. Noticing that others had removed their jackets and hung them over the backs of their chairs, the new employee did the same. At 10 A.M., everyone got up for coffee break at a wagon brought to the floor. Afterward, the eager newcomer returned to his desk and resumed studying the material he had been given. Soon his neighbor was motioning to him to put on his jacket. "Thanks, but I'm

---

[2] Individual ideas about how members ought to behave, which are not widely held by the group, are not called *norms;* rather, they are *individual beliefs.*

comfortable this way," he replied. A few minutes later the neighbor cleared his throat and said in a whisper, "It's time to put on your jacket." Enjoying being in his shirtsleeves, the newcomer smiled but continued as he was. A few minutes later the neighbor, now looking irritated, said, "Really, we all put our jackets on now; you should too!" Genuinely bewildered at this apparently irrational ignoring of the temperature but not wanting to create problems with strangers, the puzzled student put on his jacket and resisted no more. But his initial enthusiasm for banking diminished. It wasn't until many years later that he realized that putting on jackets after 10 A.M. was probably a reflection of public opening hours at the bank and that the trainees did what the loan officers were doing down on the first floor.

Norms can be useful in helping facilitate the group's work or they can hinder it. And they can be highly conscious and explicit or unconscious and automatic. Occasionally, norms can even take on the quality of *magic,* as in the bank example. That is, behavior that may once have been productive continues to be enforced even when there is no longer any use for it (except to bind members together). But whatever their degree of helpfulness and consciousness, when norms are agreed to by most members and strongly held they have a powerful impact on behavior.

At the New York Times *the cub reporters sit in the last row of desks. . . ; as they prove themselves they move up row by row. Beginning reporters who unknowingly sit at a vacant desk a row or two up from the back are politely but firmly told where they belong.*

Kim Foltz
***Harper's,* July 1974**

Norms tend to develop around particular subjects of interest to group members. Among other areas, most groups have norms about how much effort and output is expected of members, how to dress (as at the bank described above), the use and meaning of time, the degree to which expressions of feeling are allowed, how to handle conflict, and so forth. The longer groups work together, the more likely they are to develop elaborate sets of norms to guide behavior. One of the difficulties faced by temporary groups is the need to establish shared norms among members who may have quite different ideas about appropriate behavior, based on the norms of their various home groups. Can you generate a list of norms from any group(s) of which you are a member? Which norms are task-related? Which serve personal interactions of members? Which are counterproductive? Answering these questions can give you valuable insights into the group and your behavior in it. It can also be the first step in changing norms that are not useful or desirable.

Sources of Norms

Where do these powerful guidelines for behavior come from? Some are derived from the general culture of the country or region in which the group exists. Most Americans, for example, are raised with great consciousness about the value of time, and a high percentage of adults wear watches. Thus, these general attitudes about time often carry over into organizational groups, which emphasize being on time, getting right to work, and so on. In many Asian and Latin American cultures, time is not seen as a continuous line that is running out, and its value is different, so that being on time for meetings is less likely to emerge as a group norm.

Some norms originate in the culture of the particular organization (i.e., in the general practices and attitudes of the wider organization) and then are carried into particular groups. To illustrate, IBM for years stressed that male executive employees should wear white shirts and dark suits. There was general acceptance by IBM employees that this mode of dress was proper, so that in most IBM executive groups formal dress readily became the norm. Even at offsite training programs held in resort hotels, IBM salesmen were likely to be wearing dark suits and white shirts even when groups from other companies using the facilities dressed in casual clothes.

The new president of a conservative company that did not especially welcome him used his understanding of norms to test how well he was doing in winning other executives over to his side. Noting that all executives wore a tie and jacket in the office, he began to take off his jacket as soon as he got to the office and would walk around all day in shirtsleeves. By observing which executives started to take off their jackets at work, he had a quick and visible indicator of "converts" and could tell at a glance whether he was making progress in gaining allies.

Other norms may be carried into a group by members with a common background and common interests—ethnic, educational, or religious. For example, work groups with a majority of southern Europeans are likely to expect members to be readily expressive of feelings, while a group of northern Europeans may expect restraint and understatement from members. Similarly, groups composed of minority members or women are more likely to value expressiveness than groups of white males, reflecting the socialization of the wider society. Student groups in a classroom are likely to reflect the norms of the school itself. A large-city business school may encourage one to be aggressive and competitive, while a small rural liberal arts college may be more likely to encourage one to be polite and avoid conflict.

Finally, some norms arise from critical incidents or events in a group's life, which cause the group to learn "the way things ought to be." Perhaps an angry fight between two members over the correctness of a work procedure led to a reprimand from a supervisor for fighting—and from that experience the group developed a strong norm that insists "no one should air his troubles or disagree with a fellow member in front of anyone from management." Sometimes norms come from overreactions or overgeneralizations from one or two experiences—and then remain untested because "everyone knows" that dire consequences will follow if the norm is violated.

Values

Another important type of attitudes is *values*. While *norms are shared ideas of "correct" behavior in the group, values are more fundamental notions of ideal behavior, usually unattainable but to be striven for*. Values are seldom explicit but very much shape how members interpret events and form expectations about behavior.

For example, in some groups members believe that it is "right" that individuals should always put group needs ahead of their own personal interests. Individuals are expected to subordinate their desires for the betterment of the total group. An extreme version of this value is found in the traditional families in India, where even marriage and career choice are made by elders with overall family benefit in mind. The extreme opposite of such values might be found in a contemporary American family where each child is taught from an early age to listen to his or her conscience and make choices accordingly.

In a work setting, such group values as work before pleasure, friendship, and loyalty above all, the customer is always right, or everyone should look out for his own interests, strongly determine how members behave, even though they are not always attainable.

Quite often, however, conflicting values may be held by various members of a group or even by one member, and this can cause serious tension at crucial times. For instance, telling the truth is a commonly held value but so is avoiding hurting others. These two values are not always compatible. In groups there are often value differences underlying questions of how important it is to talk through strong disagreements: "majority rules" (so outvoted members should accept defeat gracefully) versus "everyone gets his day in court" (so dissatisfied members must somehow be placated).

In general, it is important to look and listen for underlying values even though groups do not always make their values explicit.

Rank or Status

Finally, an important set of attitudes has to do with internal position within the group. Few groups can (or even want to) sustain complete equality among members; over time some members are seen as better at providing what the group needs, while others are perceived as less able or willing. We will discuss the evolution and impact of differential status within groups in more detail in Chapter 5; for now, it is useful to note that groups informally recognize different rankings among members, even when group members may adopt "equality" norms that forbid discussing such differences.

THE BASIC SOCIAL SYSTEM CONCEPTUAL SCHEME

With a more developed picture of the elements of any social system, we are now ready to present the basic conceptual scheme of this book. The material that follows is designed to help you sort out the *causes* of behavior from the *symptoms* you can observe. It is hard enough to observe accurately what is going on, since people do not hold still for leisurely study, do not always say why they are behaving as they are (or do not know), or change their behavior when an outsider is watching. But even seeing accurately may not explain why a group is acting as it is—holding down production, sabotaging quality, voluntarily working extra hours without complaint, protecting one another, fighting about everything—in short, behaving in ways that are functional and should be preserved or dysfunctional and should be changed. The difficulty is in being able to analyze *all* the factors that together account for or cause the behavior. Since most behavior is caused by many interwoven forces, it is critical to identify more than just one or two. This will ultimately allow for sensible action.

REQUIRED VERSUS EMERGENT BEHAVIOR

A helpful conceptual distinction in tracing the source of behavior and attitudes is to separate out that part of a group's behavior and attitudes which is *required* or *given* by the larger system (organization) of which it is a part and that which *emerges* from the interactions of the group (see Figure 3–1). *The required system is what the organization requires of group members as part of their jobs.* It consists of the behavior and attitudes that management has determined to be required of some group of employees in order to successfully meet the organization's objectives. The requirements usually sound logical—

FIGURE 3–1 Separating the Required from the Emergent System

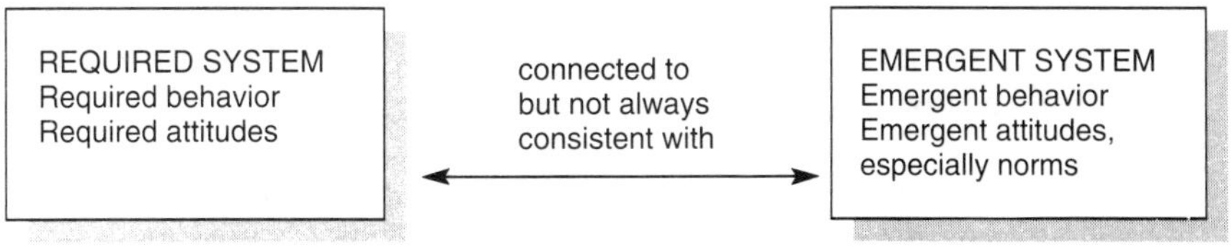

REQUIRED SYSTEM Required behavior Required attitudes	connected to but not always consistent with	EMERGENT SYSTEM Emergent behavior Emergent attitudes, especially norms

especially to the managers who have created them—and specify what people are supposed to do.

The behavioral requirements include both activities and interactions with others. These requirements usually begin with (1) *required activities,* tasks assigned to the group, such as: assemble so many parts per hour, sell so many contracts per month, make so many loans per week, and so forth. The required activities may be further broken into much more detail, such as: pull necessary parts from bins, visually inspect them as you go, assemble them in this prescribed sequence, test the assembled product, then place it on the finished goods rack. In addition, there are likely to be (2) some *required interactions:* "Get the forms from Clerk A, inquire if there are any more, and after checking them over give Agent C an assignment." (3) Finally, there will usually be some *required attitudes,* such as: "Don't be insolent when receiving instructions," or "Be loyal to our products," or "Don't make fun of the clients."

These requirements are developed by the organization and are frequently called the "formal system." They are usually contained in job descriptions and organizational rulebooks and in directions from superiors, though sometimes they are just seen as "part of the job" and are not spelled out. Written procedures, regulations, and rules—about what to do, with whom to talk, and how to feel—are a formal framework intended to guide the behavior of employees.

THE LEADER'S (SUPERVISOR'S) STYLE AND EXPECTATIONS

Sometimes job requirements are not written down but are conveyed by the supervisor or other supervisors as demands or rules about what is supposed to happen. The supervisor's style, based on assumptions about how to lead or manage, also will create required activities, interactions, and attitudes. A boss, for example, who thinks that subordinates will try to get away with murder will require many written reports, frequent meetings to check up on progress, considerable deference, and pledges of loyalty. While none of these requirements may be written down, they are nevertheless part of the required system for members of that task group.

Furthermore, a boss, as a member of management, tends to behave in keeping with the norms of his or her own reference group (other managers at the same level). These norms may then be translated into job requirements for his or her subordinates. One fairly high executive in a pharmaceutical company started out allowing his managers the freedom to govern their own working hours (within reason). Later, when he discovered that this practice was not consistent with what his peers did (even though there was no company rule about managerial hours), he made it a formal requirement that his managers all come to work at 7:30 A.M. Interestingly enough, the source of this 7:30 custom was the founder of the company, who happened to enjoy starting work early!

For analytical purposes we will treat the group's supervisor, creating and passing on requirements for job performance to group members, as outside of the group, even though, from some points of view, the boss could be considered a group member.

The boss's style in passing on demands also has an impact on the group's responses and must be taken into account. Although leadership style and its impact on performance will be examined in greater detail in Chapters 11 and 12, for now it is sufficient to call attention to possible variations in the major elements of style—how controlling, task-oriented, person-concerned, explicit, and cautious the boss is—and to suggest that you include a look at it in tracing behavior that emerges from the group.

EMERGENT BEHAVIOR

Inevitably, because people are social beings with needs greater and more complex than those of machines, a variety of unanticipated behavior and attitudes that are not required will begin to *emerge* and over time take on relatively stable patterns. On a smaller scale, this parallels the way in which the informal organization (Chapter 2) supplements the formal organization. Making frequent appointments through a secretary leads to small talk and slowly to some kind of relationship in which a greater amount of information, ideas, and feelings are exchanged than a few informational questions about the boss's availability. The worker at the opposite bench with whom coordination is necessary ventures opinions and complaints, suggests having a coffee break together, slowly becomes a friend, and perhaps visits you when you're sick. In these kinds of ways a social system elaborates itself, leading to *emergent* and lasting behavior and attitudes that go way beyond what was originally required just to do the job. Some of what emerges will be norms— a key form of attitudes—on how to do the task, how much to produce, and so on, while other norms will be related to purely social relationships, such as who has coffee with whom and who likes whom. *In both cases, it is this emergent (informal) system which gives a group its particular identity,* its view of who should do what, who should have influence, and how close members should feel.

Even the actual leadership of a group may emerge as different from the designated leader. It isn't always the formally named supervisor of a group who has the most influence over decisions and group activities; members with special expertise or skill may well become the most respected or influential persons. The member(s) who emerge with leadership influence may support or oppose, supplement or undermine, the formal supervisor. Group members may or may not be explicit about who provides the real leadership of the group, but they will usually recognize the informal leader(s) in some way—by being extra respectful, deferring slightly, or just by addressing questions or requests for help to them.

The emergent system often influences the performance of a group as much as or more than the required system. It is important to understand the significance and potency of emergent systems, since they can outweigh even formal orders issued from above. Emergent social systems acquire their own life, which is connected to but goes beyond what is required by the formal organization.

It is important to note that a well-developed emergent system with strong norms for behavior can feel to any member as if the group-approved behavior is "required" of him or her. For example, if there is a strongly enforced emergent norm that "each member must produce at least 80 parts per hour but no less than 20," this may feel like a "requirement" to the new group member, even though management may not formally require any particular hourly output. For our purposes behavior "demanded" by a group of its members is still called *emergent* provided that it is a result of group ideas, rather than formal *organizational* requirements imposed from outside the group.

When examining a required system and trying to predict likely emergent behavior, some of the questions you might ask are:

1. What tasks are required? What is it people have to do when they are working? How are they likely to feel about the tasks?
2. Who is required to interact with whom, and what relationships are likely to result?
3. What attitudes are required, and are these attitudes likely to cause resentment or enthusiasm?

BACKGROUND FACTORS

But how can we connect what emerges to what is required? Don't personalities and personal preferences make more difference than the requirements of the job? That indeed is a question worth exploring.

Personal Systems

People do bring something of their history with them when they enter a group. The values and feelings they have about what kind of behavior is proper, desirable, or possible are carried with them and influence how they react to what happens in the group, as well as whether or not they will choose to accept what happens. While we will explore in the chapters on individual behavior more about how individuals influence, and are influenced by, the world around them, at this stage of analysis we take personality characteristics as *givens* in each group. That is, the person arrives at the group with some set of attitudes which, when mixed with those of others, help create whatever emerges.

For our purposes, the individual in the group is also the "carrier" of the wider culture, insofar as he or she brings along norms, values, and perceptions that are introduced into the group through the members. For example, there are widespread beliefs in the United States about the desirability of democratic procedures, especially among peers. If several members of a student study group carry these widely held beliefs, someone is likely to suggest that the group work without a formal leader or make decisions only by informal consensus. Since many members share such beliefs, it is easy for the attitude from the wider culture to be accepted and adopted as a norm in the study group. What individuals have learned from the broader culture and their experiences in it becomes a (background) factor in determining the social system that will emerge in the group.

As suggested earlier, of special significance are the values, feelings, and attitudes of formally designated leaders, as these aspects of personality determine their leadership style. Remember that the style of a leader can have important consequences for what emerges.

The set of attitudes a person brings to the group, the way the person sees him or herself and sees what is proper behavior, we call the personal system. The sum of all the individual members' personal systems, plus that of any supervisor or designated leader, is an important background factor needed to understand what emerges in a group. All these personal systems combine with the job requirements to affect the emergent system (see Figure 3–2).

Nevertheless, job requirements and the group's emergent system often can be so powerful and overwhelming that even people with quite different personal systems will behave similarly when placed in a job. There is a tendency in organizations to overcredit individual personality defects for problems and to underestimate the impact of job requirements and the surrounding situation.

When trying to trace the source of a group's particular emergent system, some questions you might ask about the personal systems of members are:

1. How do individual members see themselves? How do these views combine to help explain the choices the group has made about how to make decisions, produce, relate to one another, and so forth?
2. Why have members accepted or rejected the group's norms? What makes individual members receptive or resistant to the group's accepted way of doing things?
3. Why do some members respond differently to the same set of requirements and leadership style?
4. Do the backgrounds of various members help explain why they initiated key or prominent events?

FIGURE 3–2   Connections of Personal Systems to Required and
                  Emergent Systems

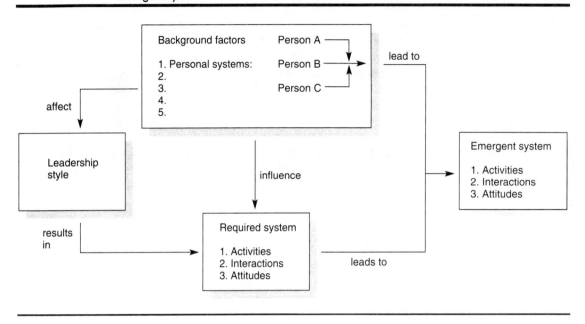

5. What is the fit between the required system and the members' personal
    systems? Are the requirements likely to be accepted as proper by the
    people who happen to be group members?

External Status

In addition to individual personality, another aspect of people that tends to
be overlooked as an influence on what emerges in a group is the person's
position or status in other settings—home, community, social groups, organizations. People's status outside the group influences how they see themselves and how others in the group see them.

To illustrate, if a student task group is formed in a course and one
member is president of student government and widely respected on campus,
other members are likely to turn to that person for leadership. In turn, the
person is likely to begin to take on leadership functions even if he or she is not
the most suited to be leader for the given task. Similarly, in an organizational
task force or committee the member who has the highest position or title in
the organization is likely to become chairperson of the group. While this does
not always happen, position outside a group initially tends to affect position
within it. In general, **the higher a person's status outside a group, the
higher a position or rank he or she will be accorded in a new group, at
least at the beginning (Homans, 1950).** Does this fit with your experience?

In tracing the sources of the emergent system, you might ask:

1. How does a member's external status relate to his or her position within the group at different times? (The next chapter will look in greater detail at member positions in the group.)
2. Is a valuable contributor being ignored because of low external status relative to other members?
3. Are some people getting more influence than their actual contribution merits because of high external status?

Organizational Culture

Culture is a catchall word summarizing the way things are generally done, the prevailing atmosphere or climate, general notions (sometimes explicit but often just understood and taken for granted) about how members of the organization are supposed to act and feel, what is rewarded, and so on. The term *organizational culture* here refers to the culture of the wider organization of which the group being analyzed is a part. One way to think of organizational culture is in terms of the social context or environment in which the work group is located. Another way of thinking about organizational culture is that just as small groups develop norms for behavior, larger organizations tend to develop general norms that apply to every member, regardless of position (Steele & Jenks, 1977).

For example, in one insurance company in New England, many employees have noted that the norms within the company included such things as: "Don't make waves," "Avoid conflicts by joking or shutting up," "Be informal and on a first-name basis with everyone," "Work long hours and don't be a clock watcher." Whether an organization's climate is friendly or hostile, whether organization members in general are trusted and assumed to be motivated or suspected and considered irresponsible, whether disagreements are buried or encouraged, whether individuality is suppressed or fostered, and so forth, all make a difference to what people bring to their work group. The organization's usual ways of handling such issues affect the beliefs and feelings with which members will approach a group. Every organization has general norms of some kind, and every group in the organization is subject to those norms and is likely to reflect them in some way.

However, the reflection may not always be a clear one, since every group tends to develop its own unique character—partly a reflection of its particular membership. Consequently, a group's norms will be an *elaboration* of, a *distortion* of, and a direct *reflection* of the culture (customs) of the larger organization.

In addition, the cultures of the region or country in which the organization is located may shape beliefs within the organization, as suggested previously in the discussion about the sources of norms. For example, a student task group will develop its emergent system in part based on the culture of

MANAGERIAL TOOLS

The Concept of Corporate Culture

In a widely read book,* Terrence Deal and Allan Kennedy describe the ways in which corporations develop complex and powerful cultures (like any society) and how these cultures influence the behavior patterns of employees at all levels. Deal and Kennedy identify five elements of culture:

1. *Business environment*—a company's place in the business world as defined by its products, competitors, customers, technology, etc.
2. *Values*—the basic concepts and beliefs of an organization, as well as its standards for achievement.
3. *Heroes*—the people who personify the culture's values and serve as role models for employees.
4. *Rites and rituals*—the systematic and programmed routines of day-to-day life in the company (including ceremonies).
5. *The cultural network*—the "carrier" of the corporate values and heroic mythology. It includes "storytellers, spies, priests, cabals, and whispers."

* *Corporate Cultures* (Reading, Mass.: Addison-Wesley Publishing, 1982).

the college as a whole, and probably in part on the culture of the region or country from which most of its members come.

In tracing the sources of the emergent system, you might ask:

1. What is the organization's culture as reflected in generally held beliefs about the way things ought to be?
2. Do any of the group's norms reflect the wider organization's culture and how the influence was transmitted?
3. Are the group's norms and procedures consistent with or in opposition to the wider organizational culture? The region or country culture?

Technology and Layout

Technology refers to the means by which work is done. It can include the machines, tools, and materials used; the sequence or flow of operations; the way in which work arrives and is processed (continuously or in batches); the pace and timing of work as controlled by machine speed or customer demands; deadlines and interdependencies with other parts of the organization; noise level; and procedures, processes, and forms used in doing work. It can also include the level and kind of expertise or technical skill needed to do the work.

In a group at a manufacturing job, the technology will usually include some machines that have to be operated by group members. In a group working in service jobs, the technology may not utilize machines but may involve meetings, discussion, and deskwork and require a few tools, such as

MANAGERIAL BULLETIN

Life at IBM

When Thomas J. Watson, Sr., died in 1956, some might have thought the IBM spirit of the stiff white collar was destined to die with him. But indications are that the founder's legacy of decorum to International Business Machines Corporation still burns bright. . . .

Besides its great success with computers, IBM has a reputation in the corporate world for another standout trait: an almost proprietary concern with its employees' behavior, appearance, and attitudes.

What this means to employees is a lot of rules. And these rules, from broad, unwritten ones calling for "tasteful" dress to specific ones setting salesmen's quotas, draw their force at IBM from another legacy of the founder: the value placed on loyalty. Mr. Watson believed that joining IBM was an act calling for absolute fidelity to the company in matters big and small. . . .

What it all amounts to is a kind of IBM culture, a set of attitudes and approaches shared to a greater or lesser degree by IBMers everywhere. This culture, as gleaned from talks with former as well as current employees, is so pervasive that, as one nine-year (former) employee puts it, leaving the company "was like emigrating."

pens, pencils, paper, forms, telephones, and a place to sit. As you can see, the technology of a service group, *when it calls primarily for talking with others,* is almost identical with the required system—that is, in describing the technology it will be necessary to include a description of many of the required activities and interactions. But this overlap should serve as an indicator of how important the technology is for explaining eventual emergent behavior.

In addition, the way in which space is used and equipment is laid out can be considered part of technology. Where machinery is located; the height of walls, desks, cabinets, or machines; the placing of seats, work stations, or offices; and general size of the spaces utilized can all affect behavior.

Both technology and layout are important background factors because they determine many things for people in the organization: amount of individual attention, involvement and judgment needed; degree of interaction, communication, and cooperation necessary to complete work; numbers of people who must be present; and the like. In turn, these constraints affect who is likely to, must, or cannot interact with whom, and when. Thus, both technology and layout set limits on what social interactions and emergent behavior are possible, and cause various interactions to occur. They also affect what behavior can be required.

For example, it is difficult to form a relationship with someone who must constantly tend a machine on the other side of a thunderously noisy nine-foot-high stamping machine; on the other hand, a quiet, open office with desks placed side by side makes conversation with neighbors easy. Three people sitting next to one another and feeding cashed checks into a microfilm

machine, so that the bank will have a record of transactions, can easily talk
with one another while working. The machines are quiet, do not require
close attention, and are located physically near one another. Contrast this
with boiler loaders standing in front of roaring furnaces, shoveling coal in as
needed, working intensively for half-hour bursts, then resting in a cooler area
for 15 minutes. At the least, if there is conversation it will come in short
snatches and have to be shouted to one another over the roar of the furnaces.
It's not hard to see that different norms and ways of working together are
likely to emerge.

Similarly, the timing of when shift members report and leave can be an
important factor in communications and, therefore, important in the emergent system. Organizations that need around-the-clock coverage and high
sharing of information (like hospitals) schedule differently from organizations that only work a second shift when there is great demand, and when the
second shift's work is self-explanatory.

All of these factors, loosely grouped under technology, shape what is and
can be required and are usually fixed or determined in advance or outside of
the group's existence. In turn, this will affect the emergent system.

When trying to trace what emerges to technology, you might ask questions like:

1. What is the effect of the technology on what activities and interactions
   are required?
2. What is the nature of the group's technology in terms of numbers of
   people needed, when they must be in certain places, how much latitude they have in physical movement, variations of work methods
   used, judgment? How does all this affect how members feel?
3. What kinds of interactions and activities are made easy or not possible,
   because of the layout, noise level, flow of work, and so forth?

4. What kind of expertise is required by the technology, and how does that affect who group members are, how they see one another, how they will be supervised, and so on?

Reward System

One of the best ways to predict behavior in any work group is to look at what behavior is actually rewarded. Most people tend to do what will get them rewarded. This can be a bit tricky because organizations (or managers, or parents) don't always actually reward what they say they will; subordinates do not always correctly interpret what is going to be rewarded; and groups of people sometimes refuse to value the organization's rewards, because the benefits of acceptance by peers outweigh those of management.

Nevertheless, it is very useful to identify the formal and informal reward systems in an organization when trying to understand group behavior. Just as technology is often determined apart from the particular members of the group, the organization's formal reward system (pay, recognition, praise, opportunities for advancement, responsibility, and the like) is usually established before the group exists. Informal reward systems, on the other hand, are often not so explicit. The particular leader, supervisor, or manager of a group may have his or her own ideas about what behavior should be rewarded. The leader's assumptions about what motivates people in general, what kind of people are in the group being led, what kinds of behavior demonstrate hard work, competence, promise, and loyalty, all can affect what rewards are available to a group.

The combination of formal and informal organizational rewards is a background factor that affects what is required and what emerges, as well as whether or not employees fully respond to offered rewards and punishments. It is important to remember that sometimes a group's emergent system will be in opposition to the organization's reward system, or at least not fully consistent with it. Workers, for example, can become quite skeptical about incentive schemes, believing fervently that, if they increase output, they will soon be required to produce the new higher amount regularly and that the incentive pay or bonus will somehow be taken away or so altered that they end up worse off than when they started. Some groups will decide that, to "protect" themselves, they should perform only to minimum expectations, rather than respond with full effort to the organization's rewards. And occasionally individuals or groups will produce much more—and try much harder—than the organization is able or willing to reward. Thus, it is necessary to probe carefully when analyzing the impact of the organization's reward system on emergent behavior.

In tracing emergent behavior to the reward system, you might ask how pay is determined and what effect that has on behavior, whether the pay system encourages competition or cooperation among members, what the available rewards are besides pay, whether good performance can be easily measured and rewarded or bad performance measured and punished, and how that will affect emergent behavior.

Summary

All of the above factors—personal system, external status, organizational culture, technology, layout, and reward system—can be thought of as background factors, preconditions to the group's existence that help determine what will be required of members and also what emerges in their behavior (see Figure 3–3). Note that these factors usually affect one another; it is by their particular combination that behavior will be determined.

FIGURE 3–3   The Connection between Background Factors and the Required and Emergent Systems

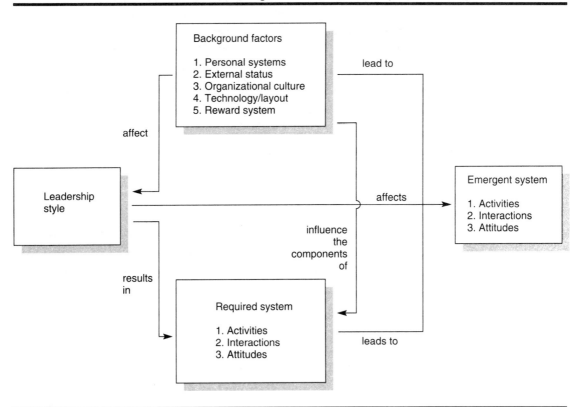

KEY EVENTS AND THE EMERGENT SYSTEM

Key events that occur during the life of a group also influence the emergent system. The background factors and the required system set the direction in which the emergent system is likely to develop, but that process of development is dynamic and interactive. Events may reinforce, modify, or undercut that ongoing direction. As we discussed earlier, norms are often created by a group's reaction to some dramatic event, such as a quarrel among members, a scolding by management, or a breakthrough on a tough issue yielding a sense of accomplishment and a norm to henceforth confront issues early. Other events may make it clearer to members that either a certain norm exists or it is really fairly unimportant and not likely to be strongly enforced. Still other events, such as one member doing a unusually good job, may determine who ends up in particular roles or who has more influence than one might have predicted from knowing the background factors alone. The emergent system is constantly evolving as time and *events* occur.

THE CONSEQUENCES OF EMERGENT SYSTEMS

All of what has been discussed so far in this chapter must be seen from the perspective of final results. The connections among background factors and required and emergent systems are important primarily in terms of the functionality or dysfunctionality of the consequences for the organization and its members. How does the behavior of any person or group help the organization *sustain its competitive position?* In the long run, that is what really matters. Does the behavior create needed products and services, build customer loyalty, keep costs competitive, attract, train, and keep people with the needed skills? We can assess the consequences for sustaining competitive position of whatever emergent system develops along several broad dimensions.

Productivity

Any work organization will be interested in overall *productivity:* how well the group does its required tasks, cost per unit of output, ability to meet deadlines, quality of output, and so on. Productivity is more than a narrow economic measure; it can be used to measure how well the group performs its required tasks to satisfy its customers inside and outside the organization. Though many managers, particularly in small private companies, maintain that productivity and, in turn, profits are all the consequences they care to know about, in fact few people with managerial responsibility actually operate only on this dimension.

MANAGERIAL BULLETIN

An Expert Cereal-Making Team at General Mills

. . . They do just about everything middle managers do, and do it very well: Since General Mills introduced teams . . . productivity has risen up to 40 percent. [Three members] operate machinery to make . . . Oatmeal Crisp. Denny . . . is a manager but he doesn't supervise in the traditional sense. He coaches the team on management techniques and serves as their link to headquarters. [Two members] help maintain the machinery, which [another] operates. Team members like the added responsibility, but also feel more pressure . . . "I work a lot harder than I used to. You have to worry about the numbers."

Satisfaction

For a variety of reasons managers also are interested in the satisfaction of members of their organization. It can affect employee commitment to the job and organization, their willingness to do more than is required, their creativity or flexibility. It can also affect turnover, the degree to which talented people stay with the organization. While there is *no necessary connection* between satisfaction and productivity (a subject we will explore later), the actual satisfaction people derive from their work and membership in a particular group is important enough in its effects on the people involved as well as on their productivity to merit close examination in each situation we study. In fact, in some work groups, achieving satisfaction (close friendship, comfortable relations) may be the only dimension *members* are interested in regardless of management's concerns or the impact on productivity! (If you are in a class task group, you might like to check whether this proves to be true.)

Development

A third dimension to which we will also pay attention is that of individual and group development/growth/learning. Except in those rare situations where the supply of employees is unlimited and they are instantly replaceable, organizations need members who are learning new skills and are flexible enough to solve problems as they arise. The knowledge of employees is an increasingly valuable asset in the information age. A group may be reasonably productive and satisfied but preventing its members from developing, from learning anything that will increase *(a)* their individual skills or abilities, *(b)* the range of resources available to the group, or *(c)* their ability to function effectively as a group in changed circumstances. For example, a student task group may be dividing up the work in a way that produces good reports or papers but teaches members no new skills. An expert report writer may be doing most of the work, using already developed abilities but leaving other members underutilized and unstretched.

Not only would this diminish individual member learning, but it would also mean that the group is giving itself less opportunity to learn to function effectively as a whole. This can easily happen to a classroom group that does well on its first project, then becomes fixated on that successful approach and never tries alternative ways of functioning.

Just as production is not necessarily correlated with satisfaction, group development can be independent of either. Conversely, development or learning can be occurring even when productivity and satisfaction are low. For example, even dissatisfied misfits in a job may be developing valuable skills; disgruntled employees often leave to start their own ventures, fueled by discontent and what they have learned from the job and from others. The dimension of development and learning is important to assess along with the other two dimensions of productivity and satisfaction. Administrators who are concerned about the long-run enhancement of their organization's human resources will also value this dimension. However, some managers, feeling under pressure for immediate results, may push productivity at the expense of satisfaction or development.

It is important to note again what was stated in Chapter 2, that it may not be possible in any given situation to achieve high performance on all three dimensions. An individual or group may make or have to make trade-offs among these dimensions. What to sacrifice for which benefits is determined by the values of the person(s) choosing. Our concern is to make any action's likely consequences along all three dimensions more explicit in advance, so that choices can be more informed. But we will offer no magical or easy solutions guaranteeing wealth, happiness, and growth to everyone.

We can complete Figure 3–3 by adding what we have just described. Whatever the emergent behavior and attitudes of a group, their functionality should be assessed along at least three broad dimensions: productivity, satisfaction, and development (see Figure 3–4).

These consequences will then be judged by those members of an organization who feel responsible for performance; as you might guess, should they judge the consequences negatively they are likely to make some changes in the required system and/or background factors. If productivity, for example, is seen as too low, changes might be made in the type of equipment used, the pay system, the closeness of supervision, the personnel, or whatever those responsible assume to make a difference. Can you see that changes in the required system might in turn affect the emergent system with new consequences for productivity, learning, or satisfaction? Adjustments in one area will lead to responses in other areas until a new equilibrium is reached in the balance among the various components of the group.

All too often, unfortunately, the consequences of change are not those anticipated by the changer; tightening up on supervision might lead to sabo-

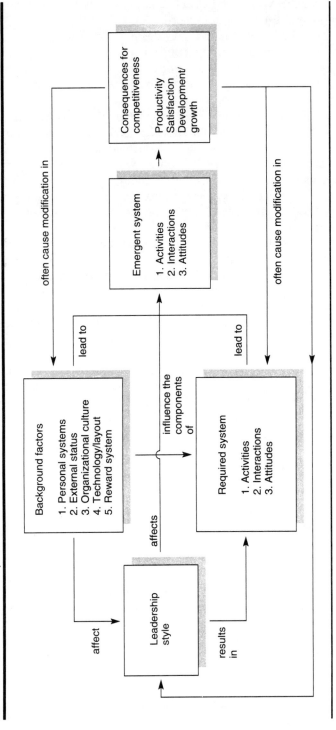

■ FIGURE 3–4   The Complete Basic Social System Conceptual Scheme

tage rather than more productivity, for example. But that is worth closer attention and will be looked at again in the book's final chapter. For now we suggest you begin to get in the habit of sorting what you observe in groups, as best you can, into the five categories we have suggested: background factors, required system, leadership style, emergent system, and competitive consequences. Then try to trace the connections among them: What causes what? What seems to be associated with what? What seems unexplainable and needs more investigation?

THE RELATIONSHIPS BETWEEN REQUIRED AND EMERGENT SYSTEMS

It is important to note again that what emerges in groups will not necessarily be supportive of the required system; in fact, emergent behavior and attitudes may well be in conflict with the required tasks imposed from above or by the situation. Sometimes work groups elaborate on ways to improve their performance, inventing improved methods, informally helping one another, and so forth. They even may develop an emergent system that compensates for deficiencies in the required system, as when norms develop in a paper mill that the nearest person to a paper break, regardless of formal position, immediately will start to rethread the paper in order to minimize waste. At other times, however, groups develop norms of limiting production, holding back effort, or even sabotaging the product. Anyone who has ever had an unfixable rattle in a car knows that auto workers may have said "nuts to you" when feeling negative and done things like toss some bolts into a panel as it was about to be permanently sealed.

A key challenge for you will be to attempt to develop a series of propositions (hypotheses, generalizations) to predict when emergent systems are likely to be in conflict with the required system and when not. Can you trace what the relationships are between leadership style, technology, task requirements, member backgrounds, and so on, and the kind of system that emerges? The more useful the generalizations you can formulate, the more effective you can be in making informed managerial choices. And, of course, you need to be ready to modify your propositions when you come across contradictory evidence.

We are suggesting that it is often possible to predict likely emergent behavior if what is "given" by the situation—the background factors, leadership style, and required system—are known in advance. Many students are surprised to learn that the particular individuals in a situation may make less difference to what happens than the situation and its requirements. The demands of the task, technology, or management style often can pull behavior from a group regardless of who the particular members are. This is often referred to as the "office making the person," elevating its occupant and forcing growth in whomever fills the leadership role. Recent history with respect to the presidency of the United States has proven, however, in a

MANAGERIAL BULLETIN

An Example of a Work Group on a College Campus

If several college students were hired by a college to be a grounds crew for the summer, the kind of work group they become can be explained and even predicted by references to the interplay of who they are (personal systems), other background factors, their boss's style, and the behavior required of them by the college. Let us assume the following:

- The students have similar interests, are all individuals with a strong sense of responsibility, need the job, and view outdoor work as a desirable summer job.
- The crew boss is an older, full-time college employee who takes pride in keeping the college grounds looking nice, has led summer crews before, and relates well with college-age people.
- The college is a prestigious institution with a tradition of maintaining a lovely campus and has a reputation for being a good place to work.
- The grounds crew is paid by the hour worked at a reasonable rate. The results of what it does or does not do are highly visible to the general public, as well as to the crew boss.
- The work required of the crew includes cutting grass, raking up clippings, picking up trash, spreading loam and wood chips, planting and watering flowers, etc. A certain amount of coordination and cooperation among the crew members is necessary for efficiency. Some care is required to not damage the shrubbery or the equipment. Since the campus is in use throughout the summer, the crew is expected to exhibit courtesy toward any pedestrians who may be passing and not spray them with water, etc. Finally, the college expects the crew to work steadily and give a full day of work, but it does not demand an unreasonable work pace.

Given these background factors and requirements, it would not be surprising if the crew developed into a hardworking and satisfied group. It's likely to develop a norm of getting the job done, even if it means working a little bit beyond the normal break time. Talking while working and even some occasional horseplay would probably go on, although not in a manner that slowed efficiency or endangered equipment. Overall, the consequences probably would include satisfactory productivity in the eyes of the college, general job satisfaction for the crew, but only a modest amount of learning of new skills by the crew members. These results are particularly likely if the interplay of background factors and requirements are reinforced by a few key events early in the life of the crew, such as the president of the college happening upon the crew just as it is finishing planting flowers under the flagpole and warmly expressing justified appreciation for a job well done.

Change a few of the factors described above and the emergent behaviors and consequences could be quite different. What if the job were a last-resort job for the students, and the college had a reputation as a low-paying, insensitive employer? What if the college's budget led to the hiring of a crew so small that the workload exceeded what it could reasonably be expected to produce? What if the president saw only the one flower out of alignment and criticized the crew for that while ignoring their overall good work? While one change in the overall array of background factors, requirements, and key events might not make a big difference in what emerged, it would not take much change in the situation from that outlined to yield quite different norms and results.

painfully glaring way that occupying even the highest political office in no way *guarantees* particularly elevated behavior. The pulls are there, however, just as in any organizational situation, and often have induced more noble and strong behavior from presidents than they had exhibited earlier in their careers.

As you move through the course, try to notice if you are increasingly able to anticipate the kinds of behavior, norms, productivity, satisfaction, and so forth, to which a given set of requirements and background factors lead. We will try to help you improve your predictive abilities by what follows.

As an aid in helping you get started—to analyze cases, your own classroom group, the group you work in—the next chapters contain a series of propositions (tentative hypotheses) based on research, empirical observation, and experience. We have tried to build them up in a logical sequence and have also attempted to show how you can connect various pieces of what is observable. That type of analysis goes beyond just using the concepts as fancy labels for behavior; it is a way of trying to *explain* what happens by referring to other connected happenings. In that way, possible choice points where your decision as a manager can make a difference to outcomes should become visible.

KEY CONCEPTS FROM CHAPTER 3

1. A group can be defined by its:
    a. Size.
    b. Degree of autonomy.
    c. Differentiation from other groups.
    d. Interrelationships of some duration.
    e. Identification of members with a group.
    f. Common goals and symbols.
2. Behavior in group.
    a. Interactions.
    b. Activities.
3. Attitudes in group.
    a. Perceptions.
    b. Feelings.
    c. Norms.
    d. Values.
4. The basic social system conceptual scheme.
    a. Background factors:
        (1) Personal systems.
        (2) External status.
        (3) Organizational culture.
        (4) Technology/layout.
        (5) Reward system.

    b. Required system.
    c. Leadership style.
    d. Key events.
    e. Emergent system.
    f. Consequences for competitiveness: productivity, satisfaction, and development.

PERSONAL APPLICATION EXERCISE

Imagining Your First Full-Time Job

- Draw a set of empty boxes representing the social system conceptual scheme.
- In the Required System box fill in the job requirements for your ideal first job—the tasks, the kinds of interactions, the rules, and so on.
- In the Background Factors box fill in a list of your traits—abilities, preferences, outstanding personality characteristics, and the like. Also, list some of the aspects of the workplace, the rewards, the technology, and so forth that would be important to you.
- In the Emergent System box list the norms and the kinds of behavior and interactions that you would expect to occur, given the contents of the first two boxes.
- Finally, describe the outcomes in terms of *your* productivity, satisfaction, and development.
- Save this product for future reference.

SUGGESTED READINGS

Bradford, L. P., and D. Mial. "When Is a Group?" *Educational Leadership* 21 (1963), pp. 147–51.

Cartwright, D., and A. Zander. *Group Dynamics: Research and Theory.* New York: Harper & Row, 1953.

Hare, A. P. *Handbook of Small Group Research.* New York: Free Press, 1962.

_____. *Handbook of Small Group Research.* 2nd ed. New York: Free Press, 1976.

Homans, G. C. *The Human Group.* New York: Harcourt Brace Jovanovich, 1950.

_____. "Social Behavior as Exchange." *American Journal of Sociology,* May 1958, pp. 597–606.

_____. *Social Behavior: Its Elementary Forms.* New York: Harcourt Brace Jovanovich, 1961.

Jones, G. R. "Task Visibility, Free Riding, and Shirking: Explaining the Effect of Structure and Technology on Employee Behavior." *Academy of Management Review,* October 1984, pp. 684–95.

Lincoln, J. R., and J. Miller. "Work and Friendship Ties in Organizations: A Comparative Analysis of Relational Networks." *Administrative Science Quarterly,* June 1979, pp. 181–99.

Luft, J. "Living Systems: The Group." *Behavioral Science* 16 (1971), pp. 302–98.

Napier, R. W., and M. K. Gershenfeld. *Groups: Theory and Experience.* Boston: Houghton Mifflin, 1973.

Orth, C. D., III. *Social Structure and Learning Climate; The First Year at the Harvard Business School.* Boston: Division of Research, Graduate School of Business, Harvard University, 1963.

Pettigrew, A. M. "On Studying Organizational Cultures." *Administrative Science Quarterly,* December 1979, pp. 570–81.

Shaw, M. E. *Group Dynamics: The Psychology of Small Group Behavior.* New York: McGraw-Hill, 1971.

Smith, P. B. *Groups within Organizations.* New York: Harper & Row, 1973.

Steele, F., and R. S. Jenks. *The Feel of the Work Place.* Reading, Mass.: Addison-Wesley Publishing, 1977.

Thibaut, J. W., and H. Kelley. *The Social Psychology of Groups.* New York: John Wiley & Sons, 1969.

Trice, H. M., and J. M. Beyer. "Studying Organizational Cultures through Rites and Ceremonials." *Academy of Management Review,* October 1984, pp. 653–69.

Wholey, D. R., and J. W. Brittain. "Organizational Ecology: Findings and Implications." *Academy of Management Review,* July 1986, pp. 513–33.

Zander, A. *Groups at Work.* San Francisco: Jossey-Bass, 1977.

Cohesiveness in Groups

"Group cohesion will be increased by acceptance of a superordinate goal subscribed to by most members."

A crucial emergent factor in any work group is the degree to which members turn out to like each other and the group as a whole. A group that is close and unified will behave differently, for better or worse, than one that is distant and fragmented. In this chapter we will look at *what* makes a group stick together. The consequence of sticking together for productivity, satisfaction, and development is ultimately a more important issue, but let us first try to understand what pulls a group together. With a better understanding of the factors that lead to closeness, a manager is more likely to succeed in efforts to increase or decrease this important emergent characteristic of groups.

In an effort to spell out the propositions about closeness, we begin with some elementary "building blocks" of relationships. While the first proposition looks obvious, it is often overlooked and is important to those that come later. Remember from Chapter 3 that technology, work layout, required interactions, and the arrangement of space affect the chances of people talking with one another; we can restate that idea more formally:

The greater the opportunity/requirements for interactions, the greater the likelihood of interaction occurring (Homans, 1950, 1961).

That leads directly to the next proposition, which is fundamental to all human relationships:

The more frequent the interaction among people, the greater the likelihood of their developing positive feelings for one another (Homans, 1950, 1961).

And, in turn:

The greater the positive feelings among people, the more frequently they will interact (Homans, 1950, 1961).

In other words, if you like someone, you will probably choose to spend more time with him or her than with someone you do not like.

People tend to approach other people they see as attractive and to avoid those they see as unattractive. Though most people have general ideas about what kind of people they do not like, these general feelings are often easily overcome when they actually interact with and get to know a particular person or group of people. While knowing someone does not guarantee liking, it is rather difficult to like someone you do not know. In fact, people are often surprised to find how likeable others are once they've had the opportunity to interact with them.

*It is easier for a man to be loyal to his club than to his planet; the bylaws are
shorter and he is personally acquainted with the other members.*

E. B. White
One Man's Meat

I know I don't like it because I've never tried it.
Ad for Guinness Stout

These propositions must be modified or at least qualified under certain
conditions. For example, when there are strong prior negative feelings on the
part of one or more interactor or when there are extreme status differences
between those interacting, interaction may only increase prior feelings of
dislike or distance and may lead to avoidance or superficial contact. When
interaction reveals strong value differences, individuals may decide to avoid
one another for fear of getting into heated arguments. Furthermore, even
positive interactions cannot increase indefinitely; at some point they will level
off and reach a kind of equilibrium where both parties are either interacting
enough to satisfy their needs or are prevented by task requirements from
interacting further.

While there are exceptions, these propositions are surprisingly applicable
to many different situations and have potent implications for managers. Consider different ways in which you might use them to design an organization:
To resolve conflicts? To help make work more interesting? These simple
propositions, when combined with others that follow (and which you develop yourself on the basis of your observations) can help explain the variety
of emergent systems you will encounter.

FACTORS THAT INCREASE COHESION

Required Interactions

The previous propositions suggest that, once there is a work reason for
people to interact, they will begin to do it more often and will develop some
liking for one another beyond the original task reason for their interaction.
Thus: **The more frequent the interactions required by the job, the more
likely that *social* relationships and behavior will develop along with task
relationships and behavior (Homans, 1950, 1961).** This is another way of

describing the relationship between required and emergent interactions discussed in Chapter 3.

When members of a group begin to like one another and like being in the group, then the group will have attraction for the members, and acceptance from the group will be seen as desirable by them. In other words: **The more attractive the group, the more *cohesive* it will be (Festinger, Schacter, & Back, 1950).** As the emerging social relationships form, the group will develop norms—ideas about what behavior is expected of group members. **The more cohesive the group, the more eager individuals will be for membership, and, thus, the more likely they will be to conform to the group's norms.** Another way of saying this is: **The more cohesive the group, the more influence it has on its members. The less certain and clear a group's norms and standards are, the less control it will have over its members (Festinger et al., 1950; Homans, 1961).**

From the point of view of a total group, finding ways of getting members to feel attracted to and willing to be influenced by the group is extremely desirable; a group can best reach its goals when it has everyone's allegiance and willingness to sacrifice personal desires on behalf of the group. From the individual's point of view, however, cohesion may be a mixed blessing in that there are personal costs in return for whatever may be the satisfaction of being an accepted member. The individual may have to forgo preferred ways of relating to others, put out greater effort than is desired, or give more time and concern than is comfortable. In Chapter 7 we will explore more of the dilemma faced by the individual trying to decide how much to give up for the closeness offered by the group; we want to note for now, however, that while membership has a price for the individual, insofar as the participation of all members is necessary or valuable for achieving the *group's* goals, the creation of group cohesiveness is important.

Common Attitudes and Values

We have already shown how cohesion is increased by frequent interaction, but a number of other factors can affect it. For example, if members of a group come to it with similar attitudes and values, cohesion is much more likely to occur rapidly. **The greater the similarity in member attitudes and values brought to the group, the greater the likelihood of cohesion in a group (Homans, 1961).**

We would caution you against assuming that cohesion based on these kinds of similarities is necessarily desirable or even easy to generate today. As discussed in Chapter 1, work force diversity related to gender, race, and national origin is increasing both naturally and deliberately as organizations globalize and as issues of social justice become paramount in the norms and policies.

MANAGERIAL BULLETIN

A Most "Proper" Manager

A manager was offered a job at an investment banking firm in Boston. The firm's executives were all "proper Bostonians," educated at Ivy League schools. The manager was subsequently told he had been hired because the firm wanted greater diversity among the people employed, and during interviews he had revealed how different he was (despite his technical competence):

1. He owned a power boat (and did not sail).
2. His MBA degree was from the University of Massachusetts, not Dartmouth or Harvard.
3. He wanted to leave early one afternoon each week to coach Little League (not play squash).

Superordinate Goal

Along the same lines, when there are differences among group members, if there is some kind of overarching goal to which group members subscribe, cohesion is likely to increase. For example, a product invention group at a large consumer goods firm consisted of members with very different backgrounds: a chemist, a marketing expert, a production engineer, and a nutritionist. Whenever they met they argued about: how to proceed, feasibility of ideas, desirability of particular products to consumers, the capacity of the company to produce certain items—even what technical language to use when discussing ideas. But all members knew that their reputations and ultimately the company's future depended upon their success in coming up with profitable new products. This commitment to the shared overall goal of new product creation pulled them past their frequent disagreements and made them fiercely loyal to their team. They prided themselves on their creativity and their collective practicality. Thus: **Group cohesion will be increased by the existence of a superordinate goal(s) subscribed to by the members (Sherif, 1967).**

A Common Enemy

Similarly, you probably have had experience with another kind of superordinate goal: dislike for a common enemy. If people have the same enemy, they are likely to feel a kinship; this general notion has long been used effectively by politicians in a number of countries to try to create a sense of national cohesion that overrides the variety of self-interests among different groups. In a smaller group as well: **Group cohesion will be increased by the perceived existence of a common enemy (Blake & Mouton, 1961).**

The common enemy may not necessarily be a hated enemy. Even friendly competition among groups usually has the effect of pushing group members to feel closer to one another. If by the time you read this you have already done a class exercise in groups, you may have noticed how the presence of other groups working on the same tasks seemed to cause people in your group to like one another more and, perhaps, even to begin to make joking comments about how much better your group was than the others. In Chapter 13 we will look more closely at relationships across groups, but for now it is important to note that the presence of competing (or even potentially competing) groups often makes members within groups feel closer to one another. In some situations, especially in competitively oriented Western society, this phenomenon is so powerful that, even when a multigroup activity is conducted in which groups are *not* being compared to one another, group members still act as if it were a competitive situation and seem to feel cohesive just by being near other groups visibly working on a similar activity.

Success in Achieving Goals and Group Status

Another factor that can lead to greater feeling of liking among group members is for the group to be successful in achieving its goals. If a group seems to be successful at getting what it wants, that makes the group more attractive to members and seems to carry over in the way that members feel about one another. Thus: **Group cohesion will be increased by success in achieving the group's goals (Sherif & Sherif, 1953).**

A connected factor affecting group cohesion has to do with the relative position of the group in relation to other groups in the same overall organization. As you might expect, the higher the status of a particular group in relation to other groups, the more attractive it will seem to members. This is apparently true for everyone but Groucho Marx, who once said, "I wouldn't want to belong to any club which would have me as a member." But for others of us less witty or perceptive: **Group cohesion is increased in proportion to the status of the group relative to other groups in the system (Cartwright & Zander, 1968).**

Low External Interactions

A related issue from a somewhat opposite point of view has to do with the amount of time that group members are required to spend away from the group. If group members by the nature of their job have to relate to many outsiders (including others in the same organization but not in the group), they are less likely to feel strong allegiance to their own group. This is very often true of certain kinds of professional employees who spend a good portion of their time dealing with the problems of nonspecialists in their organization and who also spend time at professional meetings with people from other organizations in order to keep up to date in their specialty, whether it is engineering, medicine, law, or whatever. Similarly, an organization's purchasing agent will often have to spend more time dealing with outsiders than fellow organization members, leading to reduced loyalty to his or her own department and organization. Thus: **Group cohesion will be increased when there is a low frequency of required external interactions** (Homans, 1950).

Resolution of Differences

Every group will at times have differences of opinions; how they are resolved affects cohesion. If a group has repeated problems with resolving differences among members, because of strong differences of opinion, values, or working style, the members' liking for one another will tend to decrease even when the group manages to be successful. Thus: **The more easily and frequently member differences are settled in a way satisfactory to all members, the greater will be group cohesion** (Deutsch, 1968). Nevertheless, success, even if arrived at by a cantankerous process, can soothe many bad feelings. A winning group usually overlooks its differences; a losing group often finds fault with its members.

Availability of Resources

Finally, the way members feel about each other is frequently affected by the availability of resources to the whole group. When resources, such as money, supplies, prestige, or recognition, are scarce, group members are likely to feel competitive with one another. Conversely, when there is an abundance of whatever resources the group needs, members are likely to see each other more charitably and, therefore, like each other more. **Group cohesion will increase under conditions of abundant resources.** For example, when the staff of an innovative health center saw government grants rolling in, the members felt close to the other "pioneers" on the staff. When government money dried up and even weekly paychecks were in jeopardy, dissension and anger toward one another broke out.

The preceding propositions all relate to group integration. The cohesiveness or attractiveness of a group and the power of its norms to regulate behavior are major aspects of emergent systems and are important factors for diagnosing and predicting group behavior. As explained, cohesiveness is influenced by background factors, such as similarity in member attitudes, and by attributes of the required system, such as the necessity for interaction. By carefully tracing what is brought to the work group and what is required of it, it is possible to make sense of the degree of closeness that emerges. But keep in mind that "nothing is as simple as it seems" (see Chapter 1). Cohesiveness is the result of many factors; a careful analysis requires that you think in terms of multiple causality.

While all of the above propositions have been phrased in terms of what positively increases cohesion, they are also intended to be reversible in terms of what decreases cohesion. As a manager you may wish at any given time to increase or decrease cohesion among a particular group and may be able to affect differing aspects of the conditions cited by the propositions. Deciding in which direction cohesion should be pushed and then how to do it requires a careful assessment of existing conditions.

> The manager of a large department store was faced with customer complaints about waiting time for service. Upon investigation, he found that many of the full-time salespeople congregated near the fitting rooms for conversation. They enjoyed one another's company so much that they found it difficult to interrupt the gossip and joking to go wait on customers. The manager had to find a way to decrease the group's cohesion without creating major resentment that would interfere with selling enthusiasm. How might such a problem be approached? Would it be wise to crack down and prohibit all social talk? What would be the effect of physically rearranging the work area?

CONSEQUENCES OF COHESION FOR PRODUCTIVITY, SATISFACTION, AND DEVELOPMENT

Productivity

Since a cohesive group is one in which members adhere to the norms, it should not be surprising that in such a group norms are likely to develop not only in regard to general behavior but also about member productivity. The group will usually arrive at a strong sense of how much each member should produce and how much variation from that level will be tolerated, and then encourage the members to produce at or near that level. Whether production is measured in widgets/hour as in a manufacturing group or in "sufficient hours spent preparing an analysis" as in a student task group: **The more cohesive the group, the more *similar* will be the output of individual members (Homans, 1950).**

Another way of looking at the effect of cohesiveness on productivity is in terms of how much effort members will make to see that the productivity norms, high or low, are followed. As you might expect: **The more cohesive the group, the more it will try to enforce compliance with its norms about productivity.** Cohesive groups will work hard to get members to increase output if it is lower than the group thinks appropriate and also will supply pressure to hold down the output of members who embarrass the group by producing "too much." Cohesiveness does not cause *high* productivity, merely similar levels of it among group members.

You may remember from Chapter 3 that a group's idea of what is the proper amount to produce may be only vaguely related to higher manage-

MANAGERIAL BULLETIN

"Revolution at Corning Ceramics Plant"

Everyone is assigned to a team of about six workers, who together set goals and schedules, and even assign each other jobs. And although that method is proving efficient, it's also the source of numerous conflicts.

"People problems are the issue," says a . . . kiln operator. For instance, some teams have felt pulled down by one lazy member. "If there's a conflict, . . .

we're expected to resolve it" instead of turning to a supervisor. "If someone isn't feeling well or pulling their weight, we can't let it go on or it'll just be a bigger problem," she adds, noting how it's difficult to confront a co-worker.

SOURCE: Alecia Swasy and Carol Hymowitz, "The Workplace Revolution," *THE WALL STREET JOURNAL*, February 9, 1990.

ment's or the rest of the organization's ideas of the proper amount. In general, if the group feels in sympathy with or supported by "higher management" (or those who define good performance), it will have a tendency to enforce a fairly high level of productivity on its members and vice versa. Since a cohesive group will bring member productivity into line: **The greater the cohesion of the group, the higher productivity will be if the group supports the organization's goals, and the lower productivity will be if the group resists the organization's goals (Zaleznik, Christensen, & Roethlisberger, 1958).**

A cohesive group that wants to produce more will pull even its weaker members along quite effectively. But the group that sticks together can thus be irritatingly resistant to efforts to increase its productivity when, for whatever reason, it does not wish to raise output. What does this suggest to you, as a future manager, about your relationships to task groups reporting to you and about the conditions under which their cohesiveness might be desirable?

Another way in which cohesiveness may not lead to higher productivity arises when members come to like each other so much that they prefer to socialize, rather than work, as was the case with the department store salespeople mentioned earlier. Conversely, a group that is not cohesive could still be productive if its members were highly individualistic and driven to work hard by their needs and values—and the work itself did not require great cooperation and interdependence. In some respects, it's like the difference between a basketball team and a baseball team. The former depends upon a constant spirit of teamwork while the latter emphasizes individual effort on behalf of the team.

Group cohesiveness can also either enhance or stifle productivity, depending upon the members' willingness to be open with one another. On the one hand, in a cohesive group members feel close enough to one another to be able to discuss issues and problems frankly. Closeness should

MANAGERIAL BULLETIN

NBA Update

GENEROUS: The Atlanta Hawks have a team rule that if a player is given a gift for appearing on a postgame show, he has to turn it over to a teammate. "It's part of our new closeness," guard **Doc Rivers** said. "If a guy's named player of the game and gets something, he's got to give it up to the guys on the bench who cheer for him." It's as good a reason as any to explain a team that has won 14 consecutive games at home after losing six in a row at the Omni earlier in the season.

SOURCE: *USA Today,* February 1, 1991.

MANAGERIAL TOOLS

Quality Circles and Productivity

The Quality Circles approach—voluntary groups of about 10 workers who meet with a supervisor to make suggestions about how to solve shop floor quality problems—provides an excellent example of how groups of workers can become highly productive as a result of having common goals, achieving success, and having frequent required interactions. While this technology was developed for the purpose of improving product quality on the production floor, extra benefits—increased worker commitment, higher morale, lower turnover, and the like—are predictable from the propositions about cohesion and realized when the results are supported by the organization. All of these outcomes benefit productivity. Indeed, companies like Toyota, where almost all employees participate in QC programs, report greater numbers of useful suggestions per worker than companies without formal programs. Many companies have found that equivalent "problem-solving teams" among white-collar workers (technicians, administrators, sales support, and so on) can yield similar benefits if managed well.

make explorations of issues easier, since all members can presumably be trusted with information and with members' feelings.

On the other hand, when people feel attracted to a group, they may see the risk of offending someone they like as greater than if the others didn't matter. Holding back opinions, feelings, or ideas, because the approval of others is so important that it can't be tested, can lead to unproductive decisions.

When cohesiveness is a result of great similarity in member attitudes, values, and external status, it can lead to decreased productivity over time (Gillespie & Birnbaum, 1980). The similarities apparently act as a filter against disconfirming information and events, so that the ease of working together is overwhelmed by the problems of collective resistance to disconfirming inputs. While managers often fear that heterogeneity in a task group

MANAGERIAL TOOLS

Groupthink

Where groups become very cohesive, there is danger that they become victims of their own closeness.

Symptoms

1. Illusions of the group as invulnerable.
2. Rationalizing away data that disconfirm assumptions and beliefs.
3. Unquestioned belief in group's inherent morality.
4. Stereotyping competitors as weak, evil, stupid, and so on.
5. Direct pressure on deviants to conform.
6. Self-censorship by members.
7. Illusion of unanimity (silence equals consent).
8. Self-appointed "mind guards"—protecting group from disconfirming data.

Prevention Steps

A_1. Leader encourages open expression of doubt.
A_2. Leader accepts criticism of his or her opinions.
B. Higher-status members offer opinions last.
C. Get recommendations from a duplicate group.
D. Periodically divide into subgroups.
E. Members get reaction of trusted outsiders.
F. Invite trusted outsiders to join discussion periodically.
G. Assign someone the role of devil's advocate.
H. Develop scenarios of rivals' possible actions.

SOURCE: Adapted from Irving Janis, *Victims of Groupthink* (Boston: Houghton Mifflin, 1972).

will lead to conflict among members and to low group productivity, it is important for them to realize that too much homogeneity can eventually result in mediocre group performance. Some diversity in points of view can increase creativity in problem-solving.

Very cohesive groups run the risk of falling victim to "groupthink" (Janis, 1972). Groupthink is a mode of thought and behavior that occurs "when the members' strivings for unanimity override their motivation to realistically appraise alternative courses of action." As a result, the group easily overestimates its own capabilities, cuts itself off from new information, and becomes smug about its own views and judgments. Even very high-level groups of managers can fall prey to this avoidance of discomfort from disagreement; Janis studied President Kennedy and his advisers making the disastrous decisions to invade Cuba at the Bay of Pigs, finding that the few with dissenting opinions were ridiculed and treated as weaklings, until everyone went along. Fortunately, Kennedy learned from the experience and handled the Cuban Missile Crisis more effectively. In fact, he used some of the "prevention steps" outlined in the Managerial Tools above. Overcohesiveness can be stifling to a group's effectiveness if members hesitate to risk offending someone—or the group has fallen into groupthink.

A variation on groupthink, in which fears of displeasing others leads to a poor decision, have been dubbed "The Abilene Paradox," from one family's decision to spend the day in Abilene when no individual member actually wanted to go (Harvey, 1988). Yet each, thinking he or she was the only one who did not want to go, never spoke up. In many organizations, cohesive groups end up making equally poor decisions, because no one tests the apparent agreement for fear of being odd person out or of disrupting "harmony." Cohesion does not always lead to effectiveness.

Satisfaction

A cohesive group will by definition have a high overall level of satisfaction; presumably, a group attractive to its members is satisfying. Individual members, however, may very much feel that the norms of the group call for behavior that is not easily given. Belonging to a close cohesive group can be a warm supportive experience; but, for some, the embrace of the group may feel a bit suffocating. Should that happen to many members of the group, its cohesiveness may well begin to suffer as members struggle to assert their own individuality. But the positive feelings from being a member of a cohesive group can be sufficient for some people to offset even low pay, unpleasant physical conditions, harsh bosses, and so forth. That is why commitment of members to the group, leading to lower turnover, follows from cohesion. And this can occur even without commitment to the organization as a whole.

Development and Learning

A cohesive group can provide excellent opportunities for members to help and learn from one another. In fact, that can be part of what attracts members. The sharing of knowledge, skills, and experiences can be very rewarding and growth-promoting. Some groups, however, achieve cohesion only at the expense of individual growth. The group becomes so anxious to maintain a

MANAGERIAL BULLETIN

"Food, Cohesion, and Productivity"

As their number grew from 6 to 25, [mortgage traders] became louder, ruder, fatter, and less concerned with their relations with the rest of the firm. Their culture was based on food . . .

"We made money no matter what we looked like," says a former trader. . . .

Each Friday was "Food Frenzy" day . . . during which all trading ceased, and eating commenced. . . .

A customer would call in and ask us to bid or offer bonds, and you'd have to say, "I'm sorry, but we're in the middle of the feeding frenzy. I'll have to call you back."

[Yet] no one made as much money as mortgage bond traders.

SOURCE: Michael Lewis, *Liar's Poker* (New York: W. W. Norton, 1989).

certain kind of harmony that it suppresses individual knowledge and differences for fear of making some members feel unequal or inadequate.

Cohesion achieved in this way may not hinder the group from producing adequately and may be reasonably satisfying to members who want the security of minimal competition and differences among peers, but it can serve to "freeze" growth at a particular point. A student task group can, for example, see to it that everyone does his or her share of assignments, warmly socialize in and out of class, and support all members with liking and warmth, yet still prevent maximum individual learning. A quieter member who would learn valuable debating skills from being prodded to defend his/her ideas may be allowed to make contributions behind the scenes and thus never be forced to practice new skills. Or an argumentative member with a unique point of view might be cajoled into "not pushing so hard, for the good of the group," and thus never really be faced with the consequences of such a style nor have a chance to think through and persuade others about his or her views.

On the other hand, if a group lacks cohesiveness, individual and group learning may be inhibited. It often takes at least a minimally supportive environment for members to take any risks in expressing ideas, defending unpopular views, and so forth. Also, if a group lacks cohesiveness it will probably have difficulty looking at its own process or confronting conflicts and thereby be less able to "learn" as a group or develop its capacity to function effectively. Therefore the degree of cohesiveness in a group can have either positive or negative consequences for development; it takes careful analysis of the particular situation to assess the effects.

The next chapter explores further the connections between group cohesion and effectiveness by looking at the other side of cohesiveness, those forces that separate and differentiate group members. Even the most cohesive groups have differences among members that must be dealt with and that impact the group's productivity, satisfaction, and development.

KEY CONCEPTS FROM CHAPTER 4

1. Propositions on group cohesiveness:
   a. The more interactions, the more positive feelings.
   b. The more positive feelings, the more interactions.
   c. The more attractive the group, the more cohesiveness.
   d. The more cohesive the group, the more eagerness for membership.
   e. The more eagerness for membership, the more conformity to group's norms. Therefore:
   f. The more cohesive the group, the more influence it has on its members.
   g. The less clear the group's norms, the less control it has over its members.

2. Group cohesiveness is increased by:
   a. Similarity in attitudes, values, and goals.
   b. Existence of a common enemy.
   c. Acceptance of superordinate goals.
   d. Success in achieving goals.
   e. High status relative to other groups.
   f. Low number of required external interactions.
   g. Differences settled in satisfactory way to all members.
   h. Conditions of abundant resources.

3. High cohesiveness correlates with productivity, satisfaction, and development:
   a. Members' productivity similar in a cohesive group.
   b. Group productivity high if the group values productiveness.
   c. Dangers of groupthink.
   d. Member satisfaction high, by definition.
   e. Member development may be high or low.

PERSONAL APPLICATION EXERCISE

Think of a group to which you really enjoyed belonging, where members felt close to each other and wanted to be a part of the group. Which, if any, of the following factors contributed to the cohesion?

Similarity in attitudes, values, or goals? ☐

Existence of a common enemy? ☐

Acceptance of superordinate goals? ☐

Success in achieving goals? ☐

High status relative to other groups? ☐

Low number of required external interactions? ☐

Differences satisfactorily settled?   ☐

Conditions of abundant resources?   ☐

Did the cohesion feel stifling in any way? Did you see any examples of groupthink? Can you think of an example of when it caused a poor decision to be made? What were the outcomes of the cohesion for:

Productivity?	☐ High	☐ Medium	☐ Low
Satisfaction?	☐ High	☐ Medium	☐ Low
Development?	☐ High	☐ Medium	☐ Low

If any of the outcomes were less than high, what could the leader of the group have done to improve them?

SUGGESTED READINGS

B.E. Ashforth and F. Mael. "Social Identity Theory and the Organization." *Academy of Management Review* 14, no. 1 (1989), pp. 20–39.

Blake, R., and J. Mouton. "Reactions to Intergroup Competition under Win-Lose Competition." *Management Science*, July 1961, pp. 420–25.

Cartwright, D., and Z. Zander. *Group Dynamics: Research and Theory.* New York: Harper & Row, 1968.

Deutsch, M. "The Effects of Cooperation and Competition upon Group Process." In *Group Dynamics: Research and Theory*, ed. D. Cartwright and A. Zander. New York: Harper & Row, 1968.

Feldman, D. C. "The Development and Enforcement of Group Norms." *Academy of Management Review*, January 1984, pp. 47–53.

Festinger, L.; S. Schacter; and K. Back. *Social Pressures in Informal Groups: A Study of a Housing Project.* New York: Harper & Row, 1950.

Gillespie, D. F., and P. H. Birnbaum. "Status Concordance, Coordination, and Success in Interdisciplinary Research Teams." *Human Relations* 33, no. 1 (1980), pp. 41–56.

Harvey, J. B. "The Abilene Paradox: The Management of Agreement." *Organizational Dynamics* 17, no. 1 (1988), pp. 16–43.

Harvey, J. B., and C. R. Boettger. "Improving Communication within a Managerial Work Group." *Journal of Applied Behavioral Science*, March–April 1971, pp. 154–79.

Homans, G. C. *The Human Group.* New York: Harcourt Brace Jovanovich, 1950.

_____. *Social Behavior: Its Elementary Forms.* New York: Harcourt Brace Jovanovich, 1961.

Homestead, M. S. *The Small Group.* New York: Random House, 1969.

Janis, I. *Victims of Groupthink.* Boston: Houghton Mifflin, 1972.

Mudrack, P. E. "Group Cohesiveness and Productivity: A Closer Look." *Human Relations* 42, no. 9 (September 1989), pp. 771–85.

Napier, R. W., and M. K. Gershenfeld. *Groups: Theory and Experience.* Boston: Houghton Mifflin, 1973.

Schachter, S. *The Psychology of Affiliation*. Stanford, Calif.: Stanford University Press, 1959.

Seashore, S. E. *Group Cohesiveness in the Industrial Work Group*. Ann Arbor, Mich.: Survey Research Center, Institute for Social Research, 1964.

Sherif, M. *Group Conflict and Cooperation: Their Social Psychology*. Boston: Routledge & Kegan Paul, 1967.

Sherif, M., and C. Sherif. *Groups in Harmony and Tension*. New York: Harper & Row, 1953.

Skinner, B. F. *Walden II*. New York: Macmillan, 1948.

Smith, P. B. *Groups within Organizations*. New York: Harper & Row, 1973.

Steele, F. I. "Physical Settings and Social Interaction." In *Physical Settings and Organization Development*. Reading, Mass.: Addison-Wesley Publishing, 1973.

Whyte, G. "Groupthink Reconsidered." *Academy of Management Review* 14, no. 1 (January 1989), pp. 40–56.

Zaleznik, A.; C. R. Christensen; and F. J. Roethlisberger. *The Motivation, Productivity, and Satisfaction of Workers*. Boston: Harvard Business School, 1958.

Differentiation in Groups

Building Internal Structure as a Basis for Productivity

"The more an individual group member fails to conform to the group's norm, the more frequently negative sentiments will be expressed toward that person."

After looking at cohesion—what it is that makes a group stick together and be attractive to members—it is important to examine the way groups differentiate their members in terms of value to the group. Few groups have total equality among all members; some individuals obtain more respect and influence, some more liking, others less of one or the other. Over time a group will develop relative positions or "ranks" for its members—that is, members acquire different status from one another. In this chapter we will look at three key factors that determine the relative positions of group members: (1) status brought to the group from outside, (2) individual adherence to group norms, and (3) group-related roles assumed by members. These factors contribute to individual member influences, which ultimately influence group productivity, satisfaction, and development.

The notion of status differences as something to observe and discuss often makes North Americans uncomfortable, because of their widespread professed beliefs about everyone being created equal and that differences among people working together should be minimized or ignored. The United States is one of a handful of countries where such beliefs are widely espoused. In most parts of the world the ideas that some people are more worthy and esteemed than others, and that everyone has a rank or status that can be precisely identified relative to all others, are accepted as obviously true.

While Americans acknowledge broad differences in status—doctor (professional) higher than garbage collector (blue-collar), professor higher than student (sometimes?)—the idea is resisted in groups of peers or those who see themselves as "about the same." The sameness usually refers to broad categories, such as students, middle managers, or board members, and there is often resistance to the possibility that, in fact, even in a group of peers differences in status emerge, are identifiable, and have important consequences for the group and individuals in it.

For example, one of the most common norms students bring to task groups is "we are all equal," which means that no one student member is supposed to be able to dominate others, tell them what to do, or give orders. Yet it is clear that it would be extremely unlikely to have all members possessing equal skills in generating ideas, organizing, analyzing, writing, or interacting socially. As a result, once the group takes on some tasks, various members emerge with different status in the group.

No two men can be half an hour together but one shall acquire an evident superiority over the other.

Samuel Johnson
Boswell's *Life of Samuel Johnson*

MANAGERIAL BULLETIN

Leveling Those Perks

[Janet Axelrod, vice president of Lotus Development Corporation, discussing her company's aversion to executive perks on the PBS program "Adam Smith's Money World"]:

None of us had any kind of interest in being people who lived in ivory towers and traveled around in limousines. It's not just that it wasn't in our lifestyle, it wasn't what we wanted to be. And we didn't see any reason for it. It seemed like an awful money sink, and artificial separations among people.

Status-related differences between people are an unnecessary division, and none of us wanted to be divided in that way. A lot of big, heavy industry in this country was born out of this kind of robber-baron mentality, and we're not in that anymore; it's just not the way we do business.

SOURCE: "Notable & Quotable." *THE WALL STREET JOURNAL*, November 5, 1985.

Just which attributes of members will result in high ranking depends upon the norms and standards of the particular group; in some groups, status goes to those who help most with the tasks, while in others status goes to those who make members feel most comfortable and at ease. But inevitably groups do develop some informal ranking of members even if they do not discuss it directly. Though each group must be separately studied to determine the basis for status in that group, in general: **Members who contribute most to task accomplishment are accorded the most *respect* in the group, while members who contribute most to social accomplishment (development of relationships) are accorded the most *liking* in the group (Bales, 1958).** One's position on these two dimensions (respect and liking) determines a person's overall status in the group, with the weights attached to each determined by the group's emergent norms and values.

BASES OF DIFFERENTIATION

Initial Ranking: External Status and Status Congruence

While over the long run each member's status in a group will be based on the member's contribution to whatever the group values, early status in a group is usually related to the status of each group member outside the group. In a company task force set up to investigate ways of awarding bonuses to outstanding performers in the group, for example, a senior vice president will usually be given more respect at first than a personnel department assistant, despite the possibility that the personnel assistant may indeed know more about alternative bonus systems and their consequences. **The higher the background factor of external status, the higher the initial internal status of a group member (Homans, 1950).**

MANAGERIAL BULLETIN

A Vice President by Any Other Name Still Might Leave Some People Confused

Bank titles bewilder most outsiders, who assume that anybody at the bank not wielding a mop is an assistant vice president.

Now the titles are changing. But outsiders may wind up no less confused. How does "group executive," for example, improve on "executive vice president"? And how do you reply when somebody introduces himself as "vice president, branch manager, individual banking, Memphis"? . . .

The original purpose of bank titles was to give officers the authority to make loans and approve other transactions. Over the years, however, the titles proliferated since they were increasingly used to confer status. Banks relied on the vice presidential title particularly, "to make customers feel they were dealing with an important person," says George Parker, who lectures on management at Stanford Business School. "And pretty soon, a vice president wasn't such a big deal."

But it is not always obvious what attributes group members will use to rank status in the world outside the group. What some people consider high-status attributes might not be seen that way at all by others, particularly if an attribute is not judged to be relevant to the group's purposes. For example, in the bonus system task force just mentioned, being a senior vice president would probably yield a higher rank than being a personnel assistant. But within a group of workers trying to decide how to request a change in working hours, the personnel assistant's knowledge of rules and procedures, plus his or her membership on the bonus task force, is likely to result in high status there. Similarly, a high-status judge might be given little respect in a group that has crashed in the desert if his or her survival skills are comparatively low. A mechanic might be given higher status in this situation even though he or she would be seen as lower status in other circumstances.

Furthermore, many other factors may go into setting a person's status. We have been talking about profession and, by implication, income as two important factors, but there are others that often make a difference: age, sex, education (where and how long), ethnicity, marital status, and even the region of birth. In student task groups, class standing, major subject, and work experience are often important determinants, too, since careers are not yet established. Some of these factors, such as education and profession, are achievable by work and ability, while others, such as age, sex, and ethnicity, the person is born with or gets by just existing. Though the rankings may in no way be fair or just, especially to those who are low status, some kind of ranking exists everywhere. In many cultures higher status goes to those who are older, male, married, highly educated, have high incomes, and are mem-

MANAGERIAL BULLETIN

"A Difference in Societies That Can Give United States an Edge in Talks"

American officials and students of trade negotiations say that foreign officials, who are not used to dealing with career women in their own countries, often feel awkward when face to face at a negotiating table with American lawyers, economists, and other professionals who happen to be women. It's a situation that tends to favor the United States. . . . "Are they going to react to her as a man to a woman, as a man to a foreign woman, as a man to an American woman, as a man to a representative of the U.S. government?"

SOURCE: Clyde Farnsworth, *New York Times*, July 4, 1988.

bers of the dominant ethnic group. In any particular group, however, some of these factors might be reversed, as in these examples you may recognize: "never trust anyone over 30," "yuppies," "ivory-tower pointy-headed intellectuals," "nerds," "fat cats," "male chauvinist pigs," and "white trash."

In general: **The higher a person is on all of these external dimensions (or other valued ones), the higher his or her emergent status within a group, and vice versa.** To any particular group, however, one factor may be seen as overriding all others; in certain organizations, for example, if you aren't a WASP (or whatever the dominant ethnic background), being high status on all the other factors will not make up for lack of status on that dimension.

Not only can we look at how high a person is on several status factors in order to estimate likely internal status, but we can also make some predictions about emergent behavior based on how consistent a person's status ranking is *across* factors. For example, some people are high or low in status on all factors; we call that *status congruency*.

If the senior vice president in our example were a 60-year-old male, married, had an MBA, and was descended from someone who came over on the Mayflower, he would be congruently high status on all factors. Conversely, in New Hampshire at least, if the personnel assistant were female, 20 years old, French-Canadian, unmarried, new to the company, and had not gone beyond high school, she would be congruently low status on all factors. But suppose the senior vice president was a 28-year-old black woman who was completing a part-time MBA program. Or suppose the personnel assistant was a 40-year-old former philosophy professor who had changed careers and was showing great promise and potential. Can you see in these examples how the status factors of each would then be inconsistent with one another, "out of line," or *incongruent*? (See Figure 5–1). Can you imagine how difficult it might then be for the bonus system task force members to "place" or rank each one? What might be their reaction?

▓ FIGURE 5–1   Illustration of How Different People Can Be Ranked along Several Status Dimensions

PERSON	AGE	SEX	EDUCATION	ETHNICITY	PROFESSION	INCOME	
A	High	High	High	High	High	High	= High status, congruent
B	Low	Low	Low	Low	Low	Low	= Low status, congruent
C	Low	Low	High	High	High	High	= High status, incongruent
D	…	…	…	…	…	…	= and so forth

Conformity to Norms as a Determinant of Emergent Status

We have previously looked at the way norms emerge and how cohesiveness increases conformity to group norms. But no matter how attractive a group is and no matter how much members wish to belong, it is almost never possible for every member to go along with all of a group's norms. Sometimes norms call for behavior beyond the capacity of individuals in the group, as, for example, "Everyone should make creative contributions to the group's efforts." Some people have more of the skills needed by a group than do others, and when the norms call for those particular skills they are at a natural advantage. If a student task group desires high grades and must produce excellent written analyses to get them, the individual member who is good at performing such analysis and at writing clear conclusions will naturally be better able to conform to norms about contributing to the group's goals. Another member might be an excellent amateur carpenter, but not be valued as highly in the group, since such manual skills are not necessary for achieving high performance.

Other norms ask individuals to do what goes too strongly "against the grain," irritating the person's fundamental values and personality. To illustrate, some groups ask that all members act humbly even to the point of denying any needs for individual recognition. To a person raised with strong emphasis on individual competition and a belief in sinking or swimming on one's own best efforts, being modest about successes may be either impossible or seem too "wrong" to be tolerated, let alone tried. For such a person, conformity to a norm of "humility" is a virtual impossibility, even if other aspects of the group make membership attractive. In a more gentle, unjudging world, the inability or unwillingness to conform to what are, after all, only one group's particular idiosyncratic norms would go unpunished. The desirability, for example, of false humility has not been proclaimed from on high as the one true way; in fact, just around the corner (perhaps in our competitive individual's family) sits a group with equal conviction about the rightness of savoring glory when it is earned!

MANAGERIAL BULLETIN

Unusual Norms at Salomon Brothers; Groveling for Jobs

Jobs were doled out at the end of the [training] program. . . . Contrary to what we expected . . . we were not assured of employment. . . .

Each trainee had to decide for himself. . . . Those who chose to put on a full court grovel [to the managing directors who selected] from the opening buzzer found seats in the front of the classroom, where they sat, lips puckered, through the entire five-month program. Those who treasured their pride—or perhaps thought it best to remain aloof—feigned cool indifference by sitting in the back row and hurling paper wads at managing directors.

SOURCE: Michael Lewis, *Liar's Poker* (New York: W. W. Norton, 1989).

It is important to state explicitly that we are not talking about conformists and nonconformists as absolute personality types; all people have some group or groups to whose norms and values they conform, even when they are physically present elsewhere. The question is only whether a person will (or can) conform to a *particular* group's norms while a member. Nonconformity in that context is usually a sign of subscription and conformity to some other group's standards. If when in Rome a person does not "do as the Romans do," it is usually because he or she thinks that "doing as Americans/English/Germans (select your own category) do" is better, nicer, or more comfortable than going along with the present company.

Yet despite the fact that particular norms about productivity and other kinds of behavior can vary sharply from group to group, each group's ideas about proper behavior often become enshrined or "sacred," as if there were no other possible way to behave and still be a good person. Once a group has clear ideas about proper levels of productivity, for example, it will expend considerable energy trying to bring members who deviate from them (hereafter referred to as *deviants*) into line. Thus: **The more an individual group member fails to conform to the group's norms, the more frequently negative sentiments will be expressed toward him or her (Homans, 1961).**

The particular form of expression for negative sentiments can vary, depending on the general style of group members and the particular norm being enforced. Some groups may use sarcasm, irony, and indirect hints to let a member know he or she is not conforming properly, while other groups may use nods, winks, facial mugging, or "gentle love-taps" to admonish deviating members. In the classic Hawthorne experiments (Roethlisberger & Dickson, 1939) where the relationship between social relations and productivity was first explored, one work group was observed in which deviants who produced "too much" were hit on the upper arm with the fist, a process called "binging." This was a crude but effective way to see to it that no one person produced so much that management would start to ask why all workers could not do the same each day.

Whatever the particular medium of expression, every group will have ways of "punishing" its deviant members, and most will have at least some members who cannot or will not conform to its norms, leading to differences in rank. When the group expresses dislike for a member who isn't conforming, it often produces defensiveness or aggression in that member, which in turn can lead to greater punishment by the group and to new attempts to bring the member into line. After awhile, however, the group will begin to ignore the deviant as if to punish him or her by withholding what the group sees as desirable relationships. The person will then become an *isolate,* attached to the group by work assignment but essentially cut out of nonwork interactions. **The less a member conforms to a group's norms, the greater will be the interaction directed at him or her for some time. Should the interaction fail to bring the member into conformity with the norms, interaction will sharply decrease (Homans, 1961).**

While the idea of being a deviant in a group seems to have a negative connotation, there often are times when the behavior of a group violates the personal values of a member and may force that member to make a choice between conformity to group pressure for the sake of harmony and standing up for one's convictions. Making the former choice is usually easier and is likely to be supported by the other group members. The price that is paid is paid primarily by the one member. The choice to deviate by being true to personal values is the tougher decision but at least helps the individual to retain a sense of integrity. Furthermore, it is this sense of doing what is right that motivates *whistle-blowers,* those brave people who are willing to speak up and tell the truth even when they are pressured to just go along. It may, in the long run, even help the group by establishing a norm that supports individual integrity. Therefore, when you use the term *deviant,* be careful not to pre-judge it negatively; it is a relative matter that can only be judged in context—that is, by what the person is deviating from.

Conversely, the more closely a person conforms to the group's norms and carries out the group's ideas of proper behavior, the better the person will be liked by other group members and become a *regular* member of the group. **The greater a member's conformity to the group's important norms, the greater the group's liking for the member (Homans, 1961).**

The people who are best able to conform to the group's norms—because of skills, attributes, resources possessed by them, earned or otherwise—are likely to emerge as informal leaders in the group and be the most respected by other members. Just *what* the group does value varies from group to group and may not be fairly distributed among members. In one classic study, the most important attribute a work group member could have was being Irish, an attribute not easily acquired by non-Irish aspirants but possessed by enough group members to make it crucial.[1] **The member(s) who conform most closely to a group's norms have the highest probability of emerging as informal leader(s) of the group (Homans, 1961).**

Interestingly, the informal leaders of a group can end up also having the most license to break the group's norms occasionally without punishment. It is as if a person builds up credits in the "liking and conformity-to-norms account" and, thus, can be the most free to "spend" the accumulated credit when he or she desires to. Thus, we have to add the counterproposition: **Informal group leaders may occasionally violate norms without punishment, provided that they have earned their leadership by general conformity to the group's norms (Homans, 1961).**

Many task groups, however, also have some members who refuse to follow the group's norms. Students, for example, who violate student norms by preparing for every class, reading all the suggested readings as well as the required readings in the course, challenging the teacher, and filling up class time with questions and arguments will often not be swayed by any punishments their classmates can generate. What normally happens after the other members give up all efforts to bring the deviant around is that he or she ends up being isolated from the group. In Chapters 7 and 8 we will examine individual motives in a way that might help explain why a person would resist peer pressure. However, you can see that those who choose, for whatever reasons, to resist the pressure of group norms often start out as deviants and end up as isolates. (See Figure 5–2 for a summary of the link between conformity and status.)

FIGURE 5–2   Individual Conformity to Norms and Status in Group

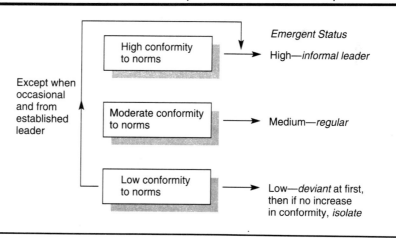

[1] A. Zaleznik, R. Christensen, and F. Roethlisberger, *The Motivation, Productivity, and Satisfaction of Workers* (Boston: Division of Research, Graduate School of Business, Harvard University, 1958).

MANAGERIAL BULLETIN

Packing Off the Peanut Packer

Elizabeth Kovacs was until recently employed by the firm of Q Peanuts as a peanut packer. She was in the habit of arriving at work up to 90 minutes before her 8 A.M. job. She used the time to sit in the canteen with newspapers and coffee and "get myself into the mood for a day's hard work."

Miss Kovacs' fellow workers, though, did not like this one bit. They prevailed on management to issue a warning to her about the insidious practice. When the warning produced no change in the lady's habits, she was fired.

SOURCE: *THE WALL STREET JOURNAL.*

External Status: How It Relates to Acceptance of Group Norms

Insofar as having a certain ethnic background, age, educational attainment, and so forth makes it likely that a person will share particular attitudes with others of the same background, external status allows group members to quickly "place" new group members. Of course, not *all* middle-aged male second-generation Lithuanian-American engineers, for example, are the same in all of their beliefs, values, and behaviors, nor are *all* Chicana women in personnel jobs the same. But within each category of people, common experiences and background can and often do lead to common tendencies, especially as compared to other groups. Most female personnel employees are probably more like one another than they are like the male engineers. Even when there are genuine differences among people within any one category, many outsiders *assume* commonalities—often by stereotypes. But apart from stereotypes, most people's values are based on how they were raised and their experiences thereafter, and various status factors do give shorthand hints at what a person's beliefs are *likely* to be. Thus, though external status may not *accurately* reflect a person's beliefs, and may even sometimes be misleading, groups in their early phases seem to rely on it to place members.

When a group's norms are strongly held, it is often extremely difficult for anyone who was raised from childhood with different beliefs to go along. A Maine native, taught Yankee independence from birth, is likely to be upset and uncomfortable in a work group of immigrant Italians who believe in helping one another on and off the job, freely borrowing and lending money, tools, and even food, and frequently stopping work to laugh and joke loudly together. The worker from Maine will probably not want or be able to go along with the others' norms and, thus, will be isolated, while the member of the Italian subgroup who is most spontaneous and generous will probably be most respected. In some other group the exact opposite could be true, and the independent Downeaster would be most respected.

It also has been observed that men and women have different ways of expressing their ideas; the former tending to be impersonal, abstract, and fact-oriented, while the latter tend to speak more from direct experience in a self-disclosing way. It is easy to see how women might be perceived as violating a norm of "rationality" in a predominantly male environment (see *Women's Ways of Knowing*).

Whatever attributes a particular group treats as high status, external status and status congruence appear to have the following consequences for internal membership rank (Zaleznik, Christensen, & Roethlisberger, 1958):

1. **High external status congruent members tend to become regular members.** It is as if a group coalesces around those whose status is uniformly high when they come to the group. Perhaps the people who come with lower external status look to those with greater status to see how things are supposed to develop, thereby helping the high-status congruent members become central.

2. **Relatively high status but incongruent members tend to end up as isolates.** Those who do not "fit" easily into one category create some confusion in others, causing neither respect nor liking. The ultimate result is often isolation, perhaps because the basically high-status person will not as strongly "need" that particular group's approval.

3. **Low external status members, regardless of congruence, tend to become deviants.** Those whose overall status is low when they enter a group seem to find difficulty in breaking free from the group but cannot fully follow norms to become regulars. They are thus likely to perpetuate within the group the low status they arrive with. Some low-status people who don't care about the group for one reason or another may become isolates, perhaps because they perceive little to lose from ignoring the group.

Roles as Differentiators of Group Members

Can you imagine what life would be like if there were no predictability to anyone's behavior? How would you behave, for example, if you could never be sure of your father's reactions? Suppose you never knew which friends you could count on for cheering up, or blowing off steam, or talking through serious problems, or playing your favorite sport? Wouldn't life be chaotic if you had to make anew every single choice of behavior every time you saw another person? It would be similar to entering a foreign culture every day of your life. While the spontaneity of it all could be exciting, it might paralyze many and wear out the rest.

As people interact, however, individuals slowly arrive at patterned behavior, where each party begins to learn the other's likes and dislikes, needs, sensitive areas, and so forth and can begin to accommodate to one another. A person comes to expect certain behavior and attitudes from others, and they come to expect particular behavior and attitudes from him or her. When you know the types of behavior or pattern expected of you in a particular situation, you have learned a role and automatically know what to do when in that situation. The way you then behave is not necessarily how you always are, but it is likely to be repeated whenever you are with that particular group of people or in that situation. This kind of "specialized" behavior is another way of differentiating members, resulting in a consistent place in the group for all who take on a patterned role. Here is an example of the role behavior of a young faculty member in a business school:

> At faculty meetings I find myself frequently raising challenging, possibly unanswerable questions about curriculum and educational philosophy, making my colleagues uncomfortable but sometimes forcing them to deal with issues on a more fundamental level. They now more or less expect this of me, that I'll take the role of the "resident radical" who tries to pull the rug out from under their assumptions, and thus they relate to me with a kind of stubbornness, which "pulls" even more questioning from me. Every group which discusses complex issues needs to have the status quo challenged; something about my personality lets me step in to fill that role, and the challenging function is thus taken care of.
>
> But at another meeting I attend, where I am on the board of directors of a community social agency, my behavior is quite different. Because there are many people on the board with low educational levels and little knowledge about organizations, there is great need for expert information on how to set organizational goals and how to make decisions. Because I have some knowledge of these matters and am seen by other board members as a "business professor," at board meetings I tend to be much more in the role of "expert advice-giver" and "problem solver," so I probably act more responsibly and less mischievously than at faculty meetings.
>
> In each case the group has a good sense of what to expect from me and vice versa, which is convenient and saves considerable time and confusion about who will do what. Particular types of behavior are almost automatically called forth.
>
> At the same time, having well-established roles also acts as a constraint on the choices made by me and the others. At faculty meetings it is hard for me to get in on proposing realistic solutions to curriculum problems, because others assume that if I am proposing something it's probably too "far out." Conversely, by my questioning role I probably prevent others from being as critical and assumption-examining as they might like to be.
>
> Similarly, there are times when I'd prefer to miss agency board meetings and relax with my family, or times when I would like to just joke around or toss out wild ideas, and many instances when I wish others would speak up more; but the responsibility of the role I'm in keeps me behaving in a helpful, problem-solving way. And, conversely, it is possible that some of the low-participating community members might feel freer to make constructive suggestions if I didn't preempt that role.

As with other kinds of deviance, behaving in ways not expected by others will cause discomfort in group members and lead to attempts to force the person back into the role. This can be uncomfortable for the individual trying to expand the role as well as for group members affected by the changes.

Thus, while our various roles are convenient they restrict our possible behaviors insofar as we choose to continue in them. Role behavior makes life more predictable and constrained by differentiating people according to particular behaviors expected of them and then reinforcing each role occupant for consistently taking that role. We expand on this in Chapter 10.

Though the patterns may vary to a greater or lesser degree, work group members inevitably acquire roles bringing their own styles and preferences to the group's requirements. Members respond to the needs of the group with their own personal styles and fairly rapidly begin to develop repetitive patterns of behavior. As group members notice one another's emerging patterns, they acquire expectations of how each person will behave, which reinforce whatever behavioral tendencies were exhibited, and soon a whole network of expectations is created, which helps make each person's participation predictable.

Few people have either so limited a repertoire of possible behaviors within them or so clear a notion of what they will not do that they can completely resist responding to others' expectations of them. Whether the behavioral pattern originates from within or from the strong expectations of others, when a person is treated as if he or she were *supposed* to act in a certain way, frequently that person will begin to do so, that is, produce the expected pattern.

Conformity to expectations by others is not inevitable, of course, and sometimes people resist being drafted into roles that do not fit. In our classes, for example, we often see athletes, treated at first as if they are only "jocks" uninterested in learning, struggle to not accept such a demeaning role and to become contributing group members. Roles assigned on the basis of external characteristics like sex, age, or appearance are probably less difficult to resist than those based on actual behavior, but they are by no means easy to escape. It takes a very determined person to continue to refuse to be what others expect, and such determination is rare. We will explore this question more closely in Chapters 8 and 10, especially in relation to conditions under which refusal is most likely. At present we can say that, for most people concerned with readily finding a comfortable place in a group, acceptance of particular roles is likely if the roles are not too incongruent with how they view themselves.

For example, early in the life of a new group there will often be some uncomfortable silences, since members do not know one another and feel cautious about risking opinions without being sure of reactions. Inevitably some member will become uncomfortable enough to think up something to say just to ease the tension. It only takes a few such events to initiate expectations of the silence breaker. In some groups that member will then usually be expected to be an idea initiator and be appreciated for that. In another group with different needs, the silence breaker might be seen as bidding for leadership and be "assigned" (often implicitly) the role of "aspiring leader." Of course, the style and particular words used by silence breakers make a difference about how they will be perceived. If it is done with some humor that member may come to be seen as a great tension releaser and be expected to take that role, to fulfill that function whenever the atmosphere in the group becomes tense. On the other hand, the person who breaks silence by nervous chattering may not be so appreciated even when members notice and expect it.

In general, *roles in groups can be categorized by whether they serve to (1) help accomplish the group task (task-oriented), (2) help maintain good relationships among members (socially oriented), or (3) express individual needs or goals unrelated to the group's purposes (self-oriented).*

Any role behavior reflects the person's personality and needs, but from the group point of view the behavior will be seen as more valuable if it also fulfills a need of the group for getting the job done or for sustaining satisfying relationships.

Furthermore, one person might take on several of these roles or at different times several members might perform in the same role. How widely distributed and firmly established roles are is an interesting indicator of the degree of crystallization or fluidity of a group's structure. Sometimes particular individuals acquire a "monopoly" on a role, and no one else can take it even though for the task at hand the other(s) would be best suited. **A group will be less effective if some or many capable members are prevented from taking needed roles.**

The following roles have been found useful and common in successful task groups:

Roles relating to accomplishing the group's tasks:[2]

1. Idea initiator: Proposes tasks or goals, defines problems, suggests procedures or ideas for solving problems.
2. Information seeker: Requests facts, seeks information about a group concern, asks for expression of feelings, requests statements or estimates, solicits expressions of value, seeks suggestions and ideas.
3. Information provider: Offers facts, provides information about a group concern, states beliefs about matters before the group, gives suggestions and ideas.
4. Problem clarifier: Interprets ideas or suggestions, clears up confusion, defines terms, indicates alternatives and issues, gets group back on track.

---

[2] Adapted from K. Benne and P. Sheats, "Functional Roles of Group Members," *Journal of Social Issues* 4, no. 2 (1948), pp. 41–49.

5. Summarizer: Pulls together related ideas, restates suggestions after the group has discussed them, offers a decision or conclusion for the group to weigh.

6. Consensus tester: Asks to see if group is nearing decision, sends up "trial balloons" to test a possible conclusion.

Roles related to the group's social relationships:

1. Harmonizer (joker or soother): Attempts to reconcile disagreements, reduces tension, gets members to explore differences.

2. Gatekeeper: Helps keep communication channels open, facilitates everyone's participation, suggests procedures that permit sharing of what members have to say.

3. Supporter: Exudes friendliness, warmth, and responsiveness to others; encourages, supports, acknowledges, and accepts others' contributions.

4. Compromiser: When own idea or status is involved in a conflict, offers compromise, yielding of status, admitting error or modifying position in interest of maintaining group cohesion.

5. Standards monitor: Tests whether group is satisfied with way it is proceeding, points out explicit or implicit operating norms to see if they are desired.

The variety of self-oriented roles is endless. Some (like "group clown") may be tolerated or neglected, while others (like "wet blanket," "playboy," "dominator," "self-confessor," or "bragger") may prove to be extremely annoying to other members and hinder group functioning. **In an effective task group, there will be a relatively low amount of self-oriented role behavior and a balance between task- and social-related roles as necessary.**

Sometimes self-oriented behavior may be quite functional for a group, serving to release tension or to smooth over differences. Reactions of group members to the self-oriented behavior of a "fight picker" or a "show-off" will depend on the frequency of the behavior and its timing. For example, a good wisecrack in the presence of a disliked authority figure may be gratefully appreciated, but constant joking when others want to work can become quite irritating.

The various roles that members take on become part of how they are ranked by the group. In some groups, idea initiators are most valued. As pointed out previously, high task contributors are usually respected, while high social contributors are usually liked; but each group will weigh the value of these patterns by its own standards and goals. **In general: The more a member fills both the task and social roles, the higher will be his or her status in the group. Members who only take either task or social roles tend to become overspecialized; their emergent status then depends on how highly the group values their "specialty."**

MANAGERIAL TOOLS

Some Dysfunctional Group Roles

Most people have had experience with group members whose behavior seems to serve mainly as an obstacle to getting anything done. In moderation their role behavior may be, and often is, helpful to the group; in excess it blocks progress. Below are listed a few of these roles (you can probably add to the list yourself):

- *Nitpicker:* Argues endlessly about the meanings of words and seems to dwell on nonessentials.
- *Endless talker:* Seems unable to let go of a topic and move on, going over the same points repeatedly.

- *Group humorist:* Uses every opportunity to make a joke, fool around, and distract group from its task.
- *Over-organizer:* Spends more time talking about what the group should be working on than working on it.
- *Topic jumper:* Cannot seem to stick to the point, goes off on tangents, jumps ahead, or goes back to a point already adequately discussed.

At times you may find yourself playing multiple roles in a group, some of which may even conflict. For example, if you happen to be the best-informed member of a group working on a specific task, you are likely to be both an idea initiator and an information provider with little difficulty, but you could find it hard to also be a gatekeeper. The first two roles supplement one another, but the third one requires a different orientation toward the other members of the group. However, if you *can* learn to master such a combination of roles, it can certainly enhance your status as a group leader as well as a contributing member.

BEHAVIOR AS A RESULT OF STATUS DIFFERENTIATION

The status or rank of a group member may not be explicit or directly discussed by group members, but it is usually inferred from observing member behavior. In general: **Lower-status members defer to higher-status members, allowing higher-status members to *(a)* initiate interactions, *(b)* make statements without being challenged, and *(c)* administer informal rewards or punishments. Higher-status members will usually talk more, talk "for the group" in public situations, make more contacts with outsiders, and usually have the widest number of connections within the group (Whyte, 1955).** Even body posture and seating arrangements can reflect status differences: Higher-status members sit at or near the head of the conference table (or where they sit becomes the head); if the group is talking informally they will be at the physical center of the grouping; they are looked at when others are speaking; they tend to sit more erectly or confidently. They can even interrupt others or change the subject.

In general, at least in the United States, there are strong expectations about how high- and low-status people are supposed to behave. In a given situation people who are clearly higher status are expected to be "nice" and not lord it over others. It is a form of noblesse oblige, with expressions of the person's higher status being subtle and designed to not make others feel bad even though they are lower status. In turn, lower-status people are expected to "know their place" and not presume on the privileges of those with higher status; those who do not properly defer are considered "uppity." Because of the democratic ideals in the United States, little of this is talked about directly; but if you have trouble believing it, try testing it in a social or work situation.

A principle of organization [necessary for] advanced social life . . . in higher vertebrates is the so-called ranking order. Under this rule every individual in the society knows which one is stronger and which weaker than itself, so that everyone can retreat from the stronger and expect submission from the weaker.

Konrad Lorenz
On Aggression

Influence

No matter how egalitarian the ideals of a work group, it is unlikely that all members can contribute equally along those dimensions—task or social—that the group values. Even where external status is roughly equal, as the group interacts some members will have better ideas, warmer personalities, or whatever is seen as desirable. As others perceive these differential talents, their possessors will be allowed more say about what the group should do, directions it should take, how decisions should be made, and so forth. *This ability to affect the behavior of others in particular directions* we define as *influence*.

Whether it is explicitly acknowledged or not, as a result of external status, adherence to norms, and roles taken, every member will have some differential degree of influence on others in the group. Some members will be more listened to or taken into account than others; and, in most groups, after awhile everyone knows reasonably accurately the relative standing of members in terms of influence. In student and other peer groups these differences are often denied, or at least talking about them is seen as taboo for fear of hurting feelings. Nevertheless, differences inevitably exist and can be documented by an observer. Since internal influence in a group correlates with

FIGURE 5–3   Determinants of Group Status and Influence

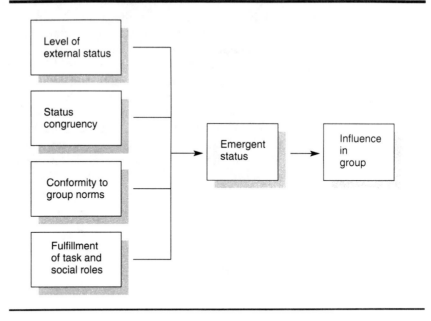

internal status, it can be noted by the same kinds of behavior: deference, assertion, physical spacing, and so on. Just as the thoughtful manager will want to know about status differentials in groups, so will he or she want to be a careful observer of influence differentials and of how influence is acquired within a group.

In general, we can predict that: **When members have congruently high external status, conform to the group's norms, and fulfill task and social roles, they will be accorded high emergent status and, therefore, have high influence within the group.** (See Figure 5–3.) If some of these factors are different, an altered proposition would be necessary to predict amount of influence within the group. Can you assess the relative influence of members of task groups to which you belong and then trace the influence to the factors discussed in this chapter?

The process of sorting out member influence and status is so important to a group's development that everything can be viewed from this perspective.[3] A group can be visualized as beginning with members sizing one another up and jockeying to find a satisfactory position in the group. The work of the group will become the means for jostling or infighting until each member has a relative position or rank with which he or she is satisfied.

_____

[3] The following formulation was originally suggested by one of our students, Nfor Susungi.

Though not everyone can be simultaneously at the top in terms of influence, stability can be achieved when all members accept the rank allotted them. If anyone is unhappy with his or her emergent position, new struggles will break out. The efforts to alter status then surface through attempts to conform more closely to norms, to change them, or to shift roles.

When you join a new group, you have some choice about the nature and degree of status you achieve. While you cannot change your external status, if you are willing to go along with group norms, take on task and social roles, and avoid self-serving behavior, you are likely to gain status and influence. Furthermore, while at first it may seem difficult to take initiative and speak up, a failure to do so will certainly limit your influence. On the other hand, talking too much can shut people off, and while it makes you visible for the moment, it may hurt you in the long run.

A group will not reach a stable equilibrium, where all its energies can be focused on its task, until its internal rankings are essentially accepted by all. Then a kind of cohesion can be reached. In this view, a group cannot be fully productive until it has arrived at a somewhat "crystallized" or accepted structure. Until differences of opinion about "proper" ranking are settled by the members of a group, it is less likely to be fully productive, since so much energy and attention must go into coping with individual restlessness.

On the other hand: **A structure that is too crystallized, where everyone "knows his place" only too well, can also have difficulties in producing, especially when tasks are changing and quick responsiveness is needed.** You might find comfort and security in knowing your niche in a group, but you might also find it somewhat limiting when it comes to challenge and new learning.

When a member tries to change rank, his or her influence is tested; a successful alteration of position indicates that the person had more influence than he or she was being credited with, while an unsuccessful attempt confirms or lowers the person's position. However, it can often be worth the risk of testing your influence; you lose little and you might discover that it is greater than you thought.

Subgroup

If group members are differentiated by how closely they adhere to group norms, there is a good possibility that they will form subgroups based on their degree of conformity to the norms. In addition, other kinds of subgroupings often emerge on the basis of mutual personality attractions, previous friendships, common interests outside the group, shared positions on crucial issues, and so on. In a classroom task group, for example, subgroups may develop among those who are serious scholars, those who are fraternity/sorority members, the athletes, the campus activists, and others.

As soon as more than two people are in a group, the possibility exists of some of them joining up and then taking sides. **The greater the numbers of people in a group, the more likely is subgroup division.** It is rare that a group does not develop some cliques.

The worst cliques are those which consist of one man.
George Bernard Shaw

For the manager the important issues is not whether subgroups exist but the basis for their formation and the consequences for group functioning. If the subgroups exist, because of differing but complementary task abilities, they may be quite functional for accomplishing group goals. Even if based primarily on social considerations, they may or may not hinder communications among members, foster cooperation or conflict, prevent or facilitate accomplishment of tasks, increase or decrease satisfaction, and so forth. Though it is certainly easier to assess the consequences of subgroup formation than do anything about it, it is an important factor in determining member standing and resultant productivity, satisfaction, and development.

One of the most serious subgroup problems rises when the smallest subgroup has only one member who is made to be a "subgroup," because he or she is visibly different from the others. The lone woman in an all-male group or the lone person of color in an all-white group—whom we can refer to as the *token* when the person is treated as a symbol rather than as an individual—often has special problems exactly because he or she has no (or very few) other subgroup members who are obviously alike and, therefore, appears to be even more different from the others than may actually be the case. While members of the dominant subgroup sometimes may actually have more in common with one another than with the token, often it may only be an untested assumption that the token is significantly different. In either case, their attitude can make it difficult for the token to know how to behave. When a joke is made about Speedy Gonzales, does the only Puerto Rican laugh, become angry, or pretend he hasn't heard it? None of these responses is very satisfactory, so, even if the token has many other things in common with the others, he or she often has a hard time establishing the common bonds (Kanter, 1977). This can lead to communication and cooperation barriers, which affect the group's ability to coordinate its work.

It could be important and useful for you to test some of the above notions in groups of which you are a member. Often such problems exist just below the surface and need to be brought into the open.

CONSEQUENCES OF MEMBER DIFFERENTIATION FOR PRODUCTIVITY, SATISFACTION, AND DEVELOPMENT

In Chapter 4 we looked at how cohesiveness is connected to a group's production, pulling individual member output toward what the group's norms define as appropriate. Even noncohesive work groups, however, develop at least rough ideas about what is too much work and what is too little. Different groups have particular nicknames, richer than *deviants* or *isolates,* for people who don't carry their own load or for those who are so gifted or willing to work so hard that they make others look bad by their output. Those members who produce "too much" are often seen as "rate busters" or, as they are known in student circles, "curve breakers." Conversely, "slackers" or "goof-offs" are those who just cannot or will not produce at a pace satisfactory to the particular group's members. In general, then, a person's standing in a group is partly determined by how closely he or she conforms to the group's norms and is particularly affected by adherence to norms about individual output. Conversely, once a person's rank is established a particular level of output is likely to follow. Of course, the degree of required task interdependence will affect individual freedom to vary production, with jobs that can be done alone more easily subject to individual variation.

An interesting irony of the above observations is that: **In a high-producing group the isolates and/or deviants are likely to be low producers, while in a group that holds down productivity the isolates are likely to be high producers!** A person may choose not to conform to avoid working so hard or so little, or may be pushed into isolation out of inability to produce near the group's desired rate. Similarly, a person who desires to be an accepted member will, if possible, adjust productivity upward or downward to meet the group's norms. Whatever the cause, there is no doubt that rank within the group is connected to productivity.

A dramatic example of just how powerful a force is exerted upon members to produce according to group norms was reported in *Street Corner Society,* a detailed study of a group of young underemployed men who "hung around" together (Whyte, 1955). One of the valued skills in the group turned out to be bowling ability. But other qualities, such as social skills, intelligence, and power of self-expression, were dominant in giving members status; as you might expect, bowling expertise is not perfectly correlated with ability to argue well or talk to many people. One of the lower-status members of the gang was the "best" bowler when measured by scores attained when bowling casually; but whenever the gang bowled competitively his scores would inevitably fall below those of the gang's leaders!

The low-status expert bowler may not have been fully aware of why he didn't do as well when competing with the others, but the pressure and razzing from the gang to have his "productivity" fall into line affected him enough temporarily to alter his ability to produce. In general, under competitive stress the gang's bowling scores almost always perfectly reflected their relative status, even though some lower-ranking members had more ability than they could deliver when being "kept in their places" by the others.

In a work group some of the differentiation of members will follow from the task requirements. If various members are required to do different tasks some group valuation of the respective worth of each task will probably emerge. Those who do jobs that the group sees as crucial to its success will probably be given higher status than others.[4] When the group ranks members by the difficulty of the task each performs, the group is likely to be relatively high in output. Thus: **The more that member differentiation is based on task requirements, the more productive the group is likely to be.**

On the other hand, if member rank is largely based on external status the group is only likely to be high producing if by coincidence the factors that determine external status are also those that would determine genuine contributions to the group's tasks. **The more that member differentiation is based on external status, the less productive the group is likely to be (unless external status happens to coincide with needed group skills).**

Summary Productivity Proposition

Differentiation, of course, need not be inconsistent with group cohesion. Though cohesive groups sometimes cling together and enforce false equality,

---

[4] This has its parallel in organizations, where members of groups associated with that company's important priorities (e.g., sales, engineering, and so on) tend to be highly influential.

MANAGERIAL TOOLS

High-Performing Teams

As reflected in some of the trends noted in Chapter 1, the concept of a high-performing team has emerged as an important part of an effective organization. In fact, some companies, usually in the high-tech area, try to conceive of their total organization as a high-performing team. This brings to mind a small group of people performing a task rapidly and cooperatively, like a basketball team in a fast break. That metaphor is often used to describe the way a team of workers on a shop floor can operate when given the opportunity to take charge of their own operations and output.

High-performing teams can be developed in many different kinds of organizations and at almost any level of operation. Think of a medical team dealing with an emergency situation, a research and de-

velopment group pressing to stay at the forefront of competitive technology, or a group of high-level managers making decisions on competitive prices in a rapidly changing, turbulent world market. All these situations demand a strong commitment of team members to the task and to working as a team. Exchange of information must be free and open, and there needs to be a willingness to keep the group's goals ahead of any personal goals or issues. The different talents and knowledge of all members need to be tapped. Leadership may be constantly shifting as the task demands, and any formal team leader is more likely to be playing an integrative role than a directing role, paying as much attention to group process as to group task.

even when differentiation would be appropriate, as in the case of groupthink, a group can be both differentiated and attractive to members. A highly differentiated group can be quite cohesive if all members believe that their positions accurately reflect their contributions, satisfy their needs, and lead to effective performance. In fact, if the group's tasks can best be done by each member *first* working on different aspects of the tasks and *then* coordinating individual efforts, the more differentiated *and* the move cohesive the group needs to be in order to produce at a high rate. Furthermore, if the group supports the organization's goals it will pull the highest possible productivity from its members. **The greater the differentiation *and* cohesion of a group with norms supporting the organization's goals, the greater its productivity is likely to be (Lawrence & Lorsch, 1967).**

Satisfaction and Development

As suggested earlier, a group that is highly differentiated but in which each member accepts his or her status can be highly satisfied. Where differentiation, however, is a result of factors that some members do not accept as appropriate, considerable dissatisfaction can result. For example, if a work group automatically assigns low status to its female members, forcing them to do all the menial tasks and ignoring their contributions to the important jobs, there can only be general satisfaction if the women accept their lower ranking. If, as increasingly is the case, however, they want to be accorded whatever status they earn by merit rather than automatically being given low (or high) status merely because of sex, the group will have dissension and low satisfaction.

When group members take on roles and ranks that restrict them to merely doing what they know well, growth will naturally be limited. A group highly differentiated on the basis of adherence to norms that support maximum productivity can be very efficient but can limit chances for members to learn new jobs, try new skills, or be creative about work processes. **If the group's tasks are routine a rigid structure may be most productive but least growth-promoting. Tasks calling for creativity and responsiveness, however, are not likely to be performed well by a rigidly differentiated group.** Furthermore, as we indicated with respect to a crystallized group, rigid differentiation is likely to be quite frustrating to members who want to learn and grow. For example, a group trying to think up a new commercial product, like a labor-saving small appliance, would have difficulty being imaginative if only the marketing person could give input on what customers might like, only the production manager could comment on how items can be built, and so forth. A free flow of ideas is called for regardless of the members' status and position in order for the group to be creative.

On the other hand, an insufficiently differentiated group may be highly productive at creative tasks, stimulate great learning by members, but be anxiety provoking at the same time. The lack of clear positioning can cause considerable uncertainty and nervousness for some members, even while allowing them maximum opportunities for growth.

Finally, as you might expect by now, an underdifferentiated group will probably be quite ineffective at performing routine tasks, thereby dragging down morale when results are poor, and probably leading to little growth except for those few members who can take advantage of the looseness to pursue their own ends.

The degree of differentiation and cohesion in a group then are important emergent outcomes of the way the group works together. They greatly affect a group's performance, satisfaction, and learning. While we have tried to show how cohesion and differentiation come about, a more detailed look at how groups function as they go about their business can be useful in assessing their effectiveness. In the next chapter we examine more closely the working processes of groups to help you more readily judge what is effective group behavior as it is occurring in the emergent system.

KEY CONCEPTS FROM CHAPTER 5

1. Overall status in group determined by:
   a. Respect: accorded to high task accomplishment.
   b. Liking: accorded to high social accomplishment.

2. Initial ranking.
   a. The higher the background of external status, the higher the initial internal status of a group member.
3. Status affects behavior.
   a. The higher a person is on dimensions valued by the group and the more norms are conformed to, the higher his or her status within the group and vice versa. Members who conform are regulars; the greatest conformers become informal leaders who may violate group norms. Consistency of relative positions on dimensions determines degree of status congruence.
   b. Deviant: member who does not conform to group's norms; most negative attitudes expressed to that member.
   c. Isolate: conforms even less to group's norms; interactions with isolate very infrequent.
4. Roles determine status and group effectiveness.
   a. Task-oriented.
   b. Socially oriented.
   c. Self-oriented and other dysfunctional group roles.
   d. The pressure of balancing multiple roles.
5. The greater the number of people in a group, the more likely is subgroup formation.
6. Influence.
   a. The ability to affect the behavior of others in particular directions.
   b. Affected by rank.
7. Differentiation and cohesion are related to productivity, satisfaction, and development.
   a. Relation to task requirements.
   b. Relation to external status.
   c. Relation to support of organization's goals.

PERSONAL APPLICATION EXERCISE

Looking at the Structure of a Group

Most students in task groups tend to view all members as equal, even when it is obvious that there are differences in many respects. There is a simple exercise, which has been around for many years, that you might try with a group of which you are a member. It involves a series of lineups.

You begin with everyone lined up according to height. It is quick and nonthreatening. You might follow that with a lineup on weight. Not as simple as height, but also not very controversial. Then try a lineup on who talks the most. This provides some useful feedback. Then move to dimensions like degree of influence in the group, closeness to the group norms, contribution to group goals, supportiveness of other members, and so on.

The important thing is to make sure you choose dimensions that are relevant to the group and will help the group to get a better understanding of its structure. Furthermore, the exercise usually gives members feedback that can help them improve their contributions to the group.

Even though this exercise is fun, it does generate important data.

SUGGESTED READINGS

Bales, R. F. "Task Roles and Social Roles in Problem-Solving Groups." In *Readings in Social Psychology.* 3rd ed., ed. E. Maccoby, T. M. Newcomb, and E. L. Hartley. New York: Holt, Rinehart & Winston, 1958.

Bales, R. F., and F. L. Strodtbeck. "Phases in Group Problem Solving." *Journal of Abnormal and Social Psychology* 46 (1951), p. 485.

Belenky, M. F.; B. McV. Clinchy; N. R. Goldberger; and J. M. Tarule. *Women's Ways of Knowing: The Development of Self, Voice and Mind.* New York: Basic Books, 1986.

Benne, K., and P. Sheats. "Functional Roles of Group Members." *Journal of Social Issues* 4, no. 2 (1948), pp. 41–49.

Grinnell, S. B. "The Informal Action Group: One Way to Collaborate in a University." *Journal of Applied Behavioral Science* 5 (1969), pp. 75–103.

Hollander, E. P. *Leaders, Groups, and Influence.* New York: Oxford University Press, 1964.

Hopkins, T. H. *The Exercise of Influence in Small Groups.* Totowa, N.J.: Bedminster Press, 1964.

Homans, G. *The Human Group.* New York: Harcourt Brace Jovanovich, 1950.

_____. *Social Behavior: Its Elementary Forms.* New York: Harcourt Brace Jovanovich, 1961.

Jacobs, T. O. *Leadership and Exchange in Formal Organization.* Springfield, Va.: National Technical Information Service, U.S. Department of Commerce, 1970.

Kahn, R. L.; D. M. Wolfe; R. P. Quinn; and J. D. Snoek. *Organizational Stress: Studies in Role Conflict and Ambiguity.* New York: John Wiley & Sons, 1964.

Kanter, R. M. *Men and Women of the Corporation.* New York: Basic Books, 1977.

Lawrence, P. R., and J. Lorsch. *Organization and Environment.* Homewood, Ill.: Richard D. Irwin, 1967.

Maier, N. R. F. "Assets and Liabilities in Problem Solving: The Need for an Integrated Function." *Psychological Review* 74 (1967), p. 244.

_____. "Male versus Female Discussion Leaders." *Personnel Psychology* 23 (1970), pp. 455–61.

Roethlisberger, F., and W. Dickson. *Management and the Worker.* Cambridge, Mass.: Harvard University Press, 1939.

Thompson, V. A. *Modern Organization.* New York: Alfred A. Knopf, 1961.

Whyte, W. F. *Street Corner Society.* Rev. ed. Chicago: University of Chicago Press, 1955.

Zaleznik, A.; R. Christensen; and F. Roethlisberger. *The Motivation, Productivity, and Satisfaction of Workers.* Boston: Division of Research, Graduate School of Business, Harvard University, 1958.

Developing Group Effectiveness

Emergent Processes

"The greater the time pressure, the more appropriate it will be for a group to make decisions by a vote or even by the unilateral decision of its leader."

Do you think you could tell from observing a group how well it is working? What criteria would you use? We have suggested that you judge by the outcomes—productivity, member satisfaction, and development. While these are the ultimate criteria of group effectiveness, it would be hard for a group to improve its operations as it went along if this were the only way to make judgments. To wait for the final outcomes to occur can be too late. Nor is progress toward those final outcomes necessarily an adequate basis for corrective action, since progress may become visible only when it is too late to take such action. Therefore, it is important for a group to have some basis for evaluating its emergent processes as it carries out a given task. The group needs to raise such questions as: "Are we working in the right way?" "Does everyone adequately understand his or her job?" "Are we avoiding important issues?" and "How do people feel about the objectives of the work?" To the extent that a group has available some set of criteria by which to assess its processes, it is in a stronger position to improve the way it goes about a task.

The effectiveness of any group depends upon several factors. Appropriate human and technological resources are background factors that establish both the possibilities and the limits for productive outcomes. Further, the policies and directives that make up the required system have direct influence over the effectiveness of a working group. Accordingly, most managers pay a great deal of attention to both background and required aspects of a work setting; they take great pains to select the right people for a job and to spell out job requirements and specifications. Yet the emergent processes of a work group, which are equally important, are often overlooked except when they overtly disrupt the work. Even when managers recognize the importance of dealing with emergent processes, they often lack a useful set of criteria by which to judge.

> For example, the top planning group of an aerospace firm was having a great deal of trouble producing useful plans. Their meetings often wandered from their stated agenda to rambling discussions of new books about youth in America, psychological interpretations of current events, and so on. In the meantime corporate profits were steadily declining. Though the vice president for planning was not happy with the way the group worked, he would not risk pushing the group to examine its own processes, partly because he did not know how to judge them himself. Meetings got worse and worse, frustration grew, and finally individual members began to quit for other jobs.

As major corporations experiment with the use of self-managing work teams and incorporate them into their means of production, the demands on managers and workers alike to develop their skills in group process will increase. Such companies as Digital Equipment Corporation, General Electric, and Corning Glass (see the Managerial Bulletin box) are among many to move in this direction.

MANAGERIAL BULLETIN

Corning Executive Norman E. Garrity Promotes Self-Managing Work Teams

The best way to empower employees, Garrity decided, was to eliminate several tiers of managers and install self-managing teams of workers who would receive extensive training. His chance to test these concepts came in 1987, when Corning decided to expand production of ceramic "substrates," the filters that serve as the core of catalytic converters used in cars. Instead of expanding an old filter plant at Erwin, New York, Garrity persuaded the company to reopen a closed plant in Blacksburg and start from scratch with a new work force and "world-class" labor and manufacturing practices.

SOURCE: John Hoerr, "Sharpening Minds for a Competitive Edge," *Business Week*, December 17, 1990.

While Chapters 4 and 5 examined the emergent *properties* of a group (its structure or state of integration/differentiation at any point in time), this chapter will focus upon the emergent *processes* (the dynamics) of a group as it functions. In short, the chapter will use a kind of social-psychological "microscope" to examine *how* a group operates.

As a starting point, we will look at issues faced by every working group, how these issues determine the criteria by which to evaluate the appropriateness of a given group's process, and how these evaluations need to take into account the particular situation of the group (e.g., example, its purpose, size, composition, surrounding circumstances, and so forth). While it will not be possible to cover all the varieties of situations and show how the criteria apply in every case, we will give you a general sense of how to fit the two together. One section of the chapter uses two contrasting case examples to demonstrate how to consider situational factors when evaluating a group's process.

ISSUES FACING EVERY WORK GROUP

Every work group has to deal with the same general issues regardless of whether it is a group of machinists on a shop floor, surgeons and nurses in an operating room, executives at a strategy meeting, or students on a project. It is the *way* in which a group goes about dealing with each of these issues and resolving the accompanying dilemmas that constitutes the group's emergent system and, thus, its effectiveness. While the dilemmas are similar for all groups, there are many possible ways of resolving them; and while groups vary in what the members consider desirable or preferable, different circumstances call for different approaches.

⬚ FIGURE 6–1   Issues Facing Any Work Group

ISSUE	QUESTIONS
1. Atmosphere and relationships.	What kinds of relationships should there be among members? How close and friendly, formal or informal?
2. Member participation.	How much participation should be required of members? Some more than others? All equally? Are some members more needed than others?
3. Goal understanding and acceptance.	How much do members need to *understand* group goals? How much do they need to *accept* to be *committed* to the goals? Everyone equally? Some more than others?
4. Listening and information sharing.	How is information to be shared? Who needs to know what? Who should listen most to whom?
5. Handling disagreements and conflict.	How should disagreements or conflicts be handled? To what extent should they be resolved? Brushed aside? Handled by dictate?
6. Decision making.	How should decisions be made? Consensus? Voting? One-person rule? Secret ballot?
7. Evaluation of member performance.	How is evaluation to be managed? Everyone appraises everyone else? A few take the responsibility? Is it to be avoided?
8. Expressing feelings.	How should feelings be expressed? Only about the task? Openly and directly?
9. Division of labor.	How are task assignments to be made? Voluntarily? By discussion? By leaders?
10. Leadership.	Who should lead? How should leadership *functions* be exercised? Shared? Elected? Appointed from outside?
11. Attention to process.	How should the group monitor and improve its own process? Ongoing feedback from members? Formal procedures? Avoiding direct discussion?

Figure 6–1 shows 11 issues facing every work group.[1] Corresponding to each issue, we have listed sets of questions with which a group must cope. We suggest that you study the chart carefully, see how it applies to any group of which you are a member, and evaluate how well that group has gone about dealing with the issues. Even before we go into detail on these 11 criteria of an effective group, you can probably discover some useful ways to apply them for yourself.

[1] A number of years ago, Douglas McGregor, a leading organizational theorist, described 11 criteria of an effective working group. While his studies were specific to certain kinds of groups (mainly executives), the issues inherent in McGregor's criteria serve as a useful framework for this chapter. See D. McGregor, *The Human Side of Enterprise* (New York: McGraw-Hill, 1960).

Every one of these issues can be related to some key aspect of a group's activities, interactions, attitudes, and norms. In examining group process, you might be looking at who is doing what, how he or she is doing it, who is interacting with whom, what seem to be the prevailing feelings, what kind of norm(s) has emerged in relation to a given issue, and so forth. Which of these questions demands attention depends entirely upon the particular situation, its complexity, and its history. For the sake of convenience throughout this chapter we will use the word *process* as a general term referring to any one or more of these emergent aspects of a group. It will be your job to determine *which* aspect of group "process" needs evaluation in any given set of circumstances. However, it is important to pay particular attention to group *norms,* since these govern the internal workings of a group. Because norms are difficult to change, their functionality needs to be examined as they emerge and before they become set in concrete. In fact, the 11 issues can be thought of as a classification system for group norms and, therefore, serve as a systematic guide to their evaluation.

WHAT THE WORK SITUATION REQUIRES

Many factors can be used to determine differences in what kind of group process is appropriate to the job. We will focus on *five* that tend to have direct and important consequences. These are:

Size of the work group.

Distribution of resources (expertise) in the group.

Complexity and/or diversity of the task.

Time pressure on the group to produce.

Degree of task interdependence required.

As we discuss each of these factors, we will generate propositions that describe the effects that each factor has on a work group. After we have discussed the factors, we will look at two examples that represent sharp contrasts in relation to all five of them. Then, using the examples as a point of reference, we will discuss each of the 11 criteria (Figure 6–1) and see how they describe effective working groups of very different kinds.

Size of the Work Group

From your experience in groups of varying sizes, have you noticed how small groups have a different "feel" than large groups? The small group allows closer relationships, a deeper knowledge of the members, and a better sense of the whole picture at any given time. These are seen as advantages by many people, and consequently they prefer working in a small group. Others are happier in a less intimate atmosphere, prefer the greater anonymity of the larger group, and like the security of knowing there are more people to do the work and carry out necessary group maintenance tasks.

Obviously, there has to be a trade-off in the various advantages of large versus small groups, many of which are primarily a matter of personal preference and many a matter of the inherent constraints posed by size. For example, it takes greater effort and more formal procedures to make sure that everyone in a large group is fully informed in matters concerning them. It also takes more time and effort to coordinate the work of more people. While these issues influence the ease of conducting the group's operations, they may or may not detract from its ultimate effectiveness. Remember, our primary concern here has to do with the utilization of resources in carrying out a task. In this regard we can say that, in most instances: **The smaller the group, the fewer total resources there are available for work; however, it is easier to obtain full participation and coordination of individual effort (Bales & Borgatta, 1955; Seta, Paulus, & Schkade, 1976).** There may be rare exceptions to this proposition. John F. Kennedy once joked at a dinner of outstanding contributors to American life, "Never before have so many brains and talents been present in the same room at one time with the possible exception of the day when Thomas Jefferson dined alone!" Normally, however, fewer people mean fewer work resources, with the result that each carries a greater burden.

Distribution of Resources (Expertise) in the Group

Suppose an instructor assigned you to a group of students to work on a problem involving the use of quantitative analysis. It's likely that you would depend upon the group member(s) who knew such methods best to take the most active part in the task. If the relevant abilities were evenly distributed among the members, the load would not fall upon any one or two individuals but could be shared by all. The proposition in this regard follows very directly from the example. **The more evenly distributed are the resources (levels of expertise) of a group among its members, the more appropriate is total member participation.** This does not rule out the option of assigning specific jobs to only one or two members; it indicates only that the degree to which the assignments can appropriately be spread around depends upon the distribution of resources. It can be as wasteful to give specific work to members who are unable to do that particular task as it is to ignore the most expert member. It also can be appropriate at times to have someone other than the most expert member carry out a task, in order to develop the individual's skills and, thus, enhance the group's development.

Complexity and/or Diversity of the Work

Suppose the task assigned in the example above were simply to determine the probability of occurrence of an event using some clearly specified information. While it would certainly take some ability to complete the assignment, it is likely that any one person who had studied probability could do it. If the assignment were much more complicated (like determining various production costs for a given product based upon information on personnel turnover, salary levels, overhead rates, market demand, and fluctuations in availability and costs of raw materials), the task might better be handled by the combined talents of several people. The proposition that follows from this is: **The greater the task complexity/diversity, the more appropriate it is to utilize the resources of a number of people (Heise & Miller, 1951).** It allows for the handling of a greater *amount* and *diversity* of information and in more complicated forms. Simple tasks call for simple information and fewer resources for completion.

In developing a plan of action for completing a complex task, groups are sometimes unable to work out every specific step ahead of time and to anticipate every contingency that might arise. Under such circumstances it becomes important for those who are implementing different aspects of the plan to "make the plan work" by adjusting and adapting to the contingencies encountered and coordinating their alterations with those responsible for other parts of the plan. Yet this kind of creative and responsible behavior is likely to be impossible if the individual lacks knowledge about the rationale behind the plan, nor is that person likely to be attentive to "making the plan work" if lacking in commitment to the plan. Thus, another important proposition is: **The more likely it is that unexpected contingencies demanding immediate adaptation will occur in carrying out a task, the greater the need for members to have full information about the work plan's rationale and be committed to the objectives of the plan (Steers, 1977).** Since the commitment to a course of action often rests on involvement in the development of the planned action and a consequent sense of ownership of the plan, a corollary proposition follows from the above: **The greater the need for individual members to make adjustments to a plan of action, the greater the need for them to share in the original planning and decision making.**

Time Pressure on the Group to Produce

This factor poses a paradox. When the time pressure is greatest, very often decisions are most critical. When decisions are most critical, the multiple resources of a group are most needed, and, thus, the working process of that group is of greatest import. Yet the pressure to produce often makes it impossible to take the time to examine group process even if it is operating poorly. Failure to take the time to look at process perpetuates that dysfunctional process; stopping to work on process eats up valuable time and can increase the stress with respect to the task. While either option is costly, the easiest time to work on group process issues is when there is adequate opportunity to deal with them fully; under pressure this is not likely to occur. Therefore, the proposition we suggest in this instance is that: **The greater the time pressure, the less appropriate it is for the group to work on process issues (Isenberg, 1979).** One implication of this statement is that, when time demands are at their lowest levels, the group should examine its ways of working to prepare itself to deal more effectively with the periods of high pressure. When there are impending deadlines, a group needs to function well reflexively, though it is often only under pressure that group members realize what they have not settled! Thus, it seems most useful to work on group processes early and on low-risk tasks where time is not crucial, then build on this base for key tasks or time constraints, or both.

Time can also affect decision making and leadership. When time pressure is great, there is often insufficient opportunity for the whole group to talk things through thoroughly to a consensus. A quicker means of reaching a decision may be needed. The proposition that follows is: **The greater the time pressure, the more appropriate it will be for a group to make decisions by vote or even by the unilateral action of its designated leader rather than by consensus.** (We will have more to say about the impact of time on leader behavior in Chapter 12.)

Degree of Task Interdependence Required

A group of auto workers assembling a new car probably has its individual tasks pretty well routinized. They may talk a lot to each other, but it is not required in order to do the work. Their interactions depend more on personal preferences, mutual attractions, interests outside the task, and so forth—what we have called *emergent factors*. There is some degree of interdependence among the tasks each is performing, because some jobs cannot proceed until others have been completed. However, the bases of the interdependence are clear-cut and require relatively little exchange of information in an ongoing manner. By way of contrast, a group of friends playing touch football constantly needs to exchange information on strategy, weak spots in the other team, mistakes in their own play, and so on. These exchanges are demanded by the nature of their task almost from moment to moment. The player throwing a pass needs to be able to anticipate where the receiver will be and who will be blocking the onrushing opponents. Whether or not the auto workers ever develop any degree of friendship, mutual understanding seems only peripherally related to task accomplishment. In the case of the touch football team, it is extremely useful for the members to know a great deal about each other's abilities, as well as to develop a sense of confidence in and support for each other. The degree of required interdependence leads to what we might call a *team*, which goes a step beyond what we call a *group*.

The proposition that applies in this instance is: **The greater the degree of task interdependence required, the more important it is for group members to maintain continuing exchanges with and have knowledge of each other as persons.** The proposition refers primarily to task-related information. Whether or not personal friendships as opposed to working colleagueships develop in the course of the interactions is again a matter of member preferences and opportunities. It is not critical to the group's success, though likely when there is high interdependence. Think, for example, of fire fighters, whose very lives depend on one another's skill, knowledge, and performance. It is not surprising that while they work together their families become close, spend time together, and form relationships beyond what is directly required by work.

When You Put All the Factors Together

It is not easy to manage a group well. (For some ideas on how to manage a single meeting, see the next Managerial Tools box.) Each of the five factors can vary and can yield a tremendous variety of possible combinations. You find small groups with an imbalanced distribution of resources, working on simple tasks under high pressure (as in a group monitoring an automated chemical process) or large groups with high task interdependence working on complex tasks under little pressure (as in a corporate research lab). There are obviously too many possible combinations to explore each one. It might be useful and fun for you to generate different combinations and to see if you can think of groups that fit; or you might take a look at some groups you know and see if you can describe them in terms of these five factors. Later, as we discuss the kinds of group processes that are appropriate to a given set of circumstances, you can determine how those processes apply to your own examples. For illustration, we will utilize two case examples of a highly contrasting nature. In this way we can highlight the importance of considering the situation when you determine what kind of group processes are appropriate.

THE CASE OF THE STRATEGIC PLANNING TEAM

Imagine that you are observing a group of five senior corporate executives who are developing a long-range plan for the company. Each individual brings equally important but special expertise to the team, and they share the goal of making sure that the plan reflects their different perspectives in a balanced way. One executive is a marketing specialist, another has financial expertise, a third deals with human resource allocations, a fourth is in charge of manufacturing, and the fifth heads up research and development. Clearly, the plan must pay attention to all aspects of the situation, requires an integration of ideas, and must be formulated in a way that allows for many future uncertainties. There is little time pressure on the group, so it can explore issues in some depth.

MANAGERIAL TOOLS

Guidelines for Running a Meeting

Most people resent poor meetings that waste time. Careful advanced planning and preparation can help, especially when time pressures mean that attention to process during a meeting will be inappropriate. Some tips on improving meetings:

I. Plan for the meeting (chairperson).
   1. Define objectives.
   2. Think through who should attend: diverse viewpoints, knowledge, degrees of commitment.
   3. Develop agenda and estimate time for each major agenda item (all necessary resources, no unnecessary resources).
   4. Make clear what is expected from the group on each item: information sharing, advice, exploration, or decision.
   5. Schedule unimportant items last.
   6. Avoid regular meetings lasting more than 1½ hours.

II. Facilitate attendee preparation.
   1. Provide sufficient notice and directions about time and place.
   2. Circulate agenda.
   3. Circulate, as appropriate, background materials (handouts).
   4. Contact selected attendees beforehand to cultivate preparedness, interest, and so on. On major issues, it is useful to talk to everyone ahead of time, to anticipate clashes, avoid hopeless battles, and the like.

III. Provide suitable physical facilities.
   1. Adequate space and furniture.
   2. Necessary equipment (flip charts, markers, projectors with extra bulbs, blackboard).
   3. Appropriate location ("neutral" territory, away from telephone, freedom from interruption, near data files, and so on).
   4. Refreshments, if appropriate.

IV. Conducting the meeting (chairperson).
   1. Start on time.
   2. Set stage: review purpose, introduce new members, and the like.
   3. Exercise control.
      a. Follow agenda.
      b. Prevent one or two from hogging "air time."
      c. Manage time (seek decision when appropriate, move on to next item, and so on).
      d. Cut off side conversations.
      e. Appoint someone to take notes.
      f. Define issues.
      g. Ask many questions.
   Manage process.
      a. "Gate keep"—insure everyone gets a chance to speak.
      b. Stop interruptions.
      c. Initiate a "stretch," open windows, and the like.
      d. Clarify misunderstandings.
      e. Don't take silence as agreement; do not force early consensus.
      f. Stop to find out why discussion is not going well when that occurs.
      g. Summarize.
   5. Speak more to group than to individuals.
   6. Finish on time!

V. Participating in meeting (members).
   1. Prepare self for meeting (read handouts, and so on).
   2. If can't attend, inform chairperson.
   3. Be on time.
   4. Exercise self-discipline (stick to topic, do not interrupt).
   5. Practice "active listening."
   6. Contribute to managing the meeting's process.
   7. Carry out, subsequently, responsibilities assigned.

VI. Concluding the meeting.
   1. Summarize decisions reached.
   2. Review responsibility assignments and clarify next steps (who, to do what).
   3. Take time to assess the meeting's process, if necessary.
   4. Schedule next meeting (if appropriate).

VII. Follow-up.
   1. Prepare and distribute notes.
   2. Follow up on carrying out of assignments.

THE CASE OF THE RESTAURANT STAFF

Let's look at another group that differs from the first. It consists of 25 members of the staff of an upscale restaurant. The group includes various levels of expertise from the head chef and maître d' on down to the dishwashers and bus staff, as well as wide variations in experience in a food service industry. The tasks themselves are not very complex, except for the chef's; each person has a clearly defined job with a very limited range of diversity. The restaurant has an excellent reputation to maintain, and every member of the staff is under pressure to be on his or her toes at all times, paying attention to the quality of the food, the service, the cleanliness of the tables and floor, and so forth. While the job that any one person performs, especially at such levels as chef or maître d', can affect the whole operation, each person's work is sharply enough differentiated so that much of it can be performed independently of the other employees. However, key points where coordination is needed are such matters as preparing orders in time, picking up food as it is ready to be served, getting tables cleared off fast enough to prepare for the next customer, and so on. But once a system has been devised, these are routine matters and do not require elaborate or intensive discussion and analysis by the staff at the time of execution.

HOW THE CRITERIA APPLY TO EACH GROUP

The Planning Group

The executive team working on the strategic plan can be described as:

A. A small group with:
B. Evenly distributed resources,
C. Dealing with a complex and diverse task,
D. Under little external time pressure,
E. But requiring a high level of interdependence.

Under these circumstances, the appropriate group processes would tend to be as follows:

1. Informal atmosphere with close, friendly relationships.
2. Full participation of all members equally.
3. High level of goal understanding and acceptance on the part of every group member.
4. Complete sharing of all information, with every member listening to every other member.
5. Disagreements discussed and resolved, not set aside.
6. Decisions made by group consensus.
7. Criticism of performance open and direct among all group members.

8. Feelings about task expressed openly and directly.
9. Task assignments made and accepted through discussion and negotiation; as voluntary as possible.
10. Leadership shared freely and changed along with corresponding changes in situational demands.
11. Group devotes significant blocks of time to the discussion of its own process.

The Restaurant Staff

The staff of the upscale restaurant can be described as:

A. A large group with:
B. Highly differentiated resources,
C. Dealing with simple and narrow tasks, except for a few highly skilled jobs like chef,
D. Under a high level of time pressure,
E. With a relatively low level of task interdependence except at a few key points.

Under these circumstances the appropriate group processes would tend to be:

1. Formal atmosphere with task-relevant relationships.
2. Participation in discussions based upon expertise.
3. Understanding and acceptance of goals related to level and scope of job responsibilities.
4. Members obtain information from and listen to those other members possessing greater relevant knowledge.
5. Only those disagreements directly interfering with task are dealt with; final resolution determined by those members with greatest expertise.
6. Decisions made by those with relevant level of knowledge and expertise.
7. Criticism of work made by those members with the requisite knowledge and experience.
8. Feelings expressed through prescribed procedures.
9. Assignments made by those members with greatest level of knowledge and expertise.
10. Leadership on any given aspect of task determined by the relevant knowledge and experience.
11. Very little time devoted to examining group process; procedures are devised by higher-level members and carried out in a formal manner.

As you compare the two pictures just drawn, you might have some personal reactions to them. The first one portrays a kind of setting that many but not all people prefer, while the second has the ring of a small bureaucracy and may not be quite as attractive to you, though there are people who do prefer working in more structured, defined settings. What actually happens in any given situation is not just a matter of what the nature of the situation requires or calls for; it is also a matter of what other options are possible and what the members of any group might consider most desirable for them. The staff of the restaurant might very well *choose* to operate in a manner similar to that of the planning group, but it would be fighting an uphill battle in the face of what the task situation demands. For instance, try to imagine 25 people struggling to resolve all the disagreements that can occur in such a large group. How feasible would it be for such a group to arrive at a consensus on all issues? What would be the costs of ignoring the many years of experience and the levels of expertise that some individuals possess, in order to widen and maximize member participation? And what would happen if everyone criticized everyone else and freely expressed all their feelings about every aspect of their work? Though such a set of choices might be made to work, it would consume extraordinary energy, and in the long run it would be unlikely to get the work done effectively.

What both situations have in common is that they are maximizing the use of group member resources. They appropriately differ from each other in *how* they use their resources, but they can be equally high in the outcomes of productivity, worker satisfaction, and development.

PROCESS CAN BE CHANGED

Sometimes a group can improve its process by direct examination of how its members are working together (i.e., by reviewing the criteria of an effective group, discussed earlier). This can be done through informal discussion or by a more formal procedure, such as the use of an instrument. The process thermometer in the Personal Application Exercise at the end of this chapter is an example of the more formal approach. It clearly has the advantage of making sure that the group addresses all the important issues, but some groups are not comfortable with its tight structure. You might find it useful to experiment with the Process Thermometer in one of your own groups, even if not all the dimensions fit your situation.

Another way a group can change its process is by restructuring itself. A large group can subdivide into smaller groups, each of which can utilize effective small-group process criteria. Further, if the subdivisions equalize the levels of expertise in each subgrouping, then other criteria begin to change in their applications. At the restaurant, for example, it may be that wait staff in each area can usefully meet to discuss possible areas of cooperation; or chef, maître d', and key wait staff might periodically examine the way orders are transmitted. Factors like task complexity and required interdependence may be less subject to change, but even these allow the possibility of exploring

---

MANAGERIAL BULLETIN

Technology Can Change the Process

Computer-aided meetings are speedy, honest, anonymous—and silent.

There's a bloody meeting going on. "This company has no leader—and no vision," says one frustrated participant. "Why are you being so defensive?" asks another. Someone snaps: "I've had enough—I'm looking for another job." Rough stuff—if these people were talking face-to-face. But they're not. They're sitting side-by-side in silence in front of personal computers, typing anonymous messages that flash on a projection screen at the head of the room.

SOURCE: "At These Shouting Matches, No One Says a Word," *Business Week*, June 11, 1990.

An Electronic Meeting?

PROS

Speeds the process, as everyone talks at once.

Fosters honestly through anonymity.

Gives participants a sense they played a role in decision-making.

Creates a printed record of results.

CONS

Requires thinking at a keyboard.

Gives equal time to bad ideas.

Does not give credit for brilliance.

SOURCE: "Business Meeting by Keyboard," *New York Times*, October 21, 1990.

---

various forms of innovation and work variation. For example, individuals normally assigned to one kind of task can exchange jobs with others in order to learn a wider range of tasks and also gain appreciation of one another's role.

We do consider it critical, however, for a work group to remember to utilize its full range of resources in order to be effective. **If the task calls for differentiated levels of expertise in a group, then the effectiveness of that group's process will depend upon the degree to which it gives influence to appropriate members.** By way of contrast: **If the task calls for evenly distributed resources among the members of a group, then the effectiveness of the group's process will depend upon the degree to which influence is equally shared among the members.**

Task Group Effectiveness Develops over Time

In taking steps to diagnose the appropriateness of a group's process and to change that process, one must not only consider the work situation as discussed above but also one other aspect of the group: its phase of development as a task group.

No group can expect to be instantly effective. Groups are known to go through developmental phases or periods during which certain of the 11 issues are central and require resolution before the group can move on to deal with other issues and eventually establish its best working process. You as an individual can probably remember some stages you went through during your life when certain issues were dominant. For example, before you became an independent adult you may have had to work through a period of counterdependence, in which you were struggling to prove yourself. Similarly, groups typically have to resolve membership issues before they can focus on issues of confrontation and reach full working expectations. The time it takes for a group to work through the phases will vary with the backgrounds of its members. If the members have had little experience working in groups, the process is liable to be slow and even cumbersome. While groups composed of members who have had experience can usually proceed more rapidly, if the range of experience is great and some become impatient with the needs of others, the process may also be slow.

Furthermore, just as counterdependent feelings can be rekindled in individuals from time to time throughout life by the actions of teachers, bosses, and others, so, too, groups do not necessarily leave a given phase of development permanently. From time to time they must recycle to rework old issues that were not fully resolved or to modify their resolutions in the face of new events or new members.

Consequently, a manager who assigns people to a committee or task force needs to understand that it may take some time for that group to reach its full effectiveness. Similarly, as you seek to diagnose the groups of which you are a member, try to consider what phase they are in and what steps you can take to facilitate their appropriate movement to the next phase. Also do not be surprised if at times you and the group need to recycle and work some more on an issue that was previously resolved.

In the next section we discuss five phases of group development:

Membership.

Subgrouping.

Confrontation.

Individual differentiation.

Collaboration.

As you consider these concepts, remember that they are very general and, while descriptive of many groups, they should not be taken as inevitable for any given group. As with individuals, every group has its unique character and manner of development.

FIVE PHASES OF GROUP DEVELOPMENT

Phase I—Membership

When a group is newly formed, the members typically wonder about whether they will have a place in the group and will find acceptance in it. They wonder whether others perceive the goals of the group as they do and whether the goals of the group that emerge (are clarified) will be ones to which they can give commitment. Will the price of membership in terms of expected behavior (norms) and the benefits of membership (support, acceptance, goal accomplishment) warrant their psychological joining of the group? In short, members tend to be concerned with their own safety and place in the group, rather than with collective efforts toward the task. Issues of participation and membership, goals, and (in a covert way) evaluation are important.

The atmosphere is likely to be strained, leading to superficial and polite interaction conducted with caution. While some individuals may respond to the ambiguity of the situation with an extra amount of activity and talk (in an attempt to establish some definition), others will tend to be hesitant and reserved.

Members are likely to feel quite dependent on the designated leader if there is one (as usually is the case in businesses), or look to the wider organization for clarification if there is not. Members often approach tasks with high energy but little coordination.

Any attempt to diagnose who ultimately will exert leadership is prone to great error, although early "activists" sometimes may be propelled into leadership positions that they ultimately cannot sustain. Listening may be quite intense, as people have their antennas out to discover the rules of the road; but distortion is likely (hearing what one wants to hear for safety), and there is little sharing and testing of understanding and interpretation.

Members need to get acquainted and begin to share expectations about goals and objectives. Efforts to rush this process by demanding that people reveal intimate facts about themselves can be disastrous; but full attention to the task, with no effort to get acquainted and no sharing of self, can also be inhibitive. The need is to become acquainted with one another and begin the process of goal clarification.

Similar attempts to establish norms about handling conflict openly or allowing full expression of feelings, while given lip service, are generally premature and, therefore, ineffective during this phase. Those issues will come up later.

Phase 2—Subgrouping

As members begin to get acquainted and identify others who share some of their expectations, pairing and other subgroupings occur. The issue of relationships begins to come to center stage as individuals focus on similarities and dissimilarities and seek out others for friendship, acceptance, and support (allies on task issues).

Relationships may tend to be clinging, as members hang on to those who seem similar among potentially dangerous others. Members begin to express some feeling of warmth within the subgroupings, and the overall atmosphere can become more relaxed, even though information flow will still be somewhat guarded.

A person in the authority position is likely to be resisted regardless of what he or she says; and if there is not a designated leader, then there will be resistance to anyone who tries to take charge. Group members complain to one another about the impossible task that the organization has given them or about aspects of the wider organization. Energy for working on the task tends to sag, and, while members begin to cooperate (at least with their new-found allies), there is little planning of task activities.

Sometimes groups in this phase develop a sense of unanimity of purpose and cohesiveness that may, in fact, be phony, based on a tendency to avoid conflict and withhold evaluations.

One danger is that pairings and subgroups form so quickly after people gain some knowledge of one another in Phase 1 that there is a lack of linkages across subgroups. Knowledge of and some linkage with all group members can be most important for pooling resources and resolving the nearly inevitable disagreements and conflicts that typically emerge in Phase 3.

Another danger during Phase 2 is that the subgroups develop spokespersons, so total group discussions are conducted by only a few members, and a pattern of narrow participation is established irrespective of the requirements of the work situation. This, too, can inhibit conflict resolution in Phase 3.

Phase 3—Confrontation

During this stage, relationships between subgroupings come to the fore along with leadership and the handling of disagreement as members seek to influence the direction and operating practices of the group. Struggles for individual power and influence are common. Questions of member roles and division of labor often emerge, along with issues of relative contribution and member evaluation.

Listening is often likely to reach a low ebb, with heated exchanges revealing feelings that may have previously been avoided, suppressed, or denied.

One danger is the temptation to avoid conflict by patching things over prematurely before the issues are fully explored and by establishing norms against rocking the boat or raising controversial subjects. When this happens the disagreements and any associated bad feelings among members go underground, ready to affect future business in often indirect and insidious ways.

A second danger is that disagreement and conflict are dealt with strictly through power, so one individual or one subgroup "wins" and others "lose"; the issue remains unresolved. Someone emerges as a loser, often resulting in either withdrawal or warfare. Withdrawal reduces the group's resources and is hardly a source of satisfaction and growth for the individuals involved. Warfare, which is typically carried over to the next task facing the group, is a sure way to guarantee lowered productivity and energies devoted to attack and self-defense, rather than growth. A third danger is merely a continuation of the struggle and a lack of energy for any new projects.

There is also great opportunity in this phase. When groups are able to resolve differences (whether interpersonal or task-oriented) successfully, the payoff can be immense as the group moves on to Phase 4. Resolution can be accomplished through finding a new, integrative solution, an open discussion of differences leading to clarification of misunderstandings, or the assistance of an outsider in helping the group listen better and improve its process. Success in dealing with disagreement and conflict can build group cohesiveness, members' skills, and confidence in the group's ability to deal with future issues.

Phase 4—Individual Differentiation

During this phase, the issues of division of labor and member evaluation are likely to be dominant. Members begin to become more accepting of differences among themselves, and there emerges a deeper and genuine concern for one another. Task assignments are based on skills, interests, and desires to grow. Roles and status become differentiated, but members respect one another's contributions. Such a division of labor often rests upon a more open, yet supportive, level of member evaluation than existed during the earlier stages. As time progresses and differentiation occurs, this stage may be marked by a kind of euphoria as group members realize that it will be possible to belong to this group without having to fight to the death or totally give in to majority wishes.

The atmosphere during this period is likely to involve cohesion, satisfaction, and trust as a result of having successfully overcome the conflicts of Phase 3 (yet include some underlying tension over the process of member evaluation and differentiation); there is an overall feeling of confidence and progress.

Leadership may have evolved, with one or two individuals having dominant roles, yet without a sense of imposed domination. Instead, members see the pattern as functional. In addition, there is likely to be effective listening,

MANAGERIAL BULLETIN

At Compaq Computers Top Managers Struggle to Make Quality Decisions

To ensure that issues are thoroughly discussed, Canion will take one side and Swavely or Stimac another. The point is to keep the discussion honest, so that the group chooses the best idea—not just the one backed by the highest-ranking executive in the room. In theory, there are no winners or losers, only contributors. "We have to leave our egos at the door," says Swavely. "But we can put any question on the table without fear of being wrong."

SOURCE: "How Compaq Gets There Firstest with the Mostest," *Business Week,* June 26, 1989.

so even the least influential member has the potential to exert influence and, thereby, share leadership.

Phase 5—Collaboration

Too few groups reach this stage. In it, members focus on ways to complement one another's strengths and weaknesses and find that they can honestly level with one another without its leading to disruption. Members support one another when they genuinely agree, and they argue with one another when they genuinely disagree. Responsibility is distributed among members on the basis of individual competence, and leadership passes around the group on the basis of competence to do particular activities. The entire group achieves a cooperative and interdependent relationship with the rest of the organization, providing input to the organization as needed and taking the organization's needs into account when doing work and making decisions. The group learns how to balance individual and group efforts on tasks, allowing individual members to do tasks alone when they have highly differential expertise and doing tasks cooperatively when many opinions and points of view are needed. Learning activities are geared to optimize individual contributions, so each individual can work toward his or her higher potential.

The issue of process is central as the group seeks to maintain the effectiveness developed as a result of its successful progress through the preceding stages. There is always potential need for a group to reexamine its process as it faces new task problems and as members individually grow and develop. Furthermore, as working conditions change, aspects of issues bypassed on the way through the five stages may become important. Consequently, a typical group recycles through aspects of these five phases again and again.

Figure 6–2 outlines typical ways in which the 11 issues facing a group manifest themselves as operating characteristics during the five phases of group development.

FIGURE 6–2 Common Operating Characteristics during Stages of Group Developement

| | STAGES | |
ISSUES	I MEMBERSHIP	II SUBGROUPING
Atmosphere and relationships.	Cautiousness.	Greater closeness within subgroups.
Participation.	Superficial and polite.	In subgroups by subgroup leaders.
Goal understanding and acceptance.	Unclear.	Some greater clarity, but misperceptions likely.
Listening and information sharing.	Intense but high distortion and low sharing.	Within subgroups, similarities overperceived.
Disagreement and conflict.	Not likely to emerge; if it does, will be angry and chaotic.	False unanimity.
Decision making.	Dominated by more active members.	Fragmented, deadlocks.
Evaluation of performance.	Done by all, but not shared.	Across subgroups.
Expression of feelings.	Avoided, suppressed.	Positive only within subgroups, mild "digs" across groupings.
Division of labor.	Little, if any.	Struggles over jobs.
Leadership.	Disjointed.	Resisted.
Attention to process.	Ignored.	Noticed but avoided.

SOURCE: Adapted from Steven L. Obert, "The Development of Organizational Task Groups" (Ph.D. dissertation, Case-Western Reserve University, 1979).

HELPING GROUP MOVEMENT TOWARD GREATER EFFECTIVENESS

We started this chapter by asking how you can tell how well a group is working without waiting for the ultimate outcomes to occur. Implicitly we also were asking what a group could do to improve its way of working. We suggest that you begin by observing the group's emergent system, noting how it has resolved the 11 issues that any group faces, and then evaluating whether that process has been appropriate given the group's situation (size, resources, task, time pressure, and degree of task interdependence). Such a diagnosis sets the stage for taking corrective action if and where it is needed.

In general, the way to move the group along is to pay careful attention to the underlying concerns of group members and then either discuss these directly to allay fears or take actions that will deal with the concerns indirectly. For example, say that a group you are in is having difficulties coming to decisions, because each of three subgroups insists on its own point of view. One approach is to comment on the deadlock, ask if others agree that the struggle is between subgroups each wanting its way, and then talk about how to reach a decision that would not make one or two subgroups feel defeated.

STAGES		
III CONFRONTATION	IV INDIVIDUAL DIFFERENTIATION	V COLLABORATIVE
Close within subgroups, hostility between subgroups.	Confidence and satisfaction.	Supportive and open.
Heated exchanges.	Individuals come in and out based on expertise.	Fluid, people speak freely.
Fought over.	Agreed upon.	Commitment.
Poor.	Fairly good.	Good.
Frequent.	Based on honest differences.	Resolved as it occurs.
Based on power.	Based on individual expertise.	Collective when all resources needed, individual when one expert.
Highly judgmental.	Done as basis for differentiation but with respect.	Open, shared, developmental.
Coming out, anger.	Increasingly open.	Expressed openly.
Differentiation resisted.	High differentiation based on expertise.	Differentiation and integration, as appropriate.
Power struggles common.	Structured or shared.	Shared.
Used as weapon.	Attended to compulsively or too uncritically.	Attended to as appropriate.

The less direct approach might include such suggestions as asking members to restate other's arguments before making their own; proposing that the group divide in half, with each half composed of members from each of the subgroups so that freer discussion might take place; proposing that the group stop trying so hard to decide among the existing alternatives and begin to brainstorm new solutions that might integrate the opposing viewpoints; or arranging a break from task activities, with lots of informal interaction.

All of these steps are designed to allow a group to improve on its emergent processes and to get past a development phase in which it may have become blocked. One caution, however: A group should not try to rush too rapidly through Phases 1 to 4 in the hopes of avoiding all difficulties. Groups need time to develop, and any suggestions you make will be accepted most readily when others feel stuck and want help in moving. Also remember that circumstances change. A periodic reassessment can provide a group with the data by which to insure that its processes continue to serve its goals and objectives.

It is important to note that groups sometimes evolve without direct action by the manager, or in a way not anticipated by the manager, as a result of key events. A crisis forces the group to work long hours and deal with its

---

MANAGERIAL TOOLS

Several Ways Groups Make Decisions; Each Appropriate at Times

1. By the unilateral action of one dominating member or designated chairperson (autocratic).
2. By the unilateral action of a dominant subgroup acting as a power block by imposing its will.
3. By assumption, with silence taken as agreement, a ploy often used by a subgroup to exert dominance.
4. By default (inaction). Inaction is a decision to either stay with the status quo or allow "fate" to decide.
5. By democratic vote (dominance of the majority).
6. By unanimous agreement, perhaps resulting from a thoughtful, open discussion and exchange of ideas.
7. By consensus. *Note*, consensus is not the same as unanimity, in that some members will still not be in agreement even after prolonged discussion; but they will be willing to go along and allow the group to act as most members see appropriate. Such willingness to go along with the majority under true consensus is an outgrowth of those in the minority feeling that their views have been heard, understood, and actively considered, and that the common goals of the group can be served best by action, rather than by further discussion.

---

problems; a higher-level executive comments publicly on the group's performance; a member lets the group down by not delivering what was promised—such critical events, as mentioned previously, can propel a group backward or forward in its development.

By the time you have read this you may have had sufficient experience in a classroom task group to be able to apply the various criteria to your own experience. Can you correlate how well your group has done on group assignments with the way you have been operating? What should you change? What seems to have worked well? Why?

The performance of your group depends on your ability to analyze the task demands, determine the appropriate set of processes, discuss how they vary from what you have been doing, and make whatever changes are neces-

---

THE CITICORP TEAM

On the accomplishment at Citibank that he [Walter B. Wriston, [then] chairman of Citicorp] *is proudest of:* "We've got a management team, a group of people around the world who work together as a team. I didn't do it, but I had a part in it. At the end of a day, that's what makes a difference."

John Brooks
New Yorker
January 5, 1981

sary (consistent with your desires). As awkward as it may feel to discuss openly the way you have been making decisions, talking and listening to one another, handling disagreements, and so forth, it is in your collective interest to do so if you haven't already. The ability to find ways to correct a group's (or organization's, or individual's) process is a crucial one that can serve you well throughout your organizational career.

KEY CONCEPTS FROM CHAPTER 6

1. Group effectiveness related to emergent processes.
2. Process issues faced by every work group:
   a. Atmosphere and relationships.
   b. Member participation.
   c. Goal understanding and acceptance.
   d. Listening and information sharing.
   e. Handling disagreements and conflicts.
   f. Decision making.
   g. Evaluation of member performance.
   h. Expressing feelings.
   i. Work assignments.
   j. Leadership.
   k. Process evaluation.
3. Factors affecting appropriateness of group process:
   a. Size.
   b. Distribution of resources.
   c. Task complexity/diversity.
   d. Time pressure.
   e. Degree of interdependence.
4. The smaller the group, the fewer total resources and the more appropriate is participation by all.
5. The more evenly distributed the resources (expertise), the more appropriate is total member participation.
6. The greater the complexity/diversity, the more resources needed.
7. The greater the time pressure, the less time for process.
8. The greater the task interdependence, the greater the need for continuous exchanges and knowledge of each other on the part of group members.
9. The greater the member participation, the greater the level of commitment to goals.
10. Evaluation of group process needs to be made relative to the group's phase of development. Five phases described:
    a. Membership.
    b. Subgrouping.

    c. Confrontation.
    d. Individual differentiation.
    e. Collaboration.

PERSONAL APPLICATION EXERCISE

The Process Thermometer

The instrument below can be used by all members of a group to assess members' perceptions of how well the group is working together. To use as a group, first, individually check the one space that most closely expresses how you would describe the group on each characteristic. Then, tally the combined perceptions and jointly discuss their implications.

It is also possible to use the instrument for your own personal assessment. Fill it out as you see the group. Next to your ratings, try filling it out with what you would expect to be the *average* response of the rest of your group. Compare your personal score with the "average group score." Where are there differences? What do you think accounts for those differences? Could you talk with your group about your perceptions? Ask them if they agree with your diagnosis? Suggest possible changes in the way your group operates? Initiate a group discussion of how to change the group's processes?

These are all ways of opening discussion that can lead to healthy changes. If the group is willing to all fill out the questionnaire and then discuss the tabulated results, so much the better. But if not, you can still use it for your own diagnosis and action planning.

THE PROCESS THERMOMETER
GROUP SELF-ASSESSMENT QUESTIONNAIRE

		1	2	3	4	5	
1.	*Atmosphere and relationship:*						
	Supportive	___	___	___	___	___	Competitive (self first).
	Personal (warm and close)	___	___	___	___	___	Impersonal (cool and distant).
	Energetic	___	___	___	___	___	Lethargic.
	Cohesive	___	___	___	___	___	Fragmented.
2.	*Member participation:*						
	All equally	___	___	___	___	___	Primarily just a few.
	Easy to get "air time"	___	___	___	___	___	Hard to get "air time."
3.	*Goal understanding and acceptance:*						
	Clear (understood)	___	___	___	___	___	Unclear (vague).
	Supported by all	___	___	___	___	___	Unsupported by many.
4.	*Listening and sharing of information:*						
	Members listen carefully	___	___	___	___	___	Members don't really listen.
	Members usually understand one another	___	___	___	___	___	Members often misinterpret what others say.
	Everyone knows what's going on	___	___	___	___	___	Only a few are "in the know."
5.	*Handling disagreements and conflict:*						
	Alternate views explored	___	___	___	___	___	Alternate views brushed aside.
	Tensions confronted, dealt with	___	___	___	___	___	Tensions avoided.
6.	*Decision making:*						
	Influence is widely shared	___	___	___	___	___	A few exert a lot of influence.
	Reflective of a full discussion	___	___	___	___	___	Quickly by majority rule.
7.	*Evaluation of member performance:*						
	Feedback open and constructive	___	___	___	___	___	Feedback avoided.
8.	*Expressing feelings:*						
	Expressed openly	___	___	___	___	___	Kept bottled up.
	Personal concerns accepted	___	___	___	___	___	Only task concerns allowed.
9.	*Division of labor:*						
	Roles clearly defined and stable	___	___	___	___	___	Roles vary with individual interests.
10.	*Leadership:*						
	A clear leader(s) exists	___	___	___	___	___	Leadership functions (acts) are done by all.
	Member differentiation appropriate and accepted	___	___	___	___	___	Jockeying for position is occurring.
11.	*Attention to process:*						
	Considered legitimate	___	___	___	___	___	Not considered legitimate.
	Process often discussed in the whole group	___	___	___	___	___	Process seldom discussed in the whole group.
12.	*Consequences: The group—*						
	Is very productive	___	___	___	___	___	Is very unproductive.
	Gives me satisfaction	___	___	___	___	___	Gives me little satisfaction.
	Facilitates my learning and development	___	___	___	___	___	Restricts my learning and development.

SUGGESTED READINGS

Albanese, R., and D. D. Van Fleet. "Rational Behavior in Groups: The Free-Riding Tendency." *Academy of Management Review,* April 1985, pp. 244–55.

Argyris, C. "T-Groups for Organizational Effectiveness." *Harvard Business Review* 42 (1964), pp. 60–68.

Bales, R. F. *Interaction Process Analysis.* Reading, Mass.: Addison-Wesley Publishing, 1950.

Bales, R. F., and E. F. Borgatta. "Size of Group as a Factor in the Interaction Profile." In *Small Groups,* ed. A. P. Hare et al. New York: Alfred A. Knopf, 1955.

Bennis, W., and H. Shepard. "A Theory of Group Development." *Human Relations* 9 (1956), pp. 415–37.

Brown, K. A. "Explaining Group Poor Performance: An Attributional Analysis." *Academy of Management Review,* January 1984, pp. 54–63.

Campbell, J., and M. Dunnette. "Effectiveness of T-Group Experiences in Managerial Training Development." *Psychological Bulletin* 70 (1968), pp. 73–103.

Davis, J. H. *Group Performance.* Reading, Mass.: Addison-Wesley Publishing, 1969.

Gersick, C. J. G. "Time and Transition in Work Teams: Toward a New Model of Group Development." *Academy of Management Journal* 31, no. 1 (March 1988), pp. 9–41.

Hackman, J. R., and C. G. Morris. "Improving Groups' Performance Effectiveness." In *Perspectives on Behavior in Organizations,* ed. J. R. Hackman, E. E. Lawler, and L. W. Porter, New York: McGraw-Hill, 1977.

Hart, S.; M. Boroush, G. Enk; and W. Hornick. "Managing Complexity through Consensus Mapping: Technology for the Structuring of Group Decisions." *Academy of Management Review,* July 1985, pp. 587–600.

Heise, G. A., and G. A. Miller. "Problem Solving by Groups Using Various Communication Nets." *Journal of Abnormal Psychology* 46 (1951), pp. 327–35.

Isenberg, D. J. "Some Effects of Time Pressure on Leadership and Decision-Making Accuracy in Small Groups." Unpublished paper, Harvard University, 1979.

Jewell, L. N., and H. J. Reitz. *Group Effectiveness in Organizations.* Glenview, Ill.: Scott, Foresman, 1981.

Krantz, J. "Group Process under Conditions of Organizational Decline." *Journal of Applied Behavioral Science* 21, no. 1 (1985), pp. 1–18.

Luft, J. *Group Processes.* 3rd ed. Palo Alto, Calif.: Mayfield, 1984.

McCann, D., and C. Margerison. "Managing High-Performance Teams." *Training and Development Journal* 43, no. 11 (November 1989), pp. 52–60.

McGregor, D. *The Human Side of Enterprise.* New York: McGraw-Hill, 1960.

Miles, M. B. *Learning to Work in Groups: A Program Guide for Educational Leaders.* New York: Teachers College Press, Teachers College, Columbia University, 1959.

Patton, B. R., and K. Giffin. *Problem-Solving Group Interaction.* New York: Harper & Row, 1973.

Petrock, F. "Five Stages of Group Development." *Executive Excellence* 7, no. 6 (June 1990), pp. 9–10.

Rice, A. K. *Productivity and Social Organization: The Ahmedabad Experiment.* London: Tavistock, 1958.

Rubin, I. M., and R. Beckhard. "Factors Affecting the Effectiveness of Health Teams." *Milbank Quarterly,* July 1972.

Schein, E. *Process Consultation.* Reading, Mass.: Addison-Wesley Publishing, 1969.

Seeger, J. A. "No Innate Phases in Group Problem Solving." *Academy of Management Review,* October 1983, pp. 683–89.

Seta, J. J.; P. B. Paulus; and J. K. Schkade. "Effects of Group Size and Proximity under Cooperative and Competitive Conditions." *Journal of Personality and Social Psychology* 98, no. 2 (1976), pp. 47–53.

Shaw, M. E. *Group Dynamics: The Psychology of Small Group Behavior.* New York: McGraw-Hill, 1981.

Steers, R. J. "Antecedents and Outcomes of Organizational Commitment." *Administrative Science Quarterly* 22 (1977), pp. 46–56.

Tuckman, B. W. "Developmental Sequence in Small Groups." *Psychological Bulletin* 63 (1965), pp. 384–99.

Wanous, J. P.; A. E. Reichers; and S. D. Malik. "Organizational Socialization and Group Development: Toward an Integrative Perspective." *Academy of Management Review,* October 1984, pp. 670–83.

Watson, G. "Resistance to Change." In *The Planning of Change,* ed. Bennis, Benne, and Chin. 2nd ed. New York: Holt, Rinehart & Winston, 1969.

Zander, A. *Making Groups Effective.* San Francisco: Jossey-Bass, 1982.

CHAPTER

18

DECISION-MAKING PROCESSES

| ISSUE FOR DEBATE | *Expert Systems for Business Applications* |

```
┌─┐
  P
  R
  O
└──┘
```

Computers have been tools for making decisions for three decades. Almost all routine, repetitive decisions that deal with quantitative data and that have a definite decision procedure are programmed. The states of a decision, programmed or nonprogrammed, depend very much on whether the decision is "unstructured" or "structured."

When no standard method exists for handling a problem or when its precise nature and structure are elusive or complex, the decision will be unstructured. Highly unstructured decisions are rarely programmed. An unstructured decision might become programmable if data can be quantified, definite decision procedures can be found, and the alternative courses of action are clarified.

Recently, the success of some expert systems has caught the attention of business executives. Expert systems are software systems designed to mimic the way human experts make decisions. In one sense, building expert systems is a form of intellectual cloning. The designer builds into the system a knowledge base and an inference system. The knowledge base is derived from the expert's knowledge and experience in the field. There are two types of knowledge: (1) the facts of domain (widely shared knowledge, commonly agreed upon among practitioners) and (2) heuristic knowledge (the knowledge of good practice and good judgment in a field). The latter is the knowledge that a human expert acquires over years of work.

Expert systems utilize the knowledge base to apply a rational step-by-step structure to corporate decision making. The systems break down problems into a logical progression of specific actions and influences, which is usually represented as a decision or probability tree. Using programmed decision rules, they then generate sequential, optimized decisions based on knowledge provided by many experts. Expert systems enable companies to work faster and on a larger scale. The insurance and credit card industries are examples of sectors where expert systems are beginning to win over corporate converts due to their ability to deal efficiently with "ill-structured problems."

```
┌─┐
  C
  O
  N
└──┘
```

Very few expert systems can be applied to organizational situations. In most cases, such situations involve behavioral variables, which can slow down acceptance of the systems. Also, organizational environments change very rapidly; managers often have to handle the unanticipated. The expert system technology itself, behavioral variables, and other characteristics of managerial decisions all limit development of expert systems for organizational applications.

Consider the frequent need for unstructured decisions. It takes more than experiential knowledge to make such decisions. Unstructured decisions involve decision processes that have not been encountered in quite the same form and for which no predetermined and explicit set of ordered responses exists in the organization. However, expert systems operate according to a set of clearly specified rules. Such systems can't deal with knowledge outside their set of rules and they have a hard time managing even a profusion of rules. It's very unlikely that expert systems for highly unstructured decisions can be built, because experts have insufficient experience to provide relevant knowledge needed for building the knowledge base and set of decision rules in the expert system.

Organizational applications involve consideration of individual needs, perceptions, goals, and values. The heuristic knowledge that leads to good judgment of such human behavior is hard to define, making the task of mining knowledge from a manager's head almost impossible. Managers, experienced in and knowing the great difficulty of making unstructured decisions, will not readily relinquish decision control to a computer that's ill equipped to deal with such problems.

The time may eventually come when researchers are better able to give artificial intelligence machines, such as expert systems, more knowledge to increase their ability to reason and solve ill-structured problems. But until then, managerial decisions will continue to be made by those best equipped to make them, managers themselves.

Source: Sara Humphrey, "Tools Help Objectify Decision Making: Managers Can Quantify Risks, Rewards with Step-by-Step Analysis," *PC Week,* March 9, 1992, pp. 113–15; "Bureaucrats of the Mind—Expert Systems: A Survey of Artificial Intelligence," *The Economist,* March 14, 1992, pp. 611–12; "The Burden of Knowledge: Teaching Expert Systems How to Think," *The Economist,* March 14, 1992, pp. 612–13; Paul B. Deschamps, "Setting Up Expert Systems Failure," *Best's Review—Property Casualty Insurance Edition,* February 1992, pp. 58–61. There is much current debate about how expert systems can be applied. See discussions in *MIS Quarterly, Planning Review, Journal of Systems Management,* and *Information Systems Management.*

This chapter focuses on decision making. The quality of managerial decisions is the yardstick of the manager's effectiveness.[1] Thus, the flow of the preceding chapters leads logically to a discussion of decision making: that is, people behave as *individuals* and as members of *groups,* within an *organizational structure,* and they *communicate* for many reasons. One of the most important reasons is to make decisions. As the Issue for Debate notes, making effective decisions can be a complex process, relying on all the skills and training a manager possesses. This chapter, therefore, analyzes decision making in terms of how people decide as a consequence of the information they receive both through the organization structure and through the behavior of important persons and groups.

■ TYPES OF DECISIONS

While managers in various organizations may be separated by background, life-style, and distance, sooner or later they must all make decisions.[2] As discussed throughout this book, debate continues on whether managers should encourage subordinates to participate in decision making.[3] Likewise, depending on the organization's size and overall technical complexity, opportunities to involve subordinates in the decision process may vary.[4] However, regardless of

[1]Bernard M. Bass, *Organizational Decision Making* (Homewood, Ill.: Richard D. Irwin, 1983).

[2]Danny Samson, *Managerial Decision Making* (Homewood, Ill.: Richard D. Irwin, 1988).

[3]See John L. Cotton, David A. Vollrath, and Kirk L. Froggatt, "Employee Participation: Diverse Forms and Different Outcomes," *Academy of Management Review,* January 1988, pp. 8–22.

[4]Patrick E. Connor, "Decision-Making Participation Patterns: The Role of Organizational Context," *Academy of Management Journal,* March 1992, pp. 218–31.

organizational variations and the degree of employee participation, managers are ultimately responsible for decision outcomes. That is, they face a situation involving several alternatives, and their decision involves a comparison of alternatives and an evaluation of the outcome. In this section, we move beyond a general definition of a decision and present a system for classifying various decisions.

Specialists in decision making have developed several ways of classifying decisions. Similar for the most part, these systems differ mainly in terminology. We shall use the widely adopted system suggested by Herbert Simon.[5] It distinguishes between two types of decisions: programmed and nonprogrammed decisions.

PROGRAMMED DECISIONS

Specific procedures developed for repetitive and routine problems.

NONPROGRAMMED DECISIONS

Decisions required by unique and complex management problems.

1. **Programmed decisions**. If a particular situation occurs often, a routine procedure usually can be worked out for solving it. Thus, decisions are *programmed* to the extent that problems are repetitive and routine and a definite procedure has been developed for handling them.

2. **Nonprogrammed decisions**. Decisions are *nonprogrammed* when they are novel and unstructured. No established procedure exists for handling the problem, either because it has not arisen in exactly the same manner before or because it is complex or extremely important. Such problems deserve special treatment.

These two classifications, while broad, make important distinctions. On one hand, organization managers face great numbers of programmed decisions in their daily operations. Such decisions should be treated without expending unnecessary organizational resources on them. On the other hand, nonprogrammed decisions must be properly identified as such, since they form the basis for allocating billions of dollars of resources in our economy every year. Table 18.1 breaks down the different types of decisions, with examples of each type in different organizations. It indicates that programmed and nonprogrammed decisions apply to distinctly different problems and require different procedures.

Unfortunately, we know very little about the human process involved in unprogrammed decisions.[6] Traditionally, to make programmed decisions, managers use rules, standard operating procedures, and the structure of the organization that develops specific procedures for handling problems. More recently, operations researchers have facilitated such decisions through the development of mathematical models. In contrast, managers make nonprogrammed decisions by general problem-solving processes, judgment, intuition and creativity.[7] Informal relationships between managers, as well as formal ones, may be utilized to handle such ambiguous problems.[8] For example, a number of studies have suggested that Japanese organizations can be highly effective at

[5]Herbert A. Simon, *The New Science of Management Decision* (New York: Harper & Row, 1960), pp. 5–6.

[6]Neil M. Agnew and John L. Brown, "Executive Judgment: The Intuition/Rational Ratio," *Personnel,* December 1985, pp. 48–54.

[7]Stephen D. Brookfield, *Developing Critical Thinkers: Challenging Adults to Explore Alternative Ways of Thinking* (San Francisco: Jossey-Bass, 1987).

[8]William B. Stevenson and Mary C. Gilly, "Information Processing and Problem Solving: The Migration of Problems through Formal Positions and Networks of Ties," *Academy of Management Journal,* March 1991, pp. 918–28.

	Programmed Decisions	Nonprogrammed Decisions
Problem	Frequent, repetitive, routine. Much certainty regarding cause and effect relationships.	Novel, unstructured. Much uncertainty regarding cause and effect relationships.
Procedure	Dependence on policies, rules, and definite procedures.	Necessity for creativity, intuition, tolerance for ambiguity, creative problem solving.
Examples:		
Business firm	Periodic reorders of inventory.	Diversification into new products and markets.
University	Necessary grade point average for good academic standing.	Construction of new classroom facilities.
Health care	Procedure for admitting patients.	Purchase of experimental equipment.
Government	Merit system for promotion of state employees.	Reorganization of state government agencies.

TABLE 18 • 1

COMPARISON OF TYPES OF DECISIONS

processing information and taking action by relying on unplanned interaction around problems rather than on formal procedures and problem solvers. To date, the advances in modern management techniques haven't improved nonprogrammed decision making nearly as much as they've improved programmed decision making.[9]

Ideally, top management's main concern should be nonprogrammed decisions, while first-level managers should be concerned with programmed decisions. Middle managers in most organizations concentrate mostly on programmed decisions, although in some cases they participate in nonprogrammed decisions. In other words, the nature, frequency, and degree of certainty surrounding a problem should dictate at what level of management the decision should be made.

Obviously, problems arise in organizations where top management expends much time and effort on programmed decisions. One unfortunate result is a neglect of long-range planning. It's subordinated to other activities whether the organization is successful or is having problems. Success justifies continuing the policies and practices that achieved it; if the organization experiences difficulty, its current problems have first priority and occupy the time of top management. In either case, long-range planning ends up being neglected. Neglect of long-range planning usually results in an overemphasis on short-run control and, therefore, less delegation of authority to lower levels of management. This often has adverse effects on employee motivation and satisfaction. The Close-Up, "Even the Japanese Make Mistakes," describes pitfalls associated with making improper decisions.

---

[9]Weston Agor, "The Logic of Intuition: How Top Executives Make Important Decisions," *Organizational Dynamics,* Winter 1986, pp. 5–18.

EVEN THE JAPANESE MAKE MISTAKES

For those who think Japanese auto makers never make a wrong decision, the problems at Nissan Motor Company, Japan's number 2 auto maker, will come as a shock. The Japanese are acute judges of ever-shifting consumer demands, right? Not Nissan—it hasn't listened carefully to its customers, missing changes in their needs and failing to serve vital market segments with products such as family sedans and minivans.

And do the Japanese carefully nurture their brand names, building their aura slowly and steadily for the long term? Not Nissan. Starting with a misguided name change in 1981, a series of marketing missteps and lurching shifts in positioning have left it without a consistent image.

And you say the Japanese hone in on export markets with fierce concentration? That they're superefficient manufacturers? That their collaborative style makes for friction-free management and pacifist labor relations? Not Nissan. It hasn't paid enough attention to its most important export market, the United States, where a lackluster dealer network has hurt sales. While quality remains on a par with the best of its peers, Nissan's productivity lags and its costs are high. Having all but ignored the vaunted Japanese consensus management approach, it has suffered internal power squabbles and labor clashes.

Twenty years ago, Nissan was poised for greatness. With the sporty Datsun 240Z defining it as Japan's most exciting car maker, Nissan surged past Volks-

wagen in 1975 as the number 1 importer to the United States. But after a series of mishaps and poor decisions made by managers, Nissan lost its traction and now faces the scenario just described. From 1980 to 1992, its U.S. market share slid from 5.5 percent to 4.7 percent while Japan's overall share grew from 17.7 percent to 28.5 percent. Its profits have also steadily deteriorated. Nissan must now scratch to come up with the funds it needs to keep investing in technology, new products, and improved marketing.

But Japan bashers shouldn't get too confident, for American auto makers have made more than their share of recent mistakes. A primary example is the decision in 1988 by then Chrysler CEO Lee Iacocca to delay revamping one of his company's two most profitable lines, the Jeep Cherokee. By deciding to solely focus redesign efforts on its minivan line, Chrysler lost momentum in the very profitable off-road vehicle market. Worse yet, during Chrysler's idle time, Ford introduced its Explorer, which has since cut sharply into Jeep sales. This wrong decision ended up costing Chrysler approximately $365 million a year in lost profits up until 1992, when a new version of the Jeep finally made its way to market.

Source: "Will Nissan Get It Right This Time," *Business Week*, April 20, 1992, pp. 82–87; Joanne Lipman, "Nissan Changes Its Tune," *The Wall Street Journal*, August 25, 1992, p. B6; Clay Chandler, "A Troubled Nissan Seeks to Cooperate With Toyota," *The Asian Wall Street Journal Weekly*, May 25, 1992, p. 12; James B. Treece, "Does Chrysler Finally Have the Jeep That It Needs?" *Business Week*, January 20, 1992, pp. 84–85.

■ THE DECISION-MAKING PROCESS

DECISION

Means to achieve some result or to solve some problem; outcome of a process influenced by many forces.

Decisions should be thought of as *means* rather than ends. They are the *organizational mechanisms* by which an attempt is made to achieve a desired state. They are, in effect, an *organizational response* to a problem. Every decision is the outcome of a dynamic process that is influenced by a multitude of forces. Although this process is diagrammed in Figure 18.1, it is not a fixed procedure. It is a sequential process rather than a series of steps.[10] This enables us to examine each element in the normal progression that leads to a decision.

[10]Paul C. Nutt, "Types of Organizational Decision Processes," *Administrative Science Quarterly*, September 1984, pp. 414–50; S. Pokras, *Strategic Problem Solving and Decision Making* (Los Altos, Calif.: Crisp, 1989).

FIGURE 18 • 1

THE DECISION-MAKING PROCESS

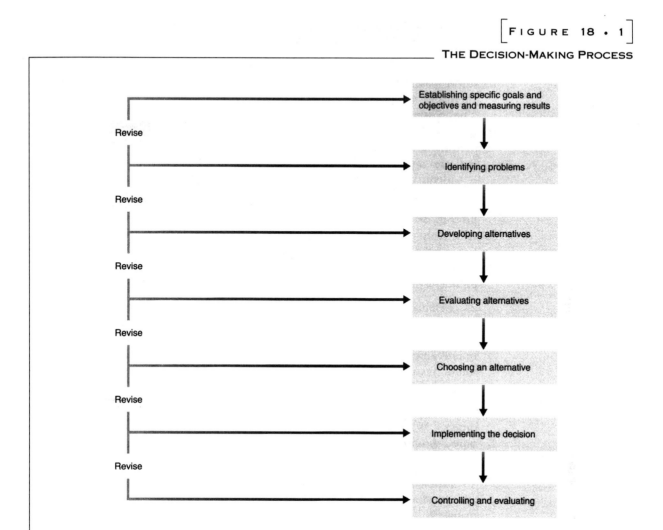

Figure 18.1 applies more to nonprogrammed decisions than to programmed decisions. Problems that occur infrequently, with a great deal of uncertainty surrounding the outcome, require that the manager utilize the entire process. For problems that occur frequently, the entire process is not necessary. If a policy is established to handle such problems, managers don't need to develop and evaluate alternatives each time a problem of this kind arises.

Establishing Specific Goals and Objectives and Measuring Results

Organizations need goals and objectives in each area where performance influences effectiveness. Adequately established goals and objectives will dictate which results must be achieved and which measures indicate whether those results have been achieved.

Identifying Problems

A necessary condition for a decision is a problem.[11] That is, if problems did not exist, there would be no need for decisions. The decision maker is a problem solver, charged with either selecting from available alternatives or inventing an alternative different in meaningful ways from previously existing alternatives.[12] The existence of a problem is indicated by a gap between the organization's goals and objectives and the levels of actual performance. Thus, a gap of 20 percent between a sales volume objective and sales volume actually achieved indicates a problem.

Identifying the exact problem can be hindered by certain factors:

1. *Perceptual problems.* As noted in Chapter 4, our individual perceptions may protect or defend us from unpleasant facts. Negative information may be selectively perceived to distort its true meaning; it may also be totally ignored. For example, a college dean may fail to identify increasing class sizes as a problem while at the same time being sensitive to problems faced by the president of the university in raising funds for the school.

2. *Defining problems in terms of solutions.* This is really a form of jumping to conclusions. For example, a sales manager may say, "The decrease in profits is due to our poor product quality," which suggests a particular solution: the improvement of product quality in the production department. Certainly, other solutions may be possible. Perhaps the sales force has been inadequately selected or trained. Perhaps competitors have a less expensive product.

3. *Identifying symptoms as problems.* "Our problem is a 32 percent decline in orders." While it is certainly true that orders have declined, the decline is really only a symptom of the true problem. The manager must identify the *cause* of the decline in orders to find the real problem.

Problems are usually of three types: opportunity, crisis, and routine. Crisis and routine problems present themselves and must be attended to by the managers.[13] Opportunities, in contrast, must usually be found; they await discovery. Often, they go unnoticed and are eventually lost by an inattentive manager. Because most crises and routine problems, by their very nature, demand immediate attention, a manager may spend a great deal of time handling them and not have time to pursue important new opportunities. Many well-managed organizations try to draw attention away from crises and routine problems and toward longer-range issues through planning activities and goal-setting programs.

Developing Alternatives

Before a decision is made, feasible alternatives (potential solutions to the problem) should be developed, and the possible consequences of each alterna-

---

[11]Russell L. Ackoff, *The Art of Problem Solving* (New York: John Wiley & Sons, 1987).

[12]Allen R. Solem, "Some Applications of Problem-Solving versus Decision-Making to Management," *Journal of Business and Psychology,* Spring 1992, pp. 401–11.

[13]Dean Tjosvold, "Effects of Crisis Orientation on Managers' Approach to Controversy in Decision Making," *Academy of Management Journal,* March 1984, pp. 130–38.

tive should be considered. For example, a sales manager may identify an inadequately trained sales force as the cause of declining sales. The sales manager would then identify possible alternatives for solving the problem, such as (1) a sales training program conducted at the home office by management, (2) a sales training program conducted by a professional training organization at a site away from the home office, and (3) more intense on-the-job training.

Developing alternatives is really a search process in which the relevant internal and external environments of the organization are investigated to provide information that can be developed into possible alternatives. Obviously, this search is conducted within certain time and cost constraints; only so much effort can be devoted to developing alternatives.[14]

However, sufficient effort should be made to develop a wide range of alternatives. Contrary to what you might think, there's a positive link between the number of alternatives considered and the speed with which decisions can be reached.[15] Not generating enough detailed and varied alternatives can actually wind up costing both time and resources, the very commodities organizations seek to conserve. One means to broaden the development of alternatives is by cultivating creativity. The Close-Up, "Enhancing Creative Decision Making," examines this issue.

Evaluating Alternatives

Once alternatives have been developed, they must be evaluated and compared. In every decision situation, the objective in making a decision is to select the alternative that will produce the most favorable outcomes and the least unfavorable outcomes. This again points up the need for objectives and goals. In selecting among alternatives, the decision maker should be guided by previously established goals and objectives. The alternative–outcome relationship is based on three possible conditions:

1. *Certainty.* The decision maker has complete knowledge of the probability of the outcome of each alternative.

2. *Uncertainty.* The decision maker has absolutely no knowledge of the probability of the outcome of each alternative.

3. *Risk.* The decision maker has some probabilistic estimate of the outcomes of each alternative.

Decision making under conditions of risk is probably the most common situation.[16] It is in evaluating alternatives under these conditions that statisticians and operations researchers have made important contributions to decision making. Their methods have proved especially useful in the analysis and ranking of alternatives.

[14]Paul Shrivastava, "Knowledge Systems for Strategic Decision Making," *Journal of Applied Behavioral Science,* Winter 1985, pp. 95–108.

[15]William Q. Judge and Alex Miller, "Antecedents and Outcomes of Decision Speed in Different Environmental Contexts," *Academy of Management Journal,* June 1991, pp. 449–63.

[16]Kenneth R. MacCrimmon and Donald A. Wehrung, *The Management of Uncertainty: Taking Risks* (New York: Free Press, 1986).

C L O S E - U P

ENHANCING CREATIVE DECISION MAKING

While dreaming and believing have a lot to do with being creative, creative decision making is a skill that can be learned and developed. Just as playing tennis makes a tennis player better, practicing creative skills results in more creativity. Executives are discovering this as they cultivate creativity daily.

The first step to being creative is to get rid of your unwritten rules. Many managers sit at their desks with pads and pens when they're ready to be creative. In reality, a walk in the park or a trip to a kids' toy store more quickly stimulates thought. In addition to getting out of their own way, here are some other tips for managers wishing to become more creative.

1. Be childlike. This perhaps is the most important tip of all because creativity seems to be connected with age. The California Raisin Advisory Board let itself be childlike when it approved the phenomenally successful concept of raisins dancing to "I Heard It through the Grapevine."

2. Be a maverick. The best ideas and decisions often come from people who don't care what other people are thinking or how they're doing things. Pringles hired creative problem solver William J. Gordon to devise a way to pack potato chips more tightly without crushing them. Someone in Gordon's creative group mentioned potato chips are like dried leaves—they crumble when crushed together. Wet leaves, however, can be packed tightly. Thus, the answer to packing chips more tightly: Shape and press potato slices together during packaging rather than after.

3. Sit on the other side of the desk. It's difficult to have new ideas if you're doing things the same way every day. The more often a manager breaks her routine, the more likely she is to have new ideas.

4. Be like Hewlett-Packard. Hewlett-Packard ran an advertising campaign with the theme "What if . . ." Asking "What if . . . ?" is an excellent way for a manager to stimulate thought in order to make better decisions.

5. Listen to others. A manager shouldn't have to feel it's his responsibility to develop the answer to each and every problem. It takes hundreds of bad ideas to come up with a good one. Therefore, the more ideas the better. At Southern California Edison, all employees are encouraged to speak up and assist managers in best determining how the business is to be run.

Source: Mary M. Byers, "Cultivating Creativity," *Association Management,* January 1992, pp. 35–37; Michael R. Peevey, "Transforming Organizational Structure," *Executive Speeches,* January 1992, pp. 6–9; Victor M. Parachin, "Seven Ways to Fire Up Your Creativity," *Supervision,* January 1992, pp. 3–4.

Pringles hired creative problem solver William J. Gordon to devise a way to pack chips without crushing them.

© Nicholas Communications, Inc.

Choosing an Alternative

The purpose in selecting an alternative is to solve a problem to achieve a predetermined objective. This point is an important one. It means that a decision is not an end in itself but only a means to an end. While the decision maker chooses the alternative that is expected to result in achieving the objective, the selection of that alternative should not be seen as an isolated act. If it is, the factors that led to and lead from the decision are likely to be excluded. Specifically, the steps following the decision should include implementation, control, and evaluation. The critical point is that decision making is more than an act of choosing; it is a dynamic process.

Unfortunately for most managers, an alternative rarely achieves the desired objective without having some positive or negative impact on another objective. Situations often exist where two objectives cannot be fully achieved simultaneously. If one objective is *optimized,* the other is *suboptimized.* For example, if production in a business is optimized, employee morale may be suboptimized, or vice versa. A hospital superintendent may optimize a short-run objective such as maintenance costs at the expense of a long-run objective such as high-quality patient care. Thus, the multiplicity of organizational objectives complicates the real world of the decision maker.

In certain situations, an organizational objective may also be at the expense of a societal objective. This is clear in the rise of ecology groups, environmentalists, and the consumerist movement. Apparently, these groups question the priorities (organizational as against societal) of certain organizational decision makers. In any case, whether an organizational objective conflicts with another organizational objective or with a societal objective, the values of the decision maker strongly influence the alternative chosen. Individual values were discussed earlier, and their influence on the decision-making process should be clear.

In managerial decision making, optimal solutions are often impossible. The decision maker cannot possibly know all of the available alternatives, the consequences of each alternative, and the probability of these consequences occurring.[17] Thus, rather than being an optimizer, the decision maker is a *satisficer,* selecting the alternative that meets an acceptable (satisfactory) standard.

Implementing the Decision

Any decision that is not implemented is little more than an abstraction. In other words, a decision must be effectively implemented to achieve the objective for which it was made. It is entirely possible for a "good" decision to be hurt by poor implementation. In this sense, implementation may be more important than the actual choice of the alternative.

In most situations, implementing decisions involves people, so the test of a decision's soundness is the behavior of the people affected by the decision. Subordinates can't be manipulated in the same manner as other resources. A technically sound decision can easily be undermined by dissatisfied subordinates. Thus, a manager's job is not only to choose good solutions but also to transform

[17]Paul Shrivastava and I. I. Mitroff, "Enhancing Organizational Research Utilization: The Role of Decision Makers' Assumptions," *Academy of Management Review,* January 1984, pp. 18–26.

such solutions into behavior in the organization. This is done by effectively communicating with the appropriate individuals and groups.[18]

Control and Evaluation

Effective management involves periodic measurement of results. Actual results are compared with planned results (the objective), and changes must be made if deviations exist. Here again, we see the importance of measurable objectives. Without them, there is no way to judge performance. Changes, if necessary, must be made in the solution chosen, in its implementation, or in the original objective if it is deemed unattainable. If the original objective must be revised, then the entire decision-making process is reactivated. The important point is that once a decision is implemented, a manager cannot assume that the outcome will meet the original objective. Some system of control and evaluation is needed to make sure the actual results are consistent with the results planned for when the decision was made.

■ BEHAVIORAL INFLUENCES ON INDIVIDUAL DECISION MAKING

Several behavioral factors influence the decision-making process. Some affect only certain aspects of the process, while others influence the entire process. However, each may have an impact and therefore must be understood to fully appreciate the decision-making process in organizations. Four individual behavioral factors—values, personality, propensity for risk, and potential for dissonance—are discussed in this section. Each has a significant impact on the decision-making process.

Values

> **VALUES**
>
> Basic guidelines and beliefs that a decision maker uses when confronted with a situation requiring choice.

In the context of decision making, **values** are the guidelines a person uses when confronted with a situation in which a choice must be made. Values are acquired early in life and are a basic (often taken for granted) part of an individual's thoughts. Values' influence on the decision-making process is profound:

In *establishing objectives,* value judgments must be made regarding the selection of opportunities and the assignment of priorities.

In *developing alternatives,* value judgments about the various possibilities are necessary.

In *choosing an alternative,* the values of the decision maker influence which alternative is chosen.

In *implementing a decision,* value judgments are necessary in choosing the means for implementation.

---

[18]Charles R. Schwenk, *The Essence of Strategic Decision Making* (Lexington, Mass.: Lexington Books, 1988).

In the *control* and *evaluation* phase, value judgments cannot be avoided when corrective action is decided on and taken.

Clearly, values pervade the decision-making process, encompassing not only the individual's economic and legal responsibilities but his ethical responsibilities as well.[19] They're reflected in the decision maker's behavior before making the decision, in making the decision, and in putting the decision into effect.[20]

Personality

Decision makers are influenced by many psychological forces, both conscious and subconscious. One of the most important of these forces is personality. Decision makers' personalities are strongly reflected in their choices. Studies that have examined the effect of personality on the process of decision making have generally focused on three types of variables:[21]

1. *Personality variables*—the attitudes, beliefs, and needs of the individual.

2. *Situational variables*—external, observable situations in which individuals find themselves.

3. *Interactional variables*—the individual's momentary state that results from the interaction of a specific situation with characteristics of the individual's personality.

The most important conclusions concerning the influence of personality on the decision-making process are:

- One person is not likely to be equally proficient in all aspects of the decision-making process. Some people do better in one part of the process, while others do better in another part.

- Such characteristics as intelligence are associated with different phases of the decision-making process.

- The relationship of personality to the decision-making process may vary for different groups on the basis of such factors as sex and social status.

- Individuals facing important and ambiguous decisions may be influenced heavily by peers' opinions.

An interesting study examined the importance of cultural influences on decision-making style differences between Japanese and Australian college

[19]Kelly C. Strong and G. Dale Meyer, "An Integrative Descriptive Model of Ethical Decision Making," *Journal of Business Ethics,* September 1992, pp. 89–94.

[20]Linda Klebe Trevino, "Ethical Decision Making in Organizations: A Person–Situation Interactional Model," *Academy of Management Review,* July 1986, pp. 601–17.

[21]P. A. Renwick and H. Tosi, "The Effects of Sex, Marital Status, and Educational Background on Selected Decisions," *Academy of Management Journal,* March 1978, pp. 93–103; A. A. Abdel-Halim, "Effects of Task and Personality Characteristics on Subordinate Responses to Participative Decision Making," *Academy of Management Journal,* September 1983, pp. 477–84. For an interesting cross-cultural study, see Frank Heller, Peter Drenth, Paul Koopman, and Veljko Rus, *Decisions in Organizations: A Three Country Comparative Study* (Newbury Park, Calif.: Sage, 1988).

students.[22] In Japan, a group orientation exists, while in Australia, the common cultural pattern emphasizes an individual orientation. The results confirmed the importance of the cultural influence. Japanese students reported greater use of decision processes or behaviors associated with the involvement and influence of others, while Australian students reported greater use of decision processes associated with self-reliance and personal ability.

In general, the personality traits of the decision maker combine with certain situational and interactional variables to influence the decision-making process. The accompanying Close-Up tells how one manager's personality significantly impacts his decision-making style.

Propensity for Risk

From personal experience, we're all undoubtedly aware that decision makers vary greatly in their propensity for taking risks. This one specific aspect of personality strongly influences the decision-making process. A decision maker with a low aversion to risk establishes different objectives, evaluates alternatives differently, and selects different alternatives from a decision maker in the same situation who has a high aversion to risk. The latter attempts to make choices where the risk or uncertainty is low or where the certainty of the outcome is high. As we'll discuss later in the chapter, many people are bolder and more innovative and advocate greater risk taking in groups than as individuals. Apparently, such people are more willing to accept risk as members of a group.

Potential for Dissonance

Much attention has focused on the forces that influence the decision maker before a decision is made and that impact the decision itself. Only recently has attention been given to what happens after a decision has been made. Specifically, behavioral scientists have focused attention on *postdecision anxiety.*

┌─ COGNITIVE DISSONANCE ─┐
Anxiety that occurs when there is conflict between an individual's beliefs and reality. Most individuals are motivated to reduce dissonance and achieve consonance.
└────────────────────────┘

Such anxiety is related to what Leon Festinger called **cognitive dissonance** over 35 years ago.[23] Festinger's theory states that there is often a lack of consistency, or harmony, among an individual's various cognitions (attitudes, beliefs, etc.) after a decision has been made. As a result, the decision maker has doubts and second thoughts about the choice. In addition, the intensity of the anxiety is likely to be greater in the presence of any of the following conditions:

1. The decision is psychologically or financially important.

2. There are a number of forgone alternatives.

3. The forgone alternatives have many favorable features.

Dissonance can, of course, be reduced by admitting that a mistake has been made. Unfortunately, many individuals are reluctant to admit that they've made

[22]Mark H. Radford, Leon Mann, Yasuyuki Ohta, and Yoshibumi Nakane, "Differences between Australian and Japanese Students in Reported Use of Decision Processes," *International Journal of Psychology,* vol. 26, no. 1, 1991, pp. 35–52.

[23]Leon Festinger, *A Theory of Cognitive Dissonance* (New York: Harper & Row, 1957), chap. 1.

A Fiery Decision Maker

To be an effective decision maker, sometimes you have to ruffle feathers. At Procter & Gamble, Chairman Edwin L. Artzt is characterized as a hard taskmaster. Managers at P&G have learned that their chairman doesn't play by the same genteel rules as his predecessors. Gone for the moment is the notion of low-profile, gray-suited leadership at the consumer products giant. Artzt wants results. If he thinks he'll get them by tweaking a manager in front of her peers, that manager had better watch out.

At a recent management dinner, Artzt wanted his top executives to stand for a moment so they could be introduced to their fellow managers. After going through many of the introductions, Artzt began looking for his executive vice president in charge of P&G's struggling food and beverage operations. Artzt finally spied the manager in the back of the room. Artzt then quipped, "I guess you can tell people's business results by where they're sitting."

Artzt aims to build a tougher, faster, more global P&G. To do this, he is promoting individual decision making and accountability—turning back the clock from the team approach of recent years. He has overhauled P&G's corporate training program in favor of a squash-the-competition version. And he is demanding that managers consistently beat the competition to market with the latest detergents, face creams, and diapers. Artzt sees lightning-quick re-

flexes as essential at a time when P&G's rivals are globalizing, streamlining, and investing in innovation. Vows Artzt, "We are going to make a quantum leap in the quality and speed of our execution."

While many inside the company feel Artzt is pushing his agenda too hard in a fashion most unlike P&G, outside analysts insist his actions make sense. P&G is embroiled in an increasingly fierce competitive battle on many fronts with formidable competitors. For example, Nestlé is giving P&G's Folgers coffee a run for its money by expanding its Hills Bros. brand into new markets. In bar soap, Lever is soaking its Lever 2000 brand with ad dollars, drowning P&G's Safeguard. All this is coming at a time when many experts feel traditional brands are losing much equity as consumers become more and more price-conscious.

Amid this upheaval, Artzt is upbeat. He maintains that his restyled personal approach is winning over employees and that his actions are beginning to pay off. Artzt says, "When all the smoke clears, people are going to say, 'Pretty damned good result.'" He may be right. But in the meantime, the smoke at P&G is getting thick.

Source: Terry Lofton, "Artzt's Gamble," *Adweek's Marketing Week,* February 17, 1992, pp. 28–29; Zachary Schiller, "No More Mr. Nice Guy at P&G—Not by a Long Shot," *Business Week,* February 3, 1992, pp. 54–56; Cyndee Miller, "Moves by P&G, Heinz Rekindle Fears That Brands Are in Danger," *Marketing News,* June 8, 1992, pp. 1, 15.

a wrong decision. These individuals are more likely to reduce their dissonance by using one or more of the following methods:

1. Seek information that supports the wisdom of their decisions.

2. Selectively perceive (distort) information in a way that supports their decisions.

3. Adopt a less favorable view of the forgone alternatives.

4. Minimize the importance of the negative aspects of the decisions and exaggerate the importance of the positive aspects.

While each of us may resort to some of this behavior in our personal decision making, a great deal of such behavior could easily harm organizational effectiveness.

Personality, specifically the level of self-confidence and persuasibility, heavily influences potential for dissonance. In fact, all of the behavioral influences are closely interrelated and are only isolated here for purposes of discussion.[24]

■ GROUP DECISION MAKING

Until now, this chapter has focused on individuals making decisions. In most organizations, however, a great deal of decision making is achieved through committees, teams, task forces, and other groups. Managers frequently face situations in which they must seek and combine judgments in group meetings. This is especially true for nonprogrammed problems, which are novel and involve much uncertainty regarding the outcome. In most organizations, decisions on such problems are rarely made by one individual on a regular basis. The increased complexity of many of these problems requires specialized knowledge in numerous fields, knowledge usually not possessed by one person. This requirement, coupled with the reality that the decisions made must eventually be accepted and implemented by many units throughout the organization, has increased the use of the collective approach to the decision-making process. As a result, many managers spend as much as 80 percent of their working time in committee meetings.

In addition to interorganizational meetings, managers are increasingly being called upon to participate in collaborative efforts between organizations.[25] Collaboration involves "a process of joint decision-making among key stakeholders of a problem domain about the future of that domain."[26] Managers participate in many forms of collaborative decision-making efforts, including those that involve dealings with other for-profit organizations and those that consist of partnering with nonprofit or government organizations. Some collaborations concentrate on advancing a shared decision among stakeholders, some focus on solving specific problems, and others are directed toward resolving conflicts among stakeholders.

Individual versus Group Decision Making

Considerable debate has taken place over the relative effectiveness of individual versus group decision making. Groups usually take more time to reach a decision than individuals do, but bringing specialists and experts together has benefits, since the mutually reinforcing impact of their interaction results in better

[24]J. Richard Harrison and James C. March, "Decision Making and Postdecision Surprises," *Administrative Science Quarterly,* March 1984, pp. 26–42. Also see James C. March, *Decisions and Organizations* (New York: Basil Blackwell, 1988).

[25]Jeanne M. Logsdon, "Interests and Interdependence in the Formation of Social Problem-Solving Collaborations," *Journal of Applied Behavioral Science,* March 1991, pp. 23–37.

[26]For examples, see B. Gray, *Collaborating: Finding Common Ground for Multi-Party Problems* (San Francisco: Jossey-Bass, 1989).

decisions. In fact, a great deal of research has shown that consensus decisions with five or more participants are superior to individual, majority vote, and leader decisions.[27]

Unfortunately, open discussion can be negatively influenced by behavioral factors, such as the pressure to conform. Such pressure may be the influence of a dominant personality in the group; or "status incongruity" may cause lower-status participants to be inhibited by higher-status participants and to "go along" even though they believe that their own ideas are superior; or certain participants may attempt to exert influence based on the perception that they are experts in the problem area.[28]

This perception of expertise also inhibits group consideration of outside assistance. Group members may show a negative bias toward advice and guidance given by nongroup members, regardless of value, preferring instead to consider only internally generated solutions to problems.[29]

Certain decisions appear to be better made by groups, while others appear better suited to individual decision making. Nonprogrammed decisions appear to be better suited to group decision making. Such decisions usually call for pooled talent in arriving at a solution; also, the decisions are so important that they are usually made by top managers and to a somewhat lesser extent by middle managers.

In terms of the decision-making process itself, the following points concerning group processes for nonprogrammed decisions can be made:

1. In *establishing objectives,* groups are probably superior to individuals because of the greater amount of knowledge available to groups.

2. In *identifying alternatives,* the individual efforts of group members encourage a broad search in various functional areas of the organization.

3. In *evaluating alternatives,* the collective judgment of the group, with its wider range of viewpoints, seems superior to that of the individual decision maker.

4. In *choosing an alternative,* group interaction and the achievement of consensus usually result in the acceptance of more risk than would be accepted by an individual decision maker. Also, the group decision is more likely to be accepted as a result of the participation of those affected by its consequences.

5. *Implementing a decision,* whether or not it was made by a group, is usually accomplished by individual managers. Thus, individuals bear responsibility for implementing the group's decision.

[27]For examples, see Barry M. Staw, "The Escalation of Commitment to a Course of Action," *Academy of Management Review,* October 1981, pp. 577–88; Max H. Bazerman and Alan Appelman, "Escalation of Commitment in Individual and Group Decision Making," *Organizational Behavior and Human Decision Processes,* Spring 1984, pp. 141–52; Barbara Bird, "Implementing Entrepreneurial Ideas: The Case for Intention," *Academy of Management Review,* July 1988, pp. 442–53; Warren E. Watson, Larry K. Michaelsen, and Walt Sharp, "Member Competence, Group Interaction, and Group Decision-Making: A Longitudinal Study," *Journal of Applied Psychology,* December 1991, pp. 803–9.

[28]Richard A. Guzzo and James A. Waters, "The Expression of Affect and the Performance of Decision Making Groups," *Journal of Applied Psychology,* February 1982, pp. 67–74; Dean Tjosvold and R. H. G. Field, "Effects of Social Context on Consensus and Majority Vote Decision Making," *Academy of Management Journal,* September 1983, pp. 500–6; Fredrick C. Miner, Jr., "Group versus Individual Decision Making: An Investigation of Performance Measures, Decision Strategies, and Process Losses/Gains," *Organizational Behavior and Human Decision Processes,* Winter 1984, pp. 112–24.

[29]Diane M. Mackie, M. Cecilia Gastardo-Conaco, and John J. Skelly, "Knowledge of the Advocated Position and the Processing of In-Group and Out-Group Persuasive Messages," *Personality and Social Psychology Bulletin,* April 1992, pp. 145–51.

Figure 18.2 summarizes the research findings on group decision making. It shows the probable relationship between the quality of a decision and the method utilized to reach the decision. It indicates that as we move from individual to consensus decision making, the quality of the decision improves. Also, each successive method involves a higher level of mutual influence by group members. Thus, for a complex problem requiring pooled knowledge, the quality of the decision is likely to be higher as the group moves toward consensus.

Techniques for Stimulating Creativity in Group Decision Making

Because groups are better suited than individuals to making nonprogrammed decisions, an atmosphere fostering group creativity should be developed. In this respect, group decision making may be similar to brainstorming. Discussion must be free flowing and spontaneous, all group members must participate, and the evaluation of individual ideas must be suspended in the beginning to encourage participation. However, a decision must be reached, and this is where group decision making differs from brainstorming.

Group decision making probably is preferable to individual decision making in many instances. However, we have all heard the statement "A camel is a racehorse designed by a committee." While the necessity and benefits of group decision making are recognized, it also can present numerous problems, some of which have already been noted. Practicing managers need specific techniques that enable them to increase the benefits from group decision making while reducing the problems associated with it.

Increasing the creative capability of a group is especially necessary when individuals from diverse sectors of the organization must pool their judgments to create a satisfactory course of action for the organization. When subordinates and peers believe that the manager in charge of the group is essentially nonbiased or "on their side," group members may express their viewpoints more freely and feel less compelled to protect themselves from potentially nonsupportive or retaliatory responses.[30] When properly utilized, three techniques—brainstorming, the Delphi process, and the nominal group technique—have been extremely useful in increasing the group's creative capability in generating ideas, understanding problems, and reaching better decisions.

Brainstorming

BRAINSTORMING

A technique that promotes creativity by encouraging idea generation through noncritical discussion.

In many situations, groups are expected to produce creative or imaginative solutions to organizational problems. In such instances, **brainstorming** often enhances the creative output of the group. Brainstorming includes a strict series of rules to promote the generation of ideas while at the same time removing members' inhibitions that usually stymie face-to-face groups. The basic rules are:

No idea is too ridiculous. Group members are encouraged to state any extreme or outlandish idea.

[30]Kathleen J. Krone, "A Comparison of Organizational, Structural, and Relationship Effects on Subordinates' Upward Influence Choices," *Communication Quarterly,* Winter 1992, pp. 1–15.

FIGURE 18 • 2

PROBABLE RELATIONSHIP BETWEEN QUALITY OF GROUP DECISION AND METHOD UTILIZED

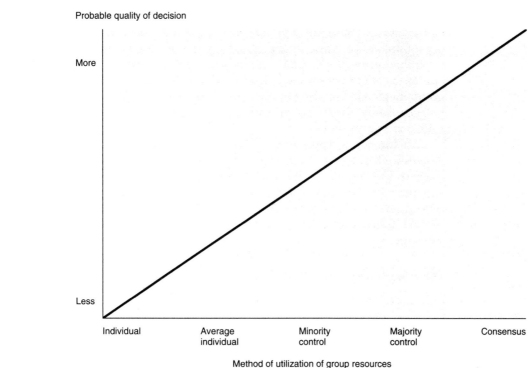

Each idea presented belongs to the group, not to the person stating it. In this way, group members utilize and build on the ideas of others.

No idea can be criticized. The purpose of the session is to generate, not evaluate, ideas.

Brainstorming is widely used in advertising, where it's apparently effective. In some other fields, it has been less successful. Brainstorming groups normally produce fewer ideas than do the equivalent number of individuals working by themselves and there's no evaluation or ranking of the ideas generated.[31] Thus, the group never really concludes the problem-solving process.

Delphi Process

This technique involves soliciting and comparing anonymous judgments on the topic of interest through a set of sequential questionnaires interspersed with summarized information and feedback of opinions from earlier responses.[32]

---

[31]R. Brent Gallupe, Lana M. Bastianutti, and William H. Cooper, "Unblocking Brainstorms," *Journal of Applied Psychology,* February 1991, pp. 137–42.

[32]Norman Dalkey, *The Delphi Method: An Experimental Study of Group Opinion* (Santa Monica, Calif.: Rand Corporation, 1969). This is the classic groundbreaking work on the Delphi method.

DELPHI PROCESS

A technique that promotes creativity by using anonymous judgment of ideas to reach a consensus decision.

The **Delphi process** retains the advantage of having several judges while removing the biasing effects that might occur during face-to-face interaction. The basic approach has been to collect anonymous judgments by mail questionnaire. For example, the members independently generate their ideas to answer the first questionnaire and return it. The staff members summarize the responses as the group consensus and feed this summary back, along with a second questionnaire for reassessment. Based on this feedback, respondents independently evaluate their earlier responses. The underlying belief is that the consensus estimate results in a better decision after several rounds of anonymous group judgment. However, while continuing the procedure for several rounds is possible, studies have shown essentially no significant change after the second round of estimation.

An interesting application of the Delphi process was undertaken by the American Marketing Association to determine the international issues most likely to have significant impact on marketing in the year 2000.[33] Twenty-nine experts on international marketing participated in the study. Major issues the experts identified included the environment, globalization, regional trading blocks, internationalization of service industries, and rising foreign direct investment.

Nominal Group Technique (NGT)

NOMINAL GROUP TECHNIQUE (NGT)

A technique that promotes creativity by bringing people together in a very structured meeting that allows little verbal communication. Group decision is the mathematically pooled outcome of individual votes.

NGT has gained increasing recognition in health, social service, education, industry, and government organizations.[34] The term **nominal group technique** was adopted by earlier researchers to refer to processes that bring people together but don't allow them to communicate verbally. Thus, the collection of people is a group "nominally" (in name only).

Basically, NGT is a structured group meeting in which 7 to 10 individuals sit around a table but don't speak to one another. Each person writes ideas on a pad of paper. After five minutes, a structured sharing of ideas takes place. Each person presents one idea. A person designated as recorder writes the ideas on a flip chart in full view of the entire group. This continues until all participants indicate that they have no further ideas to share. There is still no discussion.

The output of the first phase is a list of ideas (usually between 18 and 25). The next phase involves structured discussion in which each idea receives attention before a vote is taken. This is achieved by asking for clarification or stating the degree of support for each idea listed on the flip chart. The last stage involves independent voting in which each participant, in private, selects priorities by ranking or voting. The group decision is the mathematically pooled outcome of the individual votes.

Both the Delphi process and NGT have proved to be more productive than brainstorming.[35] Each has had an excellent success record. Basic differences between the Delphi process and NGT are:

---

[33]"Study Spots Global Marketing Trends (Global Marketing 2000: Future Trends and Their Implications, A Delphi Study)," *Marketing News,* October 14, 1991, p. 9.

[34]See Andre L. Delbecq, Andrew H. Van de Ven, and David H. Gustafson, *Group Techniques for Program Planning* (Glenview, Ill.: Scott, Foresman, 1975), for a work devoted entirely to techniques for group decision making.

[35]Brian Mullen, Craig Johnson, and Eduardo Salas, "Productivity Loss in Brainstorming Groups: A Meta-Analytic Integration," *Basic and Applied Social Psychology,* March 1991, pp. 3–23.

1. Delphi participants are typically anonymous to one another, while NGT participants become acquainted.

2. NGT participants meet face-to-face around a table, while Delphi participants are physically distant and never meet.

3. In the Delphi process, all communication between participants is by way of written questionnaires and feedback from the monitoring staff. In NGT, participants communicate directly.[36]

Practical considerations, of course, often influence which technique is used. For example, such factors as the number of available working hours, costs, and the physical proximity of participants influence selection of a technique.

Rather than to make readers experts in the Delphi process or NGT, this section has aimed to indicate the frequency and importance of group decision making in every organization. The three techniques discussed are practical devices for improving the effectiveness of group decisions.

Decision making is a responsibility shared by all managers, regardless of functional area or management level. Every day, they are required to make decisions that shape the future of their organizations as well as their own futures. Some of these decisions may have a strong impact on the organization's success, while others are less crucial. However, all decisions have some effect (positive or negative, large or small) on the organization. The quality of these decisions is the yardstick of managerial effectiveness.

---

[36]Delbecq, Van de Ven, and Gustafson, *Group Techniques for Program Planning,* p. 18.

▓ SUMMARY OF KEY POINTS

- Decision making is a fundamental process in organizations. Managers make decisions on the basis of the information (communication) they receive through the organization structure and the behavior of individuals and groups within it.

- Decision making distinguishes managers from nonmanagers. The quality of managers' decisions determines their effectiveness as managers.

- Decisions may be classified as programmed or nonprogrammed, depending on the problem. Most programmed decisions should be made at the first level in the organization, while nonprogrammed decisions should be made mostly by top management.

- Decision making should not be thought of as an end but as a means to achieve organizational goals and objectives. Decisions are organizational responses to problems.

- Decision making should be viewed as a multiphased process in which the actual choice is only one phase. The preceding phases are establishing goals, identifying problems, developing alternatives, evaluating alternatives, and implementing the decision.

- The decision-making process is influenced by numerous environmental and behavioral factors. Because of different values, perceptions, and personalities, different decision makers may not select identical alternatives in the same situation.

- A great deal of nonprogrammed decision making is carried on in group situations. Much evidence supports the claim that in most instances, group decisions are superior to individual decisions. Three techniques (brainstorming, the Delphi process, and the nominal group technique) improve the effectiveness of group decisions. The management of collective decision making must be a vital concern for future managers.

■ DISCUSSION AND REVIEW QUESTIONS

1. Biographies of successful executives often stress that they were decision makers. In your opinion, why is so much attention paid to this ability? Does everyone have the ability to make decisions?

2. In a short essay, describe whether you believe you're a decision maker and the reasons for your choice.

3. Think of a situation where you have to make a decision. Detail how you would utilize each of the seven steps in the decision-making process to reach and implement your decision.

4. Describe a situation you've encountered where a decision made by an individual would have been better made by a group. Why do you feel this way?

5. Describe two situations you faced that called for programmed decisions on your part and two that called for nonprogrammed decisions. What were some differences between them? Did this influence your decision-making approach? How?

6. Think of a major decision you made recently. It may have involved your personal life, a major purchase, and so on. Do you believe any behavioral influences affected your decision? Discuss them.

7. What is your attitude toward risk? Has that attitude ever influenced a decision you made? What are the implications of your attitude toward risk?

8. Have you ever been a member of a committee or a task force charged with making a decision? Describe the satisfactions, dissatisfactions, and problems in this experience.

9. Describe a situation where someone else made a poor decision that adversely affected you. Why was such a decision made?

10. Think of a corporate executive who, you believe, is a good decision maker. What traits make this executive effective?

■ ADDITIONAL REFERENCES

Cowan, D. A. "The Effect of Decision-Making Styles and Contextual Experience on Executives' Descriptions of Organizational Problem Formulation." *Journal of Management Studies,* September 1991, pp. 463–83.

Duxbury, L.; and G. Haines, Jr. "Predicting Alternative Work Arrangements from Salient Attitudes: A Study of Decision Makers in the Public Sector." *Journal of Business Research,* August 1991, pp. 83–97.

Falkenberg, L. "Improving the Accuracy of Stereotypes within the Workplace." *Journal of Management,* March 1990, pp. 107–18.

Fox, W. M. "The Improved Nominal Group Technique." *Journal of Management Development,* vol. 8, no. 1, 1989, pp. 20–27.

Fraedrich, J. P.; and O. C. Ferrell. "The Impact of Perceived Risk and Moral Philosophy Type on Ethical Decision Making in Business Organizations." *Journal of Business Research,* vol. 24, 1992, pp. 283–95.

Knouse, S. B.; and R. A. Giacalone. "Ethical Decision-Making in Business: Behavioral Issues and Concerns." *Journal of Business Ethics,* vol. 11, 1992, pp. 369–77.

Kraft, K. L.; and A. Singhapakdi. "The Role of Ethics and Social Responsibility in Achieving Organizational Effectiveness: Students versus Managers." *Journal of Business Ethics,* September 1991, pp. 679–86.

Liedtka, J. "Organizational Value Contention and Managerial Mindsets." *Journal of Business Ethics,* July 1991, pp. 543–47.

Mahmood, M. A.; and S. K. Soon. "A Comprehensive Model for Measuring the Potential Impact of Information Technology on Organizational Strategic Variables." *Decision Sciences,* September-October 1991, pp. 869–97.

Mentzer, J.; and N. Gandhi. "Expert Systems in Marketing: Guidelines for Development." *Journal of the Academy of Marketing Science,* Winter 1992, pp. 73–80.

Nonaka, I. "Redundant, Overlapping, Organization: A Japanese Approach to Managing Innovation Process." *California Management Review,* Spring 1990, pp. 27–38.

Nutt, Paul C. *Making Tough Decisions.* San Francisco: Jossey-Bass, 1989.

Sisodia, R. "Marketing Information and Decision Support Systems for Services." *Journal of Services Marketing,* Winter 1992, pp. 51–64.

Skivington, J. E.; and R. L. Daft. "A Study of Organizational 'Framework' and 'Process' Modalities for the Implementation of Business-Level Strategic Decisions." *Journal of Management Studies,* January 1991, pp. 45–68.

Udwadia, F. E.; and I. I. Mitroff. "Crisis Management and the Organizational Mind: Multiple Models for Crisis Management from Field Data." *Technological Forecasting & Social Change,* August 1991, pp. 33–52.

Underwood, D. "Expert Systems at Mutual Life: A Three-Pronged Approach." *Journal of Systems Management,* January 1992, pp. 13–16.

CASE FOR ANALYSIS

BREAKING THE RULES

Nancy Taggart worked in the customer service department at the Xemas Company. The Xemas Company manufactured industrial air conditioning systems and replacement parts for these systems. Xemas sold its products to large regional distributors which, in turn, supplied and supported independent dealers throughout the United States and Canada.

One night, Nancy received a call from one of Xemas's dealers who seemed unduly agitated. The dealer said he had a customer who needed a part for his air-conditioning system right away and the dealer didn't have the part in stock. He claimed he had tried to reach his distributor for the past two hours, but was unable to get through on the phone. He asked if Nancy could send the part overnight and then bill the distributor. The charge would then be included on the invoice the distributor sent the dealer at the end of the month.

Since it was past the distributor's normal operating hours, Nancy knew she couldn't reach anyone there. Furthermore, Nancy knew something was amiss, as Xemas had discontinued this type of shipping and billing practice because distributors had complained. They wanted to control all shipments to reduce the chance of selling to a bad credit risk.

But even though Nancy knew the rules, she decided to break them, based on the seemingly urgent nature of the situation. The dealer said the customer needed the part immediately. Nancy decided customer service was the most important issue involved in the situation, so she sent the part out promptly.

The next day, the local distributor was called. It turned out the dealer wasn't a regular customer of the distributor. Because of this situation, the distributor refused to pay for the part. While Xemas would try to get the dealer to pay directly to them, for the time being the company was out $150, the cost of the part. To make sure the books balanced, Nancy wrote out a personal check for $150 to cover the cost of the part and sent it to billing.

Within days, Nancy received a phone call from one of the firm's executive vice presidents, Ramon Hernandez. Ramon told Nancy that he had received a call from a supervisor in the billing department. The person he spoke to was irate and insisted that something be done about this employee, Nancy Taggart, who had broken company rules. Ramon then asked Nancy for an explanation for her actions. After hearing Nancy's story, Ramon stated that he agreed with the billing supervisor concerning the seriousness of the situation, and that actions did indeed need to be taken. He informed Nancy that she would hear from him the next day regarding those actions.

The next evening, when Nancy arrived at work, a letter awaited her from Ramon. With a feeling of dread, Nancy opened the letter. Inside was a check for $150. Attached to the check was a note from Ramon. The note stated that Nancy was going to be given both a raise and a preferred parking spot.

Discussion Questions

1. Why was Nancy rewarded for breaking the rules?

2. Describe what type of decision Nancy had to make. What decision alternatives were available to her besides the one she chose?

3. What types of behavioral factors might have influenced Nancy's decision?

Source: Adapted from David Armstrong, "Management by Storytelling," *Executive Female,* May-June 1992, p. 77; David E. Bowen and Edward E. Lawler III, "The Empowerment of Service Workers," *Sloan Management Review,* Spring 1992, pp. 31–39; Leonard L. Berry and A. Parasuraman, "Services Marketing Starts from Within," *Marketing Management,* Winter 1992, pp. 25–34.

EXPERIENTIAL EXERCISE

LOST ON THE MOON: A GROUP DECISION EXERCISE

Objective

To come as close as possible to the "best solution" as determined by experts of the National Aeronautics and Space Administration (NASA).

Related Topics

Motivation, individual differences, and group development are important topics related to this exercise.

Starting the Exercise

After reading the following scenario, you will, first individually and then as a member of a team, rank the importance of items available for carrying out your mission.

The Scenario

Your spaceship has just crash-landed on the moon. You were scheduled to rendezvous with a mother ship 200 miles away on the lighted surface of the moon, but the rough landing has ruined your ship and all of the equipment aboard, except for the 15 items listed below.

Your crew's survival depends on reaching the mother ship, so you must choose the most critical items available for the 200-mile trip. Your task is to rank the 15 items in terms of their importance for survival. Place number 1 by the most important item, number 2 by the second most important, and so on through number 15, the least important.

Work Sheet Items	1 NASA's Ranks	2 Your Ranks	3 Error Points	4 Group Ranks	5 Error Points
Box of matches	_____	_____	_____	_____	_____
Food concentrate	_____	_____	_____	_____	_____
Fifty feet of nylon rope	_____	_____	_____	_____	_____
Parachute silk	_____	_____	_____	_____	_____
Solar-powered portable heating unit	_____	_____	_____	_____	_____
Two .45-caliber pistols	_____	_____	_____	_____	_____
One case of dehydrated milk	_____	_____	_____	_____	_____
Two 100-pound tanks of oxygen	_____	_____	_____	_____	_____
Stellar map (of the moon's constellation)	_____	_____	_____	_____	_____
Self-inflating life raft	_____	_____	_____	_____	_____
Magnetic compass	_____	_____	_____	_____	_____
Five gallons of water	_____	_____	_____	_____	_____
Signal flares	_____	_____	_____	_____	_____
First-aid kit containing injection needles	_____	_____	_____	_____	_____
Solar-powered FM receiver-transmitter	_____	_____	_____	_____	_____
Total error points	Individual _____		Group _____		

Completing the Exercise

Phase I: 15 minutes. Read the scenario. Then, in column 2 (Your Ranks) of the work sheet, assign priorities to the 15 items listed. Use a pencil since you may wish to change your rankings. Somewhere on the sheet, you may wish to note your logic for each ranking.

Phase II: 25 minutes. Your instructor will assign you to a team. The task of each team is to arrive at a consensus on the rankings. Share your individual solutions and reach a consensus—the ranking for each of the 15 items that best satisfies all team members. Thus, by the end of phase II, all members of the team should have the same set of rankings in column 4 (Group Ranks). Do not change your individual rankings in column 2.

Phase III: 10 minutes. Your instructor will provide you with the "best solution" to the problem—that is, the set of rankings determined by the NASA experts, along with their reasoning. Each person should note this set of rankings in column 1 (NASA's Ranks). (Note: While it is fun to debate the experts' rankings and their reasoning, remember that the objective of the game is to learn more about decision making, not how to survive on the moon!)

Phase IV (evaluation): 15 minutes. Now, see how well you did individually and as a team. First, find your individual score by taking, for each item, the absolute difference between your ranks (column 2) and NASA's

ranks (column 1) and writing it in the first error points column (column 3). Thus, if you ranked "Box of matches" 3 and NASA ranked it 8, you would put a 5 in column 3, across from "Box of matches." Then, add the error points in column 3 and write the total at the bottom in the space for individual total error points.

Next, score your group performance in the same way, this time taking the absolute differences between group ranks (column 4) and NASA's ranks (column 1) and writing them in the second error points column (column 5). Add the group error points and write the total in the space provided. (Note that all members of the team have the same group error points.)

Finally, prepare three pieces of information to be submitted when your instructor calls on your team:

1. Average individual total error points (the average of all group members' individual totals). One team member should add these figures and divide by the number of team members to get the average.

2. Group total error points, as shown on each group member's work sheet.

3. Number of team members who had fewer individual total error points than the group total error points.

Using this information, your instructor will evaluate the results of the exercise and discuss group versus individual performance. Together, you will then explore the implications of this exercise for the group decision-making process.

ISBN 0-256-18462-3
Book #072-01179-05